The Economics of Higher Education in the United States

Walter Prescott Webb Memorial Lectures,
published for the University of Texas at Arlington
by Texas A&M University Press

The Economics of Higher Education in the United States

EDITED BY THOMAS ADAM AND A. BURCU BAYRAM

Contributors
Thomas Adam
A. Burcu Bayram
Jamie M. Brown
David C. Hammack
Jordan Hensley
Stanley N. Katz
Bruce A. Kimball
Jeremy B. Luke
Sam Stern

Published for the University of Texas at Arlington
by Texas A&M University Press
College Station

First edition

This paper meets the requirements of ANSI/NISO Z39.48–1992
(Permanence of Paper).
Binding materials have been chosen for durability.
Manufactured in the United States of America

Library of Congress Cataloging-in-Publication Data

Names: Adam, Thomas, 1968– editor. | Bayram, A. Burcu, 1979– editor.
Title: The economics of higher education in the United States / edited by Thomas Adam and A. Burcu Bayram.
Other titles: Walter Prescott Webb memorial lectures.
Description: First edition. | College Station : Texas A&M University Press, [2019] | Series: Walter Prescott Webb memorial lectures | Includes bibliographical references and index.
Identifiers: LCCN 2018055943 | ISBN 9781623497439 (book/hardcover (printed case) : alk. paper) | ISBN 9781623497446 (ebook format)
Subjects: LCSH: Education, Higher—Economic aspects. | Universities and colleges—United States—Finance. | Student aid—United States. | College costs—United States.
Classification: LCC LC67.62 .E28 2019 | DDC 378.3/80973—dc23 LC record available at https://lccn.loc.gov/2018055943

A list of titles in this series is available at the end of the book.

Contents

The Economics of Higher Education in the United States

Introduction

The Economics of Higher Education and the History of Philanthropy Research

Stanley N. Katz

I have been an admirer of Walter Prescott Webb as a historian ever since I first encountered his work in graduate school, when I was studying the western history of the United States under the tutelage of Frederick Merk in the late 1950s. I was not fortunate enough to meet Webb personally, but I had a near-miss encounter at the Palmer House in Chicago in December of 1960. I was then attending the annual meeting of the American Historical Association and looking for my first job as a historian. I had been scheduled for a job interview by the University of Toronto and met several members of their history department in a hotel room. This was the "good old days," and although our appointment was in the late morning, the two beds in the room had not yet been made or the room cleaned. The chair was the very distinguished Canadian historian Maurice Careless. The five or six of us in the room had just perched on beds or chairs to begin the interview when the phone rang, and Careless was informed that Walter Prescott Webb was waiting for him in the Palmer House lobby. Careless jumped up off the bed, saying that he had been waiting his whole life to meet Webb, and dashed out of the room. I asked the remaining department members what would happen next and was told that, so far as they knew, the interview was over. And so, it was. I never heard from Toronto again. Webb died in a car crash three years later, and I certainly never heard from him. Which means that writing this introduction is my closest encounter with Webb. What a pity!

I think that Webb would have understood that the topic of modes of funding higher education was an important one for historical inquiry. He earned a teacher's certificate and began teaching before earning his bachelor's degree at the University of Texas at Austin at the age of twenty-seven, and only then did he discover his vocation for historical research and writing. He was, that is, what we would now call an adult student and the beneficiary of a very low cost education in a state institution. Today's twenty-seven-year-olds who aspire to teaching careers are confronted with a far different economic environment. A young Texan with Webb's abilities would first have to apply and be accepted into the highly competitive environment of UT Austin (or another of the state's fine universities). He or she would then have to find a way, either through the student's own resources or from federal or state funding agencies, to pay the steep tuition and fees of the public university and would also have to compete for a place with the large cohort of out-of-state students whom UT recruits in order to secure out-of-state tuition revenue. After completing the bachelor's degree, our young Texan might then apply to do a PhD, hoping that the high tuition fees for that degree would be offset by fellowship money from either the university endowment or a private foundation.

This is the changing economic environment that the essays in this volume address. They ask, in different ways, how we have come from a political environment in which higher education was perceived as a public good, normally free to the user, to an environment in which higher education is seen as a private good, subject primarily to market forces. Almost every state university is now charging high tuition and fees (for housing, food, and student services), providing merit-based scholarships, and actively recruiting full-pay students. They are doing so because almost all states have reduced their annual financial support to historically low levels, apparently on the hypothesis that the primary beneficiaries of university education are the students themselves and that the students can and will recover the cost of their education from future earnings. The practical effect of such a higher education policy is that students from poor families are unable to afford higher education, and the state loses the capacity to channel students into training to address the state's most urgent needs.

In this perilous economic environment, states and their universities are desperately searching for sources of financial support. Some of this support comes from higher tuition (both in-state and out-of-state). Some comes from the rapidly declining federal sources of support (such as Pell grants). Some comes from (rapidly declining) federal research support provided by the National Institutes of Health (NIH) and the National Science Foundation (NSF). Some comes from the private commercial sector as research support in highly selective fields in science, technology, and engineering. Some comes from university endowments—quite a lot for UT Austin, but not so very much for most public universities. And a good deal comes from individual fundraising from alumni and others interested in the university and from applications to philanthropic foundations. What is truly novel in the current situation is the extent to which public universities are now forced to identify and solicit the financial support they need to maintain increasingly expensive educational operation.

The 2017 Webb symposium focused primarily on private-sector support for higher education and the related need of universities to accumulate wealth in the form of endowments partially to support their educational and research programs. As several of the chapters in this volume demonstrate, the formation and use of endowments has a long history in the United States, but they also show that there are now more and larger endowments, and universities are much more dependent upon endowments. The cost of higher education has risen dramatically at the same time as both states and the federal government have significantly lowered their contributions to offset that cost. There is therefore greater competition both for students and for financial support, but institutions are quite limited in the extent that they can support themselves through fees for service (for example, tuition), and thus the universities best situated to survive and thrive in this environment are those that are most successful in raising funds, especially from philanthropic resources.

And this is why I was asked to join the Webb symposium. I am now primarily a historian of philanthropy in the United States. Within the field of the history of philanthropy, my special expertise has been in private philanthropic foundations, which have been (at least until very recently) the most important institutions of large-scale philanthropy. As I will describe later, for the first half of the twentieth century the earliest group of big foundations primarily funded basic university research, and they were the most important nongovernmental supporters of higher education. But over the past half-century, these foundations have changed in fundamental ways, just as the universities have changed. So to understand the relationship of wealth to higher education, we need to look closely at the transformation of the philanthropic foundation as it enters the twenty-first century. I will now try to undertake that task by reflecting on the last forty years of research on the history of philanthropy.

Research on the History of Philanthropy: A Personal Account

I began to study grant makers, that is, American private philanthropic foundations, in the mid-1970s. The number and size of these organizations has grown substantially since Barry Karl and I started to study early-twentieth-century philanthropic foundations, but I have mostly focused on the largest grant makers. My story has two interwoven narrative threads. The first is the history of organized scholarly research on the third sector; the second reflects my current research interest in the emergence of what I term mega-philanthropy and my concern that the emergence of huge grant-making organizations poses a threat to democracy in the United States and elsewhere.

American scholars of what the rest of the world calls nongovernmental organizations have long struggled to explain exactly what phenomenon they were studying. By the 1970s we moved from the paradigm developed by Lester Salamon and others of "government by contract" as a way of explaining state/nonprofit collaboration to the paradigm of "civil society" studies. Of course, the American term *third sector* (that is, nonprofit as opposed to state and market sectors) was always contested. Years ago, insofar as anyone thought of it as a distinguishable sector, Americans called ours the *nonprofit sector*, and many still do. Later, John D. Rockefeller 3rd and others preferred the term *independent sector*, a term that seemed to have a more positive political valence in an antistatist society. The difficulty was that labeling was, at bottom, a political problem.

The noted American neoconservative scholar Irving Kristol ventured into the liberal lion's den of the Council on Foundations in 1980 to challenge the notion that "the foundation world (the nonprofit world, as we say), constitutes a 'third sector' in American society." Kristol denied the existence of a third sector: "Foundations are part and parcel of the private sector. . . . There are only two sectors in our society: the private sector and the governmental sector. The voluntary associations . . . are part of the private sector." He proceeded to attack what he saw as the "hubris" of the Ford Foundation and other large grant makers, who thought they could do "a lot of good" but were more likely to "cause a great deal of damage." He acknowledged that American foundations had come into existence early in the last century in order to do things "that the government did not do" in the nineteenth and early twentieth centuries: "That was the right thing for them to do at that time. However, the situation has changed today. . . . [Now] foundations should not be an adjunct to the government. Foundations should be an adjunct to their own, private sector." But the essence of Kristol's objection was clear: there are only two sectors, public and private, and private money should be cherished as "the life blood" of private, public-serving organizations.[1]

My own close friend and scholarly collaborator Barry Karl was also deeply skeptical of the notion of a separate nonprofit sector, but for a different reason. In his 1987 review of Woody Powell's important handbook *The Nonprofit Sector*, Barry contended that the source of American confusion about state and private provision of social services was "the very concept of not-for-profit and the view of such organizations as constituting a third or independent sector in a society supposedly divided normally between institutions organized for the purposes of making profits and tax-funded public institutions committed to providing public services." Barry objected that "third-sector or independent-sector organizations are organizations that provide public services that could be supported by public money, and . . . in many instances it is public money that third-sector agencies distribute." But in America private money, the basis of philanthropy, is a product of private enterprise that is strictly for profit. Thus, "the creation of a sanitary language designating a third or independent sector invites criticism by its very subterfuge." Barry thought we were trying to hide the private/for-profit character of philanthropy by calling it something else.[2]

But I hope we have moved beyond such crude taxonomical questions about the intellectual geography of our field. Most scholars today think of civil society as our *mappa mundi*. However, if we posit civil society as the organized space between the state and the market, we must explain its dynamic relationship to both of those sectors. That dynamic ordinarily depends upon normative assumptions. If a scholar believes that public goods are ideally the responsibility of the state, he will view some civil society activity as a placeholder for what the state ought to be doing. If he believes that public goods are ideally the responsibility of the market, he will see civil society activity as occupying space that private economic activity should control. Or the scholar might take the view that civil society is the ideal mediator between the state and market. Third sector scholars must identify where they stand on such questions.

Thus, it matters that we now live in the aftermath of the era of Margaret Thatcher and Ronald Reagan, in a post-Brexit world in which democratic values seem endangered all over the globe, not least in my own country, the United States. The emergence of neoliberalism as the dominant paradigm for much of the international political economy forces us to try to come to terms with its implications for the place of civil society in our own global conceptions. In this context, the role of philanthropy itself is being transformed in the United States and in many other countries as well. In the United States, the era of government by contract is giving way to the era of hybridity and big philanthropy, in which the private donors aim to share with the state in setting the larger public social agenda by leveraging the private power of its concentrated wealth against the public power of the state. It appears that we are redefining neoliberalism in a new age of mega-affluence, perhaps best described recently by Luc Boltanski and Arnaud Esquerre as an age of enrichment.[3] Concentrated wealth and the newly available enhanced access of such wealth to political power through big philanthropy are changing the dynamics of democracy, at least in the United States. What matters for scholars is that our debates over the nature of the sector and the terminology used to describe it have shaped the manner in which we study the sector.

The beginning phase of recent scholarship on philanthropy was the Princeton conference on the history of philanthropy that was conceived by F. Emerson Andrews of the Russell Sage Foundation, funded by the Ford Foundation, and presided over by University of Wisconsin history professor Merle Curti in December 1956. Andrews quaintly described Curti as "this delightful gentleman, small and lean, keen of eye, witty, friendly, and a thoughtful observer of the American character. Curti, Andrews went on to say, "quickly agreed that voluntary giving is an almost unique characteristic of the Anglo-Saxon peoples, and more adequate study was important for a better understanding of our whole culture."[4] Curti recruited eight senior scholars, mainly historians, from throughout the country to participate in the meeting, and the group produced a short report including suggestions for further study, a topic outline of the history of American philanthropy, and a selected bibliography. Even a brief glance at the bibliography confirms my 1999 contention that there was not at the time much in the way of serious scholarship on the main elements of the modern philanthropic grant-making system, especially what are now called private philanthropic foundations.

The Russell Sage–Ford project, while important, was limited in its long-term impact. I actually knew a good deal about it, since from 1965 to 1971 I was a colleague of Merle's at Wisconsin and was acquainted with many of the Wisconsin group. Curti, amply funded by the Ford Foundation (in the first commitment by an American foundation to fund research on the field), went on to produce a couple of very important volumes on the history of philanthropy. His colleague Irvin Wyllie and several students, funded through his Ford grant, also produced useful books on the history of US philanthropy.[5] However, none of them later produced philanthropy scholarship. This has proved to be one of our long-term challenges: how to recruit researchers to the long-term rather than to a one-shot study of the third sector. One of the ironies in our field is that while philanthropy itself has helped to create a number of new academic fields, starting with Rockefeller's support of the social sciences in the 1920s and 1930s, it has frequently been reluctant to support study of the field of philanthropy.

The post-Princeton conference history has been best chronicled by Peter Dobkin Hall in his fine *Inventing the Nonprofit Sector*. What precipitated the organization of the field and interest in its scholarly analysis was the reaction of philanthropic foundations and other nonprofits, under the leadership of the Filer Commission (instigated and funded by John D. Rockefeller 3rd), to the executive and congressional inquiries into the performance and potential abuses within the American foundation sector. These inquiries led to the Tax Reform Act of 1969, which imposed new restrictions upon private philanthropic foundations and created anxiety that further regulation might be in store for the sector. The Filer Commission funded a great deal of valuable scholarship and stimulated the creation of the first sectoral organization in the United States, Independent Sector (IS), in 1980. Hall points out, the new organization struggled to reconcile the divergent interests and attitudes of several existing charitable organizations and pledged that it would proceed "only by working through the vast network of organizations already extant." The result was the creation of an organization that represented both grant-making organizations and NGOs in an attempt to represent the totality of the field.[6]

Most important was the fact that in 1983 IS created its Research Committee, chaired by a remarkable philanthropic administrator, Robert(Bob) Payton, then president of the Exxon Education Foundation. I was one of the initial members of the committee, which began its existence by pledging not to do research itself but to encourage and support the work of others. I succeeded Bob as chair of the IS Research Committee in 1989 and remained in that position until 1993. All along, Bob Payton's dream was to use the committee to stimulate the development of an independent doctoral academic field of philanthropic studies. He also sought to assist American universities in securing funding to begin their own philanthropic research centers. The first such center had in fact already been created by President Kingman Brewster of Yale University—the Program on Nonprofit Organizations (PONPO), led in its early years by John Simon of the Yale Law School. I was delighted to work with Bob Payton in this field-building project, but I disagreed with him on one important point, since I thought the prospects were better for building the study of philanthropy from within the existing academic disciplines, since it was in disciplinary departments that almost all academic employment was likely to be found.[7] (Bob would later go on to realize part of his dream through his role in establishing what is now the Lilly School of Philanthropy in Indianapolis.)

PONPO, originally funded by John D. Rockefeller 3rd and the Rockefeller Foundation, proved to be very important in the production of nonprofit and philanthropy scholarship in the 1980s, although (as Hall notes) Yale had no dedicated faculty in the field. But there was really no academic field yet, nor were there more than a handful of scholars who considered the study of philanthropy their primary research field. PONPO also contributed importantly to the support of younger scholars who were gravitating to the field, such as the economist Henry Hansmann in the Law School; Paul DiMaggio and Woody Powell in the Sociology Department; as well as Helmut Anheier, Francie Ostrower, and Melissa Middleton Stone, then graduate students in sociology and management. There is no doubt that for many years we considered PONPO to be the leading American center of research on the sector, although by the late 1980s and early 1990s other major American centers began to emerge. Lester Salamon's center at Johns Hopkins University was one of the first. It was the research center that pioneered internationally comparative work on NGOs. Kathleen McCarthy soon began her center at the City University of New York and specialized in providing opportunities for international NGO managers. Later, the Hauser Center was inaugurated at Harvard, with links to the John F. Kennedy School and the Harvard Business School. Then the major center on philanthropy funded by the Lilly Endowment came on the scene, as well as Jim Ferris's USC Center on Philanthropy. By 1988, according to Hall's estimate, there were twenty nonprofit research centers in the United States.[8] Almost all were university-based, although Elizabeth Boris's Center on Nonprofits and Philanthropy, an important Washington, DC, think tank established in 1996 at the Urban Institute (and later also the home of the National Center for Charitable Statistics), was a valuable exception.

Meanwhile, several American philanthropic foundations had begun to follow the Ford Foundation in developing grant-making programs in philanthropy and nonprofit research. For many years Ford continued to be the leader, though other mainline foundations such as Rockefeller, Rockefeller Brothers, Carnegie, and later Packard began to support work in the field. The situation briefly improved dramatically when the Atlantic Philanthropies, under the leadership of Joel Fleishman and Harvey Dale, allocated substantial sums to fund the creation of research centers and projects both internationally and in the United States. Some of this funding went directly to nonprofit research centers, some went directly to researchers, and a good deal went to intermediate institutions such as the Nonprofit Sector Research Fund at the Aspen Institute in Washington, DC (very ably led, first by Elizabeth Boris and then by Alan Abramson, from 1991 to 2007), and the Social Science Research Council in New York.

Some years ago Peter Hall remarked: "It proved to be far easier to raise funds for special projects rather than for general support, and this difficulty inevitably drew the academic research effort away from unfundable basic research toward the 'near- and medium-term issues' that funders were more willing to underwrite."[9] I think that what Peter meant was that foundations were reluctant to support the study of the sector itself and much more likely to support the study of the impact of the sector on contemporary social and political problems. In general, I think this is still the case in the United States.

All of this raises interesting questions about the current situation of institutional leadership of third-sector scholarship in the United States. In the first half of the last century, it was first the Russell Sage Foundation and then the Ford Foundation that provided leadership, especially through their grant-making programs. Then, in the late 1960s more centralized leadership appeared under the threat of restrictive congressional legislation. The initiative was furthered by the Filer Commission, spearheaded by John D. Rockefeller 3rd; it was broadened to include donee organizations through the advocacy of Pablo Eisenberg. And then we had Independent Sector and its Research Committee, and PONPO, along with the new generation of academic third-sector research centers. At about the same time, the Association for Research on Nonprofit Organizations and Voluntary Action (ARNOVA) was created to provide an individual membership-based organization to support research, and by the early 1990s our field had also the International Society for Third-Sector Research (ISTR) as well as the serial publications *Nonprofit and Voluntary Sector Quarterly* (*NVSQ*) and *VOLUNTAS: International Journal of Voluntary and Nonprofit Organizations*.

The feel-good version of this narrative would be that over a period of about forty years a new academic field had been created and has grown into maturity. But that is not how it appears to me. I am more impressed by the number of academic centers that no longer exist or have changed their research agendas; by the radical decrease in funding available for research on the sector; and by our failure to develop sectoral research planning mechanisms. However, although several years ago I worried that we lacked a growing cadre of younger scholars committed to careers in the field, today I am heartened by their growing numbers and the quality of the work they are doing. The participants at the 2017 Webb Colloquium are proof of this. The glass now seems to me to be half-full.

My Contribution to the Field

Finally, I would like to reflect briefly on my own work in the field of third-sector studies. As I have noted a couple of times in print, my initial research in this field, in the mid-1970s, concerned the origins of philanthropic foundations in the United States and was undertaken initially at the request of a friend who was about to take an executive position with a foundation. I was fortunate enough to be able to collaborate in that project with my University of Chicago history colleague Barry Karl, who knew much more about the topic than I did.

Barry and I thought our project would be pretty straightforward and not too difficult to accomplish, but it did not take us long to see how badly we had underestimated our task. There was little in the way of general history of the American philanthropic foundation, so we had to set out to sketch the history of each of the original large foundations. This proved a daunting task since with few exceptions these organizations had done little to preserve and organize their records. The principal exception to this statement was the Rockefellers since, during the years we were beginning our research, the Rockefeller Archive Center (RAC) was opened to scholars and immediately established itself as the leading repository of foundation archives in this country (and in the world, really). Barry and I spent many months visiting major foundations to urge them to deposit their records in professional repositories, especially since the RAC was not at that time accepting much in the way of non-Rockefeller material. But now the RAC has added to and diversified its magnificent collections and has consistently supported research by individual archival researchers.

My own interests in the third sector began to broaden in the 1980s, when service on the IS Research Committee made me more aware of the breadth of the NGO sector in the United States. I was also fortunate to have been recruited by John Simon to be part of the faculty of the first Salzburg Seminar on Philanthropy, held in Austria in the summer of 1986. This gave me the opportunity to work with an international group of scholars and charitable administrators and to hold seminars with a remarkable group of young scholars and practitioners from around the world. I then met a great many people who have since risen to prominence in the third sector, not least of them Helmut Anheier, Wolfgang Seibel, and Woody Powell. I became even more aware of the organizational challenges of NGOs when I was recruited to preside over the American Council of Learned Societies (ACLS) in 1986; there is nothing like trying to run an NGO for learning how it operates. I continued to serve on the boards of a number of third-sector research organizations during my ACLS years. Most importantly, one of my primary duties at ACLS was to help manage American professorial exchange programs with socialist countries around the world, largely through American NGOs subordinate to ACLS that had been created for that purpose.

ACLS got me out of the United States and opened my eyes to the importance of the third sector in many other parts of the world, opening the present phase of my career as a scholar. Luckily, I was able to marry my institutional obligations to my scholarship. I worked with a number of US foundations and a series of Eastern European NGOs in the late 1980s and 1990s in support of democratic and constitutional reform and began to write in the field of comparative constitutionalism. It was also at that time that I began to become quite skeptical of US foundations' attempts to support incipient democratic movements in post-communist Europe, questioning whether foreign philanthropy could produce indigenous democracy.[10] I think it was also then that I began to develop deeper concerns about possible negative impacts of philanthropy upon democracy, since the consolidation of democracy has for many years been my primary intellectual and political preoccupation.

Back to my narrative. In the early 1990s I began to discuss with Benny Gidron the possibility of a major internationally comparative, empirical study of NGOs. We secured funding from Atlantic Philanthropies, recruited Zeke Hasenfeld and research teams in Northern Ireland, Israel, Palestine, and South Africa to collaborate with us, and in 2002 published *Mobilizing for Peace: Conflict Resolution in Northern Ireland, South Africa, and Israel/Palestine*.[11] After retiring from ACLS in 1997 and returning to teach at the Woodrow Wilson School at Princeton, philanthropy became my primary teaching and research subject. I began to offer regular undergraduate courses on civil society and public policy and graduate courses on nonprofits, NGOs, and philanthropy in addition to a freshman seminar I called Philanthropy: Can We Save the World Through Generosity? In other words, over a period of forty years I have moved from a narrow academic interest in the history of large philanthropic foundations in the United States to a much broader concern with philanthropy and the third sector as factors in the viability of democracy. But at the same time, during this period I have gotten my hands dirty in the business of philanthropy—I have become familiar with the management and staff of both grant-making and grant-seeking organizations, and I have joined the boards of trustees of more nonprofit organizations than I am willing to admit.

But just as I have changed over the years, the world has changed, and with it the role of the third sector. I was born during the first phase of the New Deal, when the American state began to grow in size and to assume some responsibility for social justice, especially through the creation of our social security system. I grew up during the Second World War, when the American state grew still larger. After the war, the state began to take some responsibility for funding higher education (the GI Bill) and scientific research, thereby crowding the philanthropic sector out of some of its traditional activities. And then, when I first began my teaching career, Lyndon B. Johnson launched the Great Society, vastly expanding the size of the state and broadly extending the social net through the creation of Medicare and Medicaid. However, the Johnson years would prove to be (at least until now) the apogee of US government spending for social services and the vast expansion of NGO-state collaboration in provision of social services. The decade of the 1970s, with its energy and environmental crises, laid the basis for what we call the Reagan Revolution, when Thatcherism and neoliberalism came to the United States.

The Reagan administration came into office in 1981 loudly announcing that it would reduce the federal social budget and claiming that the charitable sector could and would make up the spending gap. But there was neither the money nor the will in the private sector to meet this need, and the civic sector took a beating in the 1980s as third-sector organizations tried to replace state funding they had lost. This situation did not change much during the Clinton administration in the 1990s, since the Democrats under Bill Clinton moved significantly to the right. The impact on the third sector was to force NGOs to be more resourceful in identifying sources of funding. This led to much greater NGO reliance on fee for service and market-oriented activity and adoption of business models of management. We began to hear from the sector more about social enterprise, and we began to see more hybridity—the fusion of nonprofit and for-profit activity.

At the same time, the philanthropic foundation sector itself had also begun a transition to a more entrepreneurial model, especially among the larger organizations. Influenced by the recent business experience of new foundation creators and staff, and by the models taught in the leading US business schools, new foundations (and reformed older foundations) began to adopt the stance of "strategic" philanthropy, whose underlying model was the practices of venture capital. The new venture philanthropists tried to identify donee organizations who would agree to achieve precisely measureable goals previously specified by the funders. Their strategies were based on the perceived need to achieve clearly demonstrable impact in the near term. They prided themselves on being data-driven, evidence-based, and outcome-oriented. They also espoused narrowly focused, tailored grant-making, close relationships with donees, and a generally hard-nosed attitude towards grant-making. Many of the new funders were now on the West Coast of the United States, products of Silicon Valley. They believed in making large grants in the expectation of producing significant impact. They openly aimed to influence public policy, a trend begun by the Ford Foundation in the 1960s. Unlike the early Rockefeller and Carnegie organizations, they were not embarrassed to be what Megan Tompkins-Stange has recently called "policy patrons." All of this characterizes the current business-influenced, hedge fund–inspired philanthropy of megafoundations and the Big Bet. It is not your grandmother's philanthropy.[12]

These developments were possible because, beginning in the 1990s, the asymmetry in the distribution of wealth in the United States was approaching dimensions not seen since 1929.[13] Due partly to the emergence of the technology sector and partly to the rampant growth of the financial sector in the era of Clinton deregulation, a billionaire class began to emerge in our country (and around the world). The definitely bad news was that the lower classes did not benefit from the explosion of wealth in the country; the potentially good news was that many of the nouveaux riches became philanthropists, making possible what has become the era of the megafoundation. Even after the collapse of the dot-com balloon in the early years of the twenty-first century (and the real estate balloon a decade later), prosperity for the ultrarich continued to grow, and with it philanthropy. *Forbes* magazine recently estimated that there were 540 billionaires in the United States out of a worldwide total of 2,043—although both numbers rise each year. With the passage of the new US tax legislation in late 2017, it seems certain that both the numbers of billionaires and the asymmetry of wealth in the United States will expand substantially.

Correspondingly, the current American philanthropic world is dominated at the top by megafoundations (those with more than one billion dollars in net assets—eighty-eight and counting as of recently, up from five a decade ago), although there are literally thousands of smaller grant-making organizations in the country, and there are tens of thousands of NGOs. The rhetoric of the large grant-making organizations is increasingly that of the business community. To some extent, American grant makers have always embraced this terminology. What is new is the current glorification and romanticization of the market and the entrepreneur, especially the "social entrepreneur." To call this situation "philanthro-capitalism" would be (in my judgment) to go too far, but we certainly seem to be headed down a road on which nonprofits and for-profits are converging. Whether "the rich can save the world," as the authors of the book *Philanthrocapitalism* claim in their subtitle, seems to me quite unlikely. But there is a lot of reason to believe that philanthropists such as the Gateses and Chan-Zuckerberg think exactly that.[14]

Is it clear that scholars have the data, the conceptual apparatus, and the research tools to assess the institutions that have begun to dominate the sector in the "big bet" era of philanthropy? If it is hard enough to gain insight into the management of the Bill and Melinda Gates Foundation, how will we assess and understand the LLC recently created by Mark Zuckerberg and Priscilla Chan, which is not subject to the government reporting requirements of private philanthropic foundations? Can we gain access to their staff and decision-making processes? Where will their archives be held, and will scholars be able to access them? Will grant makers in the era after the spend-down of Atlantic Philanthropies be willing to fund critical research on philanthropy? Much more importantly, will we have both the courage and resources to scrutinize critically the emerging "policy patron" philanthropic foundations? The press, at least in the United States, seems to have abandoned its watchdog role. In this situation we will have to step up our scholarly vigilance.

None of this could have been foreseen when I began my research in this field. As I wrote the last few sentences above, I found myself asking how the funders of my current research would react to the statements I have just made about contemporary foundation practice. That is the question that Barry Karl and I asked ourselves in the 1970s, and it is a question all third-sector scholars who challenge mainstream knowledge are bound to ask. It is one of the dilemmas of much of the third-sector scholarship: How hard can we bite the hand that feeds us? Most scholars will agree with me that we have no choice but to take a deep breath and then bite, for the real danger is that we will censor ourselves. We know that speaking truth to power is our scholarly duty, but we also know that we sometimes fall short. Some will remember the moral of Walt Kelly's comic strip Pogo: "We have met the enemy and he is us."

And that is my take on the emergence of modern scholarship on the role of philanthropy in society, but the Webb Symposium was more specifically focused on the role of philanthropy and economics in the organization and behavior of higher education in the United States. There are of course only a few countries in the world in which philanthropy is a major factor in the provision of higher education. In most countries the state is the sole (or at least the dominant) provider of higher education, although there has been an international trend to shift part of the cost to users, that is, to students through tuition charges and other fees. In a few countries—the United Kingdom especially—philanthropy also plays a role. But the United States has by far the largest and most dominant private sector, one in which philanthropy plays a very large role. Given the recent spread of neoliberal political economy around the world, it may be that private-sector provision of (or funding of) higher education may soon become a more international phenomenon.

The Structure of this Book

In any case, the chapters in this volume, drawn from the Webb Symposium lectures, are extremely well informed and have much to tell us about higher education as it is structured and supported in the early-twenty-first-century United States.

Thomas Adam and A. Burcu Bayram situate our current acceptance of the notion that college students should bear the primary burden of paying for their education in the development of that practice and idea over the course of the twentieth century. They show that what we now accept as normal and inevitable is in fact a relatively recent innovation, privatizing what was historically conceived of as a public good. In the current situation in the United States, the combination of the widespread acceptance of tuition as a primary offset for the cost of undergraduate education and the decline of public support for the cost of public higher education is dramatically raising the cost of university education and therefore the incidence of debt for students. And the conservatives in control of national educational policy see nothing wrong in this situation, since they conceptualize a college degree as an individual investment in the prospective earnings of today's students—that is, a private, not a public, good.

Thomas Adam, in his chapter on national scholarship programs in the 1930s and 1940s, examines the undergraduate admissions practices of several of the most elite American universities. A problem began to develop when colleges such as those of Harvard and Princeton attempted to develop a national rather than a regional (northeastern American) student body by means of offering national scholarships, especially on the West Coast. This seemed to threaten California's Stanford University especially, but it also had the effect of heralding the beginning of a major diversification of student bodies in the elite universities. The scholarships necessary to carry out this policy were increasingly supported by charitable contributions, especially by wealthy alumni, but they were also supported by what amounted to a transfer of tuition revenues from full-pay traditional students to the new nationalized student body. As the mid-century elite universities grew in size and function, so did their urgent need for new and increased streams of funding.

Sam Stern and Jordan Hensley take us back to an earlier period and to public higher education. They profile a remarkable physician-entrepreneur of the late nineteenth–early twentieth century, Bernard Daly, who left his considerable fortune to establish the Daly Fund, a perpetuity devoted to selecting promising candidates in Daly's hometown of Lakeview, Oregon, for college scholarships. This was the origin of the American notion of "place-based" scholarships, and it has played an important role in the development of human resources in a remote and poor area in the Pacific Northwest. It was apparently Daly's thanks for the opportunity he had found as a young man and a token of support for his adopted Oregon home. It has been a model for a more recent wave of place-based educational philanthropy.

David Hammack's chapter traces the role of private philanthropy over the past century and a half of American higher education. He shows how colleges and universities accumulated funds and invested them so as to provide income for a wide range of current institutional and educational needs. To do so they behaved much like the modern philanthropic foundation, building endowments and allocating investment income to the funding of their expanding programs. By the early twentieth century the philanthropic foundation had matured as an institution, and the early large foundations devoted much of their funds to the needs of the new research universities. The foundations' role diminished after World War II, due largely to the emergence of federal funding of scientific research, but in recent decades research university endowments have often grown to such an extent that they support significant portions of annual university budgets. Nevertheless, Hammack warns us that there are limits to what universities and foundations can do to realize the democratic potential of higher education in a dramatically diversifying society.

Bruce Kimball, Jeremy Luke, and Jamie Brown trace the early-twentieth-century history of professional education (medicine, law, business) in the United States. Professional education was of course a relatively late developing aspect of higher education in this country, since the college had been its dominant activity in the eighteenth century and well into the nineteenth. Focusing on Harvard and Columbia, the authors show how university leaders came to realize the importance of storing up wealth to support graduate professional education and how their relative success in doing so shaped their futures as well as determined their current welfare. These professional schools increased their parochial wealth more quickly than did the universities in which they were loosely embedded and reflected profound differences in university leadership and management. And the three different approaches to professional training led to quite different approaches to managing and financing medical schools, law schools, and business schools. The medical schools and business schools, for different reasons, discovered that that tuition could not support their increasingly expensive educational programs, although law schools continued on the tuition-funded path. The chapter demonstrates the complications and policy implications of resource-dependent professional higher education.

These chapters, originally delivered as lectures in the Walter Prescott Webb Memorial Lecture Series at the University of Texas at Arlington in March 2017, provide a compelling series of snapshots of the intertwined problems of philanthropy and finance in the history of American higher education. The lectures focus on the United States, as did Webb, but they underscore the reality of the distinctiveness of the American experience, as Webb himself noted. For better or worse, however, in the twenty-first century the rest of the world seems to be moving in the neoliberal direction of the United States. Here and elsewhere, higher education is all too often perceived as a private good, one that primarily serves individuals—who ought to pay much or all of the cost of their own postsecondary and graduate education. The threat, from my point of view, is that higher education will be perceived as just another business, rather than as a crucial site of public engagement for the production of social capital. I think this would have surprised and disappointed Bernard Daly, just as it disappoints me.

Notes

1. Irving Kristol, "Foundations and the Sin of Pride: The Myth of the Third Sector," speech to the Council on Foundations annual meeting, 1980, https://www.hudson.org/content/researchattachments/attachment/1250/kristol_philanthropy_hudson_institute_2010.pdf.

2. Walter W. Powell, ed. *The Nonprofit Sector: A Research Handbook* (New Haven: Yale University Press, 1987); Barry Karl, "The Nonprofit Sector. A Research Handbook" (review), *Science* 236 no. 4804 (May 22, 1987): 984–85, http://science.sciencemag.org/content/236/4804/984.

3. Luc Botanski and Arnaud Esquerre, "The Economic Life of Things: Commodities, Collectibles, Assets," *New Left Review* 98 (March–April 2016), 31–54.

4. F. Emerson Andrews, *Foundation Watcher* (Lancaster, PA: Franklin and Marshall College Press, 1973), 159–60.

5. Merle Curti, *American Philanthropy Abroad: A History* (New Brunswick, NJ: Rutgers University Press, 1963); Merle Curti, *Fund Raising in the United States: Its Role in America's Philanthropy* (New Brunswick, NJ: Rutgers University Press, 1965); Merle Curti and Roderick Nash, *Philanthropy in the Shaping of American Higher Education* (New Brunswick, NJ: Rutgers University Press, 1965); Irvin G. Wyllie, *American Philanthropy: The Convergence of Public and Private Interests* (Grand Forks: University of North Dakota, 1966).

6. Peter Dobkin Hall, *Inventing the Nonprofit Sector* (Baltimore: Johns Hopkins University Press, 1992), 79.

7. To my knowledge the only current doctoral program in philanthropic studies is found at the Lilly Family School of Philanthropy, in which Bob Payton was later a professor, at Indiana University and Purdue University–Indianapolis, https://philanthropy.iupui.edu/.

8. Hall, *Inventing the Nonprofit Sector*, 251.

9. Ibid., 250.

10. "Philanthropy and Democracy: Which Comes First?" *Advancing Philanthropy*, Summer 1994, 34–39.

11. Benjamin Gidron, Stanley N. Katz, and Yeheskel Hasenfeld, eds., *Mobilizing for Peace: Conflict Resolution in Northern Ireland, Israel/Palestine, and South Africa* (Oxford: Oxford University Press, 2002).

12. Megan E. Tompkins-Stange, *Policy Patrons: Philanthropy, Education Reform, and the Politics of Influence* (Cambridge, MA: Harvard Education Press, 2016).

13. Thomas Piketty, *Capital in the Twenty-First Century* (Cambridge, MA: Harvard University Press, 2014).

14. Matthew Bishop and Michael Green, *Philanthrocapitalism: How the Rich Can Save the World* (London/: Bloomsbury Press, 2008). Of course, overall US charitable giving is also enormous. The *New York Times* reported on June 14, 2016: "Americans are now donating to charities and nonprofits at a record-high rate of more than $1 billion a day," http://www.times-standard.com/article/ZZ/20160613/NEWS/160619007.

1

The Road Toward Student Debt

The History and Politics of Paying for a College Degree

Thomas Adam and A. Burcu Bayram

During the first two decades of the twenty-first century, American colleges and universities faced substantial challenges with funding their operations. Diminishing incomes from endowments as a result of the financial crisis and cutbacks in state support have caused colleges—private and public—across the nation to raise tuition for all students significantly. From 1995 to 2015, tuition and fees at 310 national universities, all of which were included in editions of the *US News & World Report* best colleges rankings, rose considerably (Fig. 1.1). The average tuition and fee charges at private schools grew by 179 percent. Tuition and fees at public schools saw an even sharper rise. The average charges

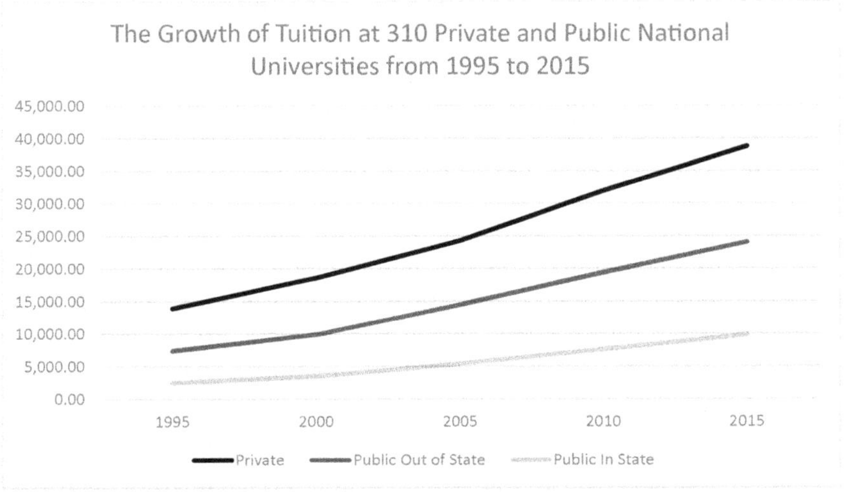

Figure 1.1. Growth of tuition at 310 private and public American universities from 1995 to 2015.

at public schools for out-of-state students grew by 226 percent, and the average charges for in-state students grew by 296 percent.[1]

These increases in tuition and fees forced students to take on more and more student loans. From 2005 to 2015, the amount of outstanding student debt more than doubled, rising from about $450 billion to more than $1.1 trillion. By 2017, outstanding student loans have reached more than $1.3 trillion and thereby have become the second largest type of household debt for American families after mortgages and home equity loans.[2]

More than 44 million Americans (14 percent of the total population) carry student loan debt. And more and more Americans have difficulties in paying back their student loans. In 2012, about 5.9 million people fell behind in their repayment of their student loans. "The amount of defaulted loans—$76 billion—is," according to the Project on Student Debt Report, "greater than the yearly tuition bill for all students at public two- and four-year colleges and universities."[3]

Economists and politicians have warned that the burden of this debt prevents young Americans from buying cars and houses and from starting a family. Economist Alvaro Mezza and others have recently established a negative correlation between increasing student loan debt and homeownership. They calculated that "a 10 percent increase in student loan debt causes a 1 to 2 percentage point drop in the homeownership rate of student loan borrowers for the first five years after exiting school." Student loan debt, thus, not only slows down the economic growth of individuals and families; it also negatively impacts the American economy by limiting the ability of Americans to participate in the consumption of goods and services. The "average student loan debt for Class of 2017 graduates was $39,400," and the average monthly student loan repayment amounts to $351.[4]

Besides these economic repercussions for individual Americans and the American economy in general, student loan debt also has a significant impact on the mental and physical health of young college-educated Americans. Increasing debt levels cause students to develop anxieties about their future. The decision about entering college, the length of college education, and opting for a graduate degree becomes as much a financial decision as it is a decision about the student's professional career and prosperity. Graduates who face the repayment of their student loans experience not only depression- and anxiety-related diseases but also diseases related to nutrition, since limited spending potentials force young Americans to forgo healthier food choices. Student debt creates a new generation of Americans that is much more susceptible to mental and physical diseases, thereby putting a higher burden on an already fragile American health care system.[5]

It is no wonder, therefore, that college affordability took center stage in the 2016 presidential election campaign. Suggestions for making college affordable and for improving public perceptions of vocational training dominated the discussions about education reform and unexpectedly propelled Bernie Sanders onto the national stage. Sanders received the support of millennials throughout the country when he made the radical but popular suggestion of providing college education at public colleges tuition-free. And even though he lost the bid for the nomination by the Democratic Party, he remains a steadfast champion of tuition-free education. During the Senate confirmation hearings of Betsy DeVos, who had been nominated by Donald Trump for the position of Secretary of the Department of Education, Sanders pointedly asked the nominee to share her views about making college education tuition free: "Will you work with me and others to make public colleges and universities tuition-free through federal and state efforts?" DeVos replied: "Senator, this is a really interesting idea and it's really great to consider and think about, but I think we also have to consider the fact that there is nothing in life that is truly free. Somebody is going to pay for it."[6]

Tuition and College Funding in Historical Perspective

Both DeVos and Sanders agreed that somebody must pay for college education. They disagreed, however, as to whom that should be. Sanders believed that the state should become responsible for financing college education. DeVos believed that it is up to students to pay for their education. Ironically, both Sanders and DeVos and many others who engaged in this debate did so without any awareness of the ways in which American colleges and universities have been funded in the past and how we ended up with the present student debt crisis.

The historical development of tuition and college expenses has received little attention among scholars of higher education and historians. Seymor E. Harris, in *The Economics of Harvard*, provides an in-depth historical study of tuition and student cost at Harvard, but little research has been done beyond this isolated case. Studies of student aid such as Rupert Wilkinson's book *Aiding Students, Buying Students* focuses on the historical dimension of student aid but does not explore the expenses of students for tuition and living. It seems that scholars who research student aid take the existence of tuition charges for granted.[7]

In two studies from the late 1920s, Walter J. Greenleaf and Ruth E. Anderson surveyed tuition costs. In 1928 Greenleaf presented his study of tuition and student expenses based upon data collected from 624 state and private colleges. This unpublished study represents the earliest systematic and national attempt at the collection of data about tuition fees. However, Greenleaf's study presented data about tuition fees without explaining the differences in tuition charges at the institutions he selected for his study. The more comprehensive and innovative study was conducted in 1929 by Ruth E. Anderson, who collected data about tuition fees at 271 endowed colleges and universities across the country. In contrast to Greenleaf, Anderson not only collected data, but she also sought to explain the different tuition fee levels by correlating tuition charges with nonfinancial factors. Her study suggests that tuition rates at private colleges were not or not only determined by the actual cost of educating students but were also related to other, noneconomic factors such as the relationship of the institution with a religious congregation, the size of the enrollment, the institution's age, and the institution's location.[8]

Both Greenleaf and Anderson were not historians and therefore did not investigate the fluctuation of tuition rates over time. Their studies were contemporary studies with an eye on tuition rates in the second half of the 1920s. They provide a starting point for a historical study, yet that study remains to be done. This essay undertakes that task based upon in-depth original archival research conducted at more than fifty university archives and special collections since 2010. This contribution provides one of the first systematic historical examinations of the road to student debt and by so doing informs current political and economic debates on one of the most important problems in American society. Without an understanding of the genealogy of how the current student debt crisis became what it is today, contemporary public and scholarly discourses will remain out of context. For as long as we do not have a comprehensive investigation into the history of college tuition, scholars and politicians will continue to claim that either college education was never free in the United States or that college education in fact had been tuition free for most students at some point in American history.

In this essay we show that the roots of the current student debt crisis are neither economic nor financial in nature but predominantly cultural. What led to the rise in college tuition and the exponential growth of student loans was a fundamental shift in the definition of college education from a public good designed to advance the welfare of societies to a private pursuit for self-aggrandizement. This cultural shift occurred at the beginning of the twentieth century in the larger context of social realignment of class and higher education.

A look into the history of American higher education reveals that tuition was neither an intrinsic part of the system nor did it mark the division between public and private colleges. Private and public colleges and universities were founded as charitable institutions supported by donors and religious associations. Often they did not charge students tuition or fees. And private and public universities were not separated by the imposition of tuition payments upon students. Private universities such as Stanford University were founded with the promise of a tuition-free education for in-state students. And several public universities and even land-grant universities charged tuition fees, since the Morrill Land-Grant Act of 1860 did not prohibit the charging of tuition to students at those institutions. In fact, land-grant universities such as Cornell University charged tuition from the outset. And public universities such as Indiana University, which was prohibited from charging tuition to residents by the state's constitution, introduced in 1880 a contingent fee of twelve dollars per year in lieu of tuition. While this fee was not called tuition, it slowly rose to reach the level of tuition charged at other public universities.[9]

Tuition fees certainly contributed to the income of colleges, but a look into the share of college incomes reveals that tuition has always represented only a *minor* share of the total college income (Fig. 1.2). Since tuition was introduced to the system of higher education in the second half of the nineteenth century, it accounted for only between 18 percent and 35 percent of overall college funding. And although tuition-based revenues for all American colleges grew in absolute numbers continuously and linearly from about $2.1 million in 1875 to about $100 million in 1925, the share tuition contributed to the

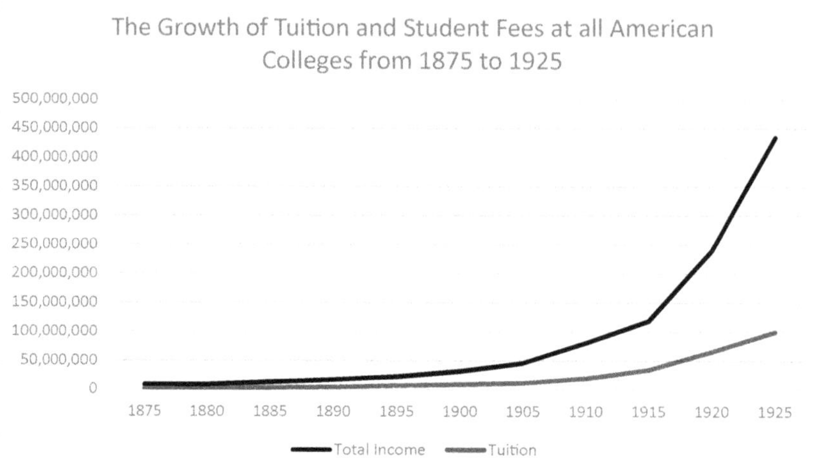

Figure 1.2. Growth of tuition and student fees at all American colleges from 1875 to 1925.

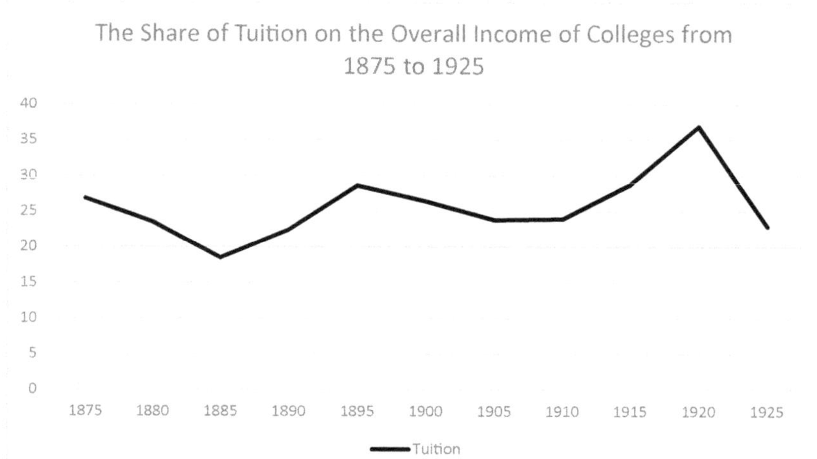

Figure 1.3. Tuition as a percentage of the overall income of colleges from 1875 to 1925.

overall income of colleges fluctuated significantly. In fact, the period from 1875 to 1925 saw several increases and decreases in the share of tuition in college income (Fig. 1.3).[10]

Even though tuition continued to increase in absolute numbers during the twentieth century, students paid only a small share of the cost for their education. In fact, tuition did not grow as fast as costs for teaching students did. The cost of educating college students rose significantly in the first half of the twentieth century, as the example

Table 1.1. Gross expense of Amherst College per student and tuition charged per student, 1900–1940

	1900	1910	1920	1930	1940
Instruction per student	$180	$212	?	$560	$520
Administration per student	$35	$60	?	$180	$180
Library per student	$14	$10	?	$26	$58
Buildings and grounds per student	$45	$46	?	$220	$210
Other expenses	$56	$0	?	$294	$232
Gross expense per student	$330	$328	$780	$1,280	$1,200
Tuition charged per student	$110	$110	$200	$400	$450

of Amherst College shows (Table 1.1). While Amherst spent only $330 per student in 1900, that amount had risen to $1,200 by 1940. The most significant factor in rising education costs was the cost for instruction. In 1900 it took only $180 per student to pay for instructors and professors. By 1940, that cost had risen to $520 per student. Amherst College absorbed only a small part of these rising costs by increasing tuition. Even though tuition fees quadrupled within just four decades from 1900 to 1940, the share students paid for their education through tuition rose only slightly from 33 percent in 1900 to 37 percent in 1940.[11]

The time from 1850 to 1910 was a period in which students could obtain a college education at the majority of colleges either free of charge or, at colleges that charged tuition, paid for by generous tuition scholarships provided by endowments and state scholarship programs. Colleges that charged tuition, such as Harvard, set those fees at comparatively low levels and abstained from increasing tuition. Charles W. Eliot, president of Harvard from 1869 to 1909, advocated for low tuition levels because he feared that increasing tuition fees would cause able but poor students to stay away from Harvard and turn that college into a resort for the rich.[12] Tuition fee levels at colleges such as Harvard remained, therefore, remarkably stable for six decades. Students at Harvard saw tuition go up only once during that period, in 1870 (Fig. 1.4).

And Harvard was not an exception. Tuition at other private colleges such as Washington University in Saint Louis and Princeton also rose very modestly during these six decades. Washington University also saw only one increase, in 1890, when tuition rose from $100 to

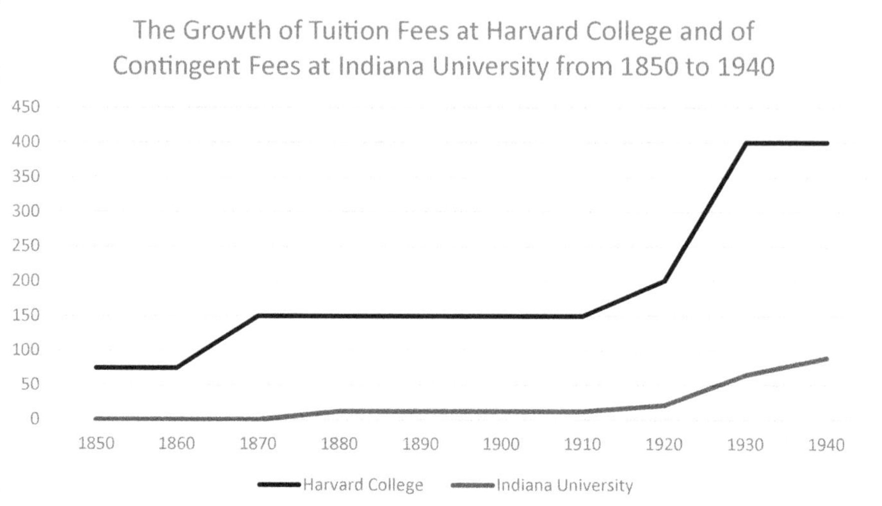

Figure 1.4. Growth of tuition fees at Harvard University and of contingent fees at Indiana University from 1850 to 1940.

$150. Princeton experienced a total of three tuition increases, bringing tuition from $50 to $75 in 1870, to $140 in 1890, and finally to $150 in 1900.[13]

Many universities, public and private, started out offering a tuition-free education. In some states, state legislature even prohibited the charging of tuition and included this stipulation into state constitutions. However, not every public university offered education free of charge. The University of Wisconsin as well as Indiana University asked their students to pay moderate fees of ten dollars and twelve dollars, respectively, per year. Other public universities, such as Oregon State University, started out with fees of eighteen dollars, then reduced them until tuition was free in 1900 before increasing them again to nine dollars by 1910. And universities such as the University of Texas and Stanford University offered college education free of charge for state residents.[14]

The 1910s and 1920s saw a sea change in attitudes towards tuition fees. The increases in tuition and fees became more frequent and steep. These increases were not merely a result of rising costs in education. Leading educators such as Trevor Arnett and donors such as William E. Harmon began to champion the idea that students should pay a larger if not the full share of what it cost to educate them. Subsequently, private universities such as Stanford, which had started out by offering tuition-free education, introduced tuition charges in 1920. Once introduced at Stanford, tuition increased rapidly. It rose to $340 in 1930 and to $520 in 1940. Stanford University was not even the most expensive college in the country. When Rollins College, Florida's oldest postsecondary institution, introduced in 1933 a tuition plan that charged students the full cost of their education, tuition (including room and board) at Rollins College was set at $1,350 per year. This made Rollins the most expensive college in the entire country.[15]

College Education as a Common Good

College education at private and public institutions had been, according to John D. Rockefeller, "practically free of charge" throughout the nineteenth century. Private colleges "were originally founded as charitable institutions, with the expectation that they would be maintained by contributions of philanthropic people." And the students trained at those institutions were expected to pay back by entering the ministry, accepting teaching positions at local public schools, or engaging "in some other professional activity in which the financial returns to them would be small but the gain to the public large."[16]

Tuition fees had become part of the American system of higher education by the early twentieth century, but paying tuition was still not an experience that every student had. Many students received tuition scholarships that covered all tuition charges. In some cases, though, such tuition scholarships, and those offered by state scholarship programs in particular, came with strings attached. Students were, for example, asked to pledge to work as a high school teacher for a certain number of years after graduation in exchange for a tuition scholarship. Such state scholarship programs proved beneficial to the students, the college, and the state. Students were enabled to obtain a college degree free of charge. Colleges received a significant form of income from the state that covered a share of their operating costs. And states were guaranteed a steady flow of teachers who contributed to the buildup of the state's school system.

In the case of the College of William and Mary, the state scholarship program of Virginia secured the very existence of that college. When it was transformed into a teacher training school in 1888, the Virginia legislature committed ten thousand dollars for a state scholarship program, which entitled "each county and city in the state" to send at no tuition cost at least one student each year to college. Each student selected for such a scholarship had to sign a pledge that stated: "In consideration of receipt from the State of Virginia of Free Tuition in the Teachers' Course, and other advantages incident to appointment as a State student of the College of William and Mary, and In compliance with the requirements of law, I hereby pledge myself to teach in the public schools of Virginia for a period of two years." It was the funds of this scholarship program that enabled the College of William and Mary, which had been brought to the brink of bankruptcy by the Civil War, to secure its continued existence.[17]

Many Midwestern states made provisions for tuition-free education from high school to college in their state constitutions. The constitution of Indiana, passed by the legislature in 1816, established in its Article VIII, section 2, that the legislature was to secure "a general system of education, ascending in regular gradation from township schools to a state university, wherein tuition shall be gratis and equally open to all." This sentiment of tuition-free education endured for most of the nineteenth century and influenced the decisions of legislators across the country. When in 1881 the Texas state legislature passed the law for the organization of the University of Texas, lawmakers insisted that men and women should be admitted to this new university "on equal terms without charge for tuition." And states such as Wisconsin that had initially mandated tuition fees for state colleges in the mid-nineteenth century abolished such tuition fees later. In 1848 the Wisconsin state legislature provided for tuition fees at the University of Wisconsin in the amount of ten dollars. That tuition fee was revoked for residents of Wisconsin by the legislature in 1878.[18]

Shifting the Burden of Paying for College Education to the Student

The notion that college education should be free to students who would benefit society led to the legal and constitutional ban on tuition at state universities and to the introduction of large-scale scholarship programs in states that permitted the charging of tuition fees, and it made college education in fact largely tuition-free up until about 1910. The introduction of tuition charges at private and public colleges and of incidental fees in lieu of tuition at public universities such as Indiana University, which was barred from charging tuition to students, reflected a fundamental change in the value attached to college education.

Considered a public good in the nineteenth century, college education was after 1910 increasingly considered a private affair. This shift in public perception impacted the funding of college education. As a public good, college education was paid for by the public through taxes and donations. As a private affair, college education had to be paid for by the individual student through tuition and student loans. This shift had various reasons, which included the secularization of college education with the shift from training ministers and teachers to educating engineers and scientists; the intrusion of Social Darwinist thinking and eugenics into higher education, which stressed the notion of "survival of the fittest"; and structural changes in the social composition of the student population from a middle-class to upper-class background. In 1927 John D. Rockefeller publicly campaigned for charging students the full cost it took to educate them. He advocated that students should also no longer receive scholarships but instead be provided with student loans. And his views resonated with the attitudes of educators, administrators, and donors across the country. "Today," Rockefeller said in 1927, "the majority of the students go to college for a good time, for social considerations or to fit themselves to earn money. The idea of service to the community is no longer the chief consideration. It would seem therefore that under these changed conditions the student might properly be expected to pay for the benefits he receives."[19]

Rockefeller's view was mirrored in the statement by Ervin T. Brown, the treasurer of Rollins College, who in 1933 justified the introduction of at-cost tuition at Rollins College by writing: "If all the people attending our endowed institutions were planning to submerge their personal welfare to the common good and take the vow of eternal poverty and service to humanity there is every reason for assuming the public should pay the entire cost of higher education, including board and room. When the present theory of college tuitions was established, this was more nearly correct. But now it is safe to assume that the vast majority of those pursuing undergraduate work are doing so for reasons which are primarily selfish."[20]

The private colleges of the 1920s were no longer populated by prospective ministers and teachers who were expected to serve the common good but increasingly by the sons of wealthy alumni who saw college as a social rather than an educational experience. Private colleges such as Amherst, Harvard, and Princeton experienced throughout the 1920s and 1930s a significant increase in the number of students who were admitted to their institution because they were related to an alumnus. From 1933 to 1940 the share of students at Amherst, which until 1975 did not admit women as students, who were relatives of Amherst alumni (not only sons) ran between 22 percent in 1934/35 and 37 percent in 1935/36 (Fig. 1.5). And at Princeton University, which admitted only men as students until 1969, the sons of alumni made up between 8.8 percent in 1927 and 15.9 percent in 1933. These colleges, thus, saw a significant increase in the self-recruitment of intellectual and economic elites.[21]

These students were increasingly coming from affluent families. Throughout the nineteenth century, colleges, including Harvard, kept tuition and fees low in order to keep their doors open to students from families with limited financial means. After 1910, more and more college students came from upper-middle-class families. Of the 147 national scholarship holders who attended Harvard College from 1938 to 1944, only 19.7 percent were students who came from lower-class families with annual incomes below $1,499. A significant share of 34.1 percent came from middle-class families with annual incomes in the rage from $1,500 to $3,999. But an astonishing share of 46.2 percent came from upper-middle-class families with annual incomes in excess of $4,000.

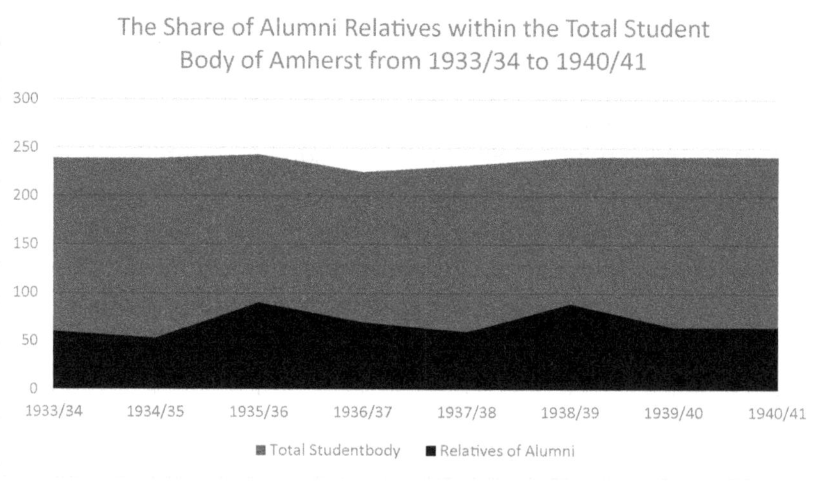

Figure 1.5. Number of relatives of alumni within the total student body of Amherst from 1933/34 to 1940/41.

These numbers are striking. First, scholarships, once intended to provide funding for students who could not afford to attend a high-priced college, were in the 1930s and 1940s given to students who came from families who could have paid for their children's college education. And children from upper-middle-class families represented the largest share among this segment of Harvard students. The doors of Harvard slowly but surely began to close for students from low-income families.[22]

And those students entering Harvard were expected to participate in social clubs and college athletics that had a high price tag. Beginning in 1880 the *Harvard University Catalogue* included estimates for "incidentals and social expenses" expected of Harvard students. From 1880 onwards these expenses were estimated to run between $40 and $200 depending on the lifestyle of the student. With tuition running at $150, these social expenses could reach an amount that was well above tuition charges (Table 1.2). These developments caused some

Table 1.2. Increase in annual student expenses at Harvard College, 1850–1900

Expense	1850	1860	1870	1880	1890	1900
Tuition	$75	$75	$150	$150	$150	$150
Room rent	$15	$20	$30–$100	$22–$175	$22–$175	$30–$200
Furniture				$10–$50	$10–$50	$10–$50
Board	$100	$140	$152–$304	$133–$304	$114–$304	$117–$390
Books and stationery	$12	$12	$16	$28–$61	$25–$61	
Incidentals and social expenses				$45–$200	$40–$200	$40–$200
Fuel and light				$11–$45	$11–$45	$11–$45
Clothing				$70–$300		
Laundry				$15–$50		
Servant				$0–$25	$0–$25	
Total	$202	$247	$348–$570	$484–$1,360	$372–$1,010	$358–$1,035

Sources: *A Catalogue of the Officers and Students of Harvard College for the Academic Year 1850–51, First Term* (Cambridge, MA: Metcalf and Company, 1850), 79; *A Catalogue of the Officers and Students of Harvard University for the Academic Year 1859–60, Second Term* (Cambridge, MA: Sever and Francis, 1860), 38; *A Catalogue of the Officers and Students of Harvard University for the Academic Year 1869–70, First Term* (Cambridge, MA: Sever, Francis, and Company, 1869), 36; *The Harvard University Catalogue, 1879–80* (Cambridge, MA: Charles W. Sever, 1879), 112; *The Harvard University Catalogue, 1889–90* (Cambridge, MA: Charles W. Sever, 1889), 160; *The Harvard University Catalogue, 1900–01* (Cambridge, MA: Published by the University, 1901), 531.

contemporary observers such as Philip A. Cowen, who worked for the Educational Research Division of the New York State Education Department, to conclude in 1930 that "some of our institutions have assumed the exclusiveness of country clubs."[23]

Scholarships as a means of supporting students in need fell out of favor with educators, politicians, and donors after 1910. After 1910 attitudes among college administrators and donors changed in favor of expanding student loan funds at the expense of scholarship funds. Capturing this transformation, Charles F. Thwing, president of Western Reserve University from 1890 to 1921, wrote in an article for *The Nation* in September 1918: "The gift was formerly the more usual; the loan is now becoming so." The new preference for student loan funds found its strongest support in the 1920s with the New York–based Harmon Foundation. Established in 1922 by the wealthy real estate developer William E. Harmon, this foundation took a leading role in collecting data about student loan funds at college campuses and in advancing a national student loan program. Challenging the position that "education is an inherent right of every man and woman capable of profiting by it" and that it "should be paid for by the state when the cost becomes too great a burden for the beneficiary," Harmon believed that "higher education is not an inherent right of the average man of adequate intelligence but rather a valuable privilege that should be paid for individually and not by society."[24]

A few years later, Walter J. Greenleaf, an associate specialist in higher education with the Department of the Interior's Bureau of Education, concluded in his report about student loan funds: "We are living in what appears to be the 'installment age' where people make large purchases by paying so much down, and so much per month. Higher education is no exception to the rule and as an investment, yields a high rate of interest with the passing years." And one unnamed university president went even further. In the Harmon Foundation–sponsored report *Student Loan Funds*, this president of an "important university" is cited as having stated: "The habit of granting free tuition and all kinds of scholarships, as a method of increasing student attendance, and of awarding all sorts of reductions and special terms to almost everyone who urgently asks for it, is a most harmful practice. It teaches young men somehow or other that the world owes them a college education, and that to require repayment in future years is somewhat harsh and unjust."[25]

By the end of the 1930s a college degree was considered a deeply personal affair. Young men and women entering college were no longer seen as doing so for the betterment of society, but rather as pursuing egoistic motives of a good job and high pay.[26] Such egoistic motivation justified in the eyes of contemporary educators, administrators, and donors that the students should pay for their college education. Brown summarized this changed perception when he wrote in 1933: "For the past ten years it has been the consensus of opinion of many leaders in the field of college financing that those who receive the benefits of higher education should pay the bill."[27] Tuition and student loans had become commonly accepted aspects of the economics of higher education. And from that moment onwards tuition charges continuously grew, and student loans became a major way to pay for them.

Student loans were of course not invented in the twentieth century but had their roots in the nineteenth century. The Harvard Loan Fund, created by Harvard alumni in 1838, was one early example of an institutional student loan fund. This loan fund resulted from the competition for students between Harvard College and Amherst College. Amherst attracted a considerable number of young but poor students, who were preparing for the ministry, from Boston and surrounding communities because it could offer significant financial support to those prospective students. Most of that support came, however, not from the college but from the American Education Society, which had been founded in Boston in 1815 to assist young men with limited financial resources to prepare for the ministry in Catholic and various evangelical denominations. The founding of this association was sparked by what was perceived by the religious leaders of Boston as a lack of educated ministers throughout the country. The Semi-Centennial Report of that society reminded its readers in 1866 of the dire situation with regards to the availability of ministers in the early decades of the American Republic. A population of roughly 8.5 million people was served by only 2,000 educated ministers, which meant that there was on average only one minister for every 4,251 people.[28]

The funds provided to students from the American Education Society were initially given in the form of scholarships. In 1819, just four years after the start of the program, the directors of the society felt, however, that their plan favored "indolence, idleness and extravagance." The scholarships were, therefore, replaced with loans, of which the beneficiaries had to repay after graduation half of the amount received.

And in 1826 the society's members changed the rules again by asking beneficiaries to refund the entire loan plus interest within a reasonable time after graduation. The scholarship program, thus, had become a student loan program that benefited students pursuing a religious training.[29]

Harvard remained, however, largely excluded from receiving funds from the American Education Society. In 1834 the society provided funding for 750 students at eleven theological seminaries, twenty-six colleges, and sixty-seven academies. The majority (421) attended colleges such as Amherst College (seventy-six students), Yale College (fifty-eight students), and Middlebury College (fifty-five students). Those three colleges received $4,714, $3,546, and $2,967, respectively, the largest shares of the $50,608 in scholarship funding. Harvard College, by contrast, received very little support by this Boston-based society. Only one student at Harvard was awarded a scholarship of $75 from the American Education Society in 1834.[30]

And since up until the Civil War Harvard's endowments for student aid were limited, it continued to lose students to Amherst and other regional colleges that benefited from the support of the American Education Society. Boston's Mayor Samuel A. Eliot and Harvard president Josiah Quincy were deeply unsettled by the luring away of young Boston men to colleges further away from Boston and Cambridge. In fall of 1838 both men entered discussions about endowing Harvard with financial means to compete for students with colleges such as Amherst, Yale, and Middlebury. The dire state of financial support for undergraduate students at Harvard College caused Quincy to consider a major fundraising effort to improve the support Harvard College could offer and thereby increase its attraction among the young men of Boston and surrounding communities. Quincy's plan to build a system of funding for students was helped by the pledge of one thousand dollars by an anonymous donor, "provided a sum not less than Ten Thousand dollars be raised." Pledged donations were, following the fundraising practice of the American Education Society, to be paid in annual installments over a period of five years. The donor further stipulated that the raised funds should be used to create a student loan fund that provided loans "never exceeding the actual quarter bills." Such a lending practice would, according to Quincy, give Harvard a competitive edge over the American Education Society. Quincy suggested "that a loan of only one hundred dollars a year, with the usual grant from the corporation, would place the reasonable expectations of the class of young men, whom I wish to see patronized—above the relative state of expectations arising from the present expenditure of the American Education Society in any other seminaries."[31]

Quincy asked Eliot to take a lead in the fundraising efforts. Eliot immediately seized the opportunity and composed a circular letter that "was sent to a selected list of Boston's richer citizens, asking them to subscribe to a fund to aid worthy students in Harvard College." The letter, which was signed by seven leading Harvard graduates, Samuel A. Eliot (1817), George Hayward (1809), Charles P. Curtis (1811), John A. Lowell (1815), John G. Palfrey (1815), William H. Gardner (1816), and Stephen C. Phillips (1819), stated:

> We are informed that a considerable number of young men of good character and indigent circumstances are, every year induced to go to other institutions for a collegiate education, though they would prefer Harvard, from the greater facility of procuring the pecuniary aid which is indispensible to them. Numerous inquiries are made of the President what assistance the college can give and when it is discovered that it is both trifling and uncertain, the inquirer seeks elsewhere for that which it would be better for him and the public if he could obtain at Cambridge. The funds which support in great part those who need assistance in other colleges are derived from the American Education Society, who devote something like $30,000 dollars a year to the support of about 600 young men. Of these scarcely any are to be found at Cambridge. The last year but one of their numerous beneficiaries entered Harvard. It is not a favorite institution with those who contribute to the funds of that Society; and it cannot be expected that its beneficiaries should ever be found at Cambridge in great numbers.[32]

The assets of the Harvard Loan Fund grew very slowly. From $11,250 at the start of the fund in 1839, the assets grew to only $29,763.99 within the next twenty years. Fifty years later, in 1889, the principal had reached $87,269.92. At the same time, Harvard administered fifty-two scholarship endowments with assets totaling $934,500.48.

The Harvard Loan Fund thus represented only 8.5 percent of the assets available for the support of needy students. Because of these very limited financial assets, until World War I the Harvard Loan Fund played a very minor role in Harvard's student aid program (Fig. 1.6).[33]

It was only after 1922 that the fund began to support a larger share of students who received financial aid. Additional donations of alumni, strategic investments of the fund's assets in stocks, and a changed climate in which student loans were seen as being of greater value than scholarships led to a significant growth in the assets of the fund and the number of students it supported. From 1922 to 1959 the principal assets of the fund grew from $238,000 to more than $2,000,000. These financial resources allowed the fund to provide an increasing number of students with student loans. In 1861 it provided 40 students combined loans of $1,600; in 1900 it supported 45 students with combined loans of $2,905; and in 1938 it aided 163 students with combined loans of $11,450.[34]

The Harvard Loan Fund was no exception. Student loan funds began to play an important role in paying for tuition, as the study of thirty-five colleges in the Greater Boston Area in 1931/32 shows. Of the 46,265 students enrolled at all thirty-five institutions, 6,116 students (13 percent) received financial aid in the form of scholarship

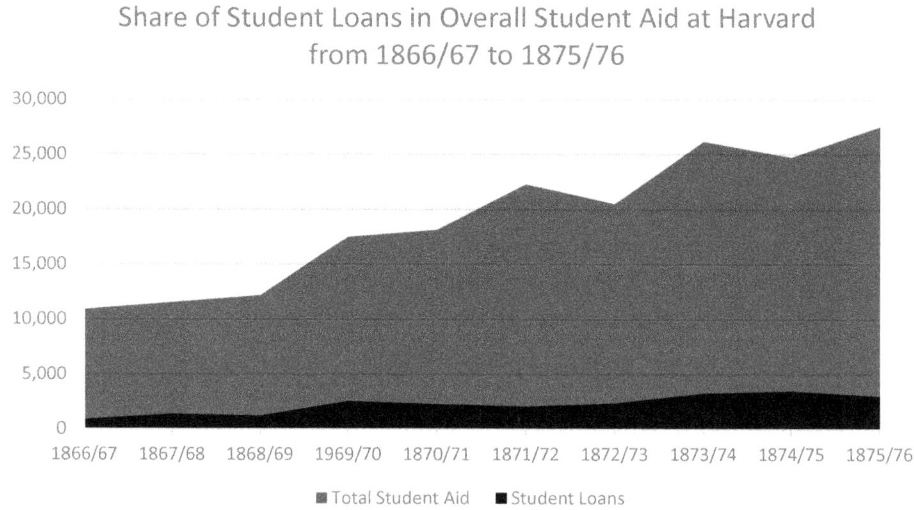

Figure 1.6. Student loans relative to overall student aid at Harvard from 1866/67 to 1875/76.

support and student loans. Student loans were provided to 2,238 of the 6,116 financially aided students (37 percent). At Harvard University the share of students who obtained loans accounted for 43 percent of all students receiving student aid. Only a fraction of these loans came from the Harvard Loan Fund. And at MIT the rate was, at 71 percent, exceptionally high. It seemed to contemporary observers that student loans would push aside scholarship aid. Scholarships were considered a remnant of the past; student loans were the future (Table 1.3).

Conclusion

In response to Senator Bernie Sanders, Betsy DeVos said that someone would have to pay for the college education of our young generation. And she strongly believes that it is the students who should shoulder the costs of their education. However, DeVos is a prisoner of a mindset in which tuition appears essential and a tuition-free education is just a dream. While she might be convinced that tuition charges could be lowered, offering education free of charge is beyond her power of imagination.

DeVos and perhaps many others in the government and the private sector at the beginning of the twenty-first century can hardly think outside the current framework of college funding that came into place nearly a hundred years ago. It was only during the 1920s and 1930s that tuition charges and student loans became an accepted and integral part of the economics of higher education. The reasons for the

Table 1.3. Student loans versus scholarship support at selected universities in the greater Boston area as of 1931/32

College	Total Student Population	Student Loans		Scholarships		Total Number of Students Aided	Total Amount of Student Aid per Year in Dollars
		Number of Recipients	Total Loan Amount per Year in Dollars	Number of Recipients	Total Scholarship Amount per Year in Dollars		
Boston University	13,909	189	$12,341	528	$45,609	719	$58,150
Harvard University	8,536	830	$221,925	913	$361,033	1,920	$639,727
Northeastern University	4,438	178	$7,291	151	$10,522	475	$32,758
MIT	3,188	592	$202,513	507	$150,367	836	$352,881

acceptance of both were not only and not even primarily financial considerations but rather cultural and social considerations. The shift in the social composition of the student body and the changing role of higher education in young men's lives caused influential donors such as Rockefeller and Harmon to call for a reevaluation of how colleges and students should be supported. Given that in the 1920s an increasing number of students came from families with ample financial means, and given that these students sought out college not for education but for social refinement, it seemed justified to Rockefeller that these young men should pay for their education.

It seems that the image of a college degree as the vehicle for individual enrichment has come to dominate the public perception of higher education ever since. College graduates' service to the community and the contribution of college graduates to the advancement of society have been pushed aside in favor of an interpretation that favors egoistic over altruistic motives. If we are looking for alternatives to the failing neoliberal funding model for college education, we will not find guidance in the system that has been in place since the 1930s. We need to look further back into the time before World War I to find an alternative with regard to the sources of funding for college education. College education in the nineteenth century was considered a public good. As a result, communities and the state considered paying the tuition bill through scholarships for students who in return promised to serve the common good by teaching high school for a certain number of years or by taking leadership positions within local communities. Tuition-free education can be realized only if college education is again reframed as a public good. For that to happen, students, communities, donors, and politicians would have to enter into a new social contract that would exchange tuition-free education for public service.

Notes

1. Travis Mitchell, Chart, "See 20 Years of Tuition Growth at National Universities," *US News & World Report*, Higher Education, July 29, 2015, http://www.usnews.com/education/best-colleges/paying-for-college/articles/2015/07/29/chart-see-20-years-of-tuition-growth-at-national-universities (accessed January 20, 2017).

2. Alvaro Mezza, Daniel R. Ringo, Shane M. Sherlund, and Kamila Sommer, "Student Loans and Homeownership," Finance and Economics Discussion Series 2016–010, 1, Washington, DC, Board of Governors of the Federal Reserve System, https://www.federalreserve.gov/econresdata/feds/2016/files/2016010pap.pdf

(accessed January 20, 2017); Michael Corkery and Stacey Cowley, "Household Debt Makes a Comeback in the US," *New York Times*, May 17, 2017, https://www.nytimes.com/2017/05/17/business/dealbook/household-debt-united-states.html (accessed August 25, 2017); Jillian Berman, "Watch America's Student Loan-Debt Grow $2,726 Every Second," *Market Watch*, January 30, 2016, http://www.marketwatch.com/story/every-second-americans-get-buried-under-another-3055-in-student-loan-debt-2015–06–10 (accessed August 25, 2017).

3. Andrew Martin, "Debt Collectors Cashing In on Student Loan Roundup," *New York Times*, September 9, 2012, A1.

4. Mezza et al., "Student Loans and Homeownership," 32; "A Look at the Shocking Student Loan Debt Statistics for 2017," https://studentloanhero.com/student-loan-debt-statistics/ (accessed July 8, 2018).

5. Katrina M. Walsemann, Gilbert C. Gee, and Danielle Gentile, "Sick of Our Loans: Student Borrowing and the Mental Health of Young Adults in the United States," *Social Science and Medicine* 124 (2015): 85–93; Katrina Walsemann, Jennifer A. Ailshire, and Gilbert C. Gee, "Student Loans and Racial Disparities in Self-reported Sleep Duration: Evidence from a Nationally Representative Sample of US Young Adults," *Journal of Epidemiology and Community Health* 70, no. 1 (2016): 42–48.

6. Bernie Sanders's questioning of Betsy DeVos is available on Youtube at https://www.youtube.com/watch?v=cjPHrKqYEgk (accessed January 20, 2017).

7. Seymor E. Harris, *The Economics of Harvard* (New York: McGraw-Hill, 1970), 53–66; Rupert Wilkinson, *Aiding Students, Buying Students: Financial Aid in America* (Nashville, TN: Vanderbilt University Press, 2005).

8. Walter J. Greenleaf, "Annual Student Expenses in State Colleges and Universities (December 1928)," six-page manuscript study, Archives of Washington University, Saint Louis; Ruth E. Anderson, "A Study of Tuition Fees in 271 Endowed Colleges and Universities," *Association of American Colleges Bulletin* 15 (May 1929): 285–332.

9. *Biennial Report of the President of the University on Behalf of the Board of Regents, to His Excellency the Governor of the State, 1886* (Sacramento: James J. Ayers 1886), 32; Lloyd Morey, "Student Fees in State Universities and Colleges," *School and Society* 28, no. 712 (August 18, 1928): 187; John Aubrey Douglass, *The Conditions for Admission: Access, Equity, and the Social Contract of Public Universities* (Stanford, CA: Stanford University Press, 2007), 19; *Fifty-Fifth Annual Report of the Indiana University, Including the Catalogue for the Academic Year 1884–1885* (Indianapolis: Wm. B. Burford, State Printer, 1885), 49.

10. Leo Jeannnot Chassee, *A Study of Student Loans and Their Relation to Higher Educational Finance* (New York: Harmon Foundation, 1926), 22, 30.

11. Alfred Sherwood Romer, 1917, Box 2, Folder 6, Amherst College Archives, Amherst, MA.

12. Harris, *Economics of Harvard*, 59.

13. The information about tuition was obtained from various annual catalogs and bulletins of these two institutions.

14. The information about tuition was obtained from various annual catalogs and bulletins of these institutions.

15. Wilkinson, *Aiding Students*, 108–9; Stanford University, *Nineteenth Annual*

Register, 1909–10 (Stanford, CA: Published by the University, May 1910), 65–66; Stanford University, *Twenty-Ninth Annual Register, 1919–20* (Stanford, CA: Published by the University), 77; Stanford University, *Fortieth Annual Register, 1930–31* (Stanford, CA: Published by the University), 137; Stanford University, *Fiftieth Annual Register, 1940–41* (Stanford, CA: Published by the University), 180; E. T. Brown, "A Daring Financial Plan: Commonsense Applied to College Financing," *The Educational Business Manager and Buyer* 11, no. 3 (March 1933): 7–8, 23.

16. "Remarks of Mr. John D. Rockefeller, Jr., acting as presiding officer at the Commencement Luncheon at Brown University, Providence, R.I., Wednesday, June 14th, 1927," 1, folder 135, Box 73, Subseries 8, Speeches, series Z, John D. Rockefeller Jr. Personal, FA 335, Office of the Messrs. Rockefeller Records (OMR), folder Colleges and Tuition, June 15, 1927, Rockefeller Archive Center, Sleepy Hollow, NY.

17. *Acts and Joint Resolutions Passed by the General Assembly of the State of Virginia during the Session of 1887–8* (Richmond, VA: J. H. O'Bannon, Superintendent of Public Printing, 1888), 512–13; Students—Teaching Pledges—1906–1920, President Tyler Papers, Archives Acc. 1984.19, University Archives, Earl Gregg Swem Library, College of William and Mary, Williamsburg, VA; *William and Mary College Catalogues No. 2*, 52–55; *Circulars of Information of the Bureau of Education No. 1, 1887* (Washington, DC: Government Printing Office, 1887), 64–66; *Catalogue of the College of William and Mary and State Male Normal College of Virginia, Session 1889–90* (Richmond, VA: Whittet & Shepperson Printers 1890), 31–32.

18. J. B. Sears, "Our Theory of Free Higher Education," *Educational Review* 65 (January 1923): 30–31; Indiana Constitution, Article VIII, section 2, http://www.in.gov/history/2874.htm (accessed November 30, 2016); *Bulletin of the University of Texas No. 140, Catalogue 1909–1910* (Austin, TX: The University, 1909), 27; *Laws of the State of Wisconsin Together with the Joint Resolutions and Memorials Passed by the Legislature at the First Session, Commencing on the First Day of June, and Ending on the Twenty-First Day of August* (Madison, WI: Rhenodyne A. Bird, 1848), 38–39; Tuition and Incidental Fees at the University of Wisconsin, 1852–1932, Compiled from Report of the Regents, University Catalogues, and Wisconsin Laws and Statutes, by Ann Neal, Wisconsin Legislative Reference Library, November 1932, 2, Subject Files, Tuition Fees, UW (folder 1), subfolder 1, University of Wisconsin Archives, Madison.

19. "Remarks of Mr. John D. Rockefeller, Jr.," 1–2.

20. Brown, "Daring Financial Plan," 8.

21. "Post War Plans for Amherst College (1944)," 19–20, Provisional Report, Alumni Committee on Admissions and Scholarships, Alfred Sherwood Romer 1917, Box 2, folder 6, Amherst College Archives, Amherst, MA; "Report of the Committee of Five," 12, 62–63, Alumni Organization Records, Box 4, folder Graduate Council Reports 1931, National Alumni Association of Princeton University, Graduate Council of Princeton University, May 15, 1931, Princeton University Archives, Princeton, NJ.

22. *The Harvard College National Scholarships: A Descriptive Report at the End of Six Years* (Cambridge, MA: Harvard University, 1941), 31–33.

23. Philip A. Cowen, *College Tuition Fees*, University of the State of New York Bulletin No. 941, February 1, 1930 (Albany: University of the State of New York Press, 1930), 6.

24. Charles F. Thwing, "Lending Money to College Students," *The Nation* 107, no. 2775, 263; Wilkinson, *Aiding Students*, 109; Harmon Foundation, *Student Loan Funds: A Study of Student Loan Funds and Their Administration Throughout the United States* (New York: Harmon Foundation, 1924), 5.

25. Student Loan Funds by Walter J. Greenleaf (Washington, DC, November 1928), 1, Georg Throop, Records, Series 03, Box 01, folder Student Loan Funds, Office of the Chancellor, Archives of Washington University, Saint Louis; Harmon Foundation, *Student Loan Funds*, 18.

26. By 1939/40 men still accounted for about 60 percent of the total student population of 1,494,000 students. Thomas D. Snyder, ed., *120 Years of American Education: A Statistical Portrait* (Washington, DC: Center for Education Statistics, 1993), 76.

27. Brown, "Daring Financial Plan," 8.

28. *Twenty-Third Annual Report of the Directors of the American Education Society, May 1839* (Boston: Perkins & Marvin, 1839), 57; Natalie A. Naylor, "'Holding High the Standard': The Influence of the American Education Society in Ante-Bellum Education," *History of Education Quarterly* 24, no. 4 (Winter 1984): 479–97; *Fiftieth Annual Report of the Directors of the American Education Society, Presented at the Annual Meeting Held in the City of Boston, May 28, 1866* (Boston: T. R. Marvin & Son, 1866), 9–10.

29. *Twenty-Third Annual Report*, 71–72.

30. Ibid., 38–40; *Eighteenth Annual Report of the Directors of the American Education Society, Presented at the Annual Meeting, Held in the City of New York, May 1834, with the Constitution and Rules of the Society* (Boston: Perkins, Marvin, & Co., 1834) 79–83.

31. *Endowment Funds of Harvard University, June 30, 1947* (Cambridge, MA: Harvard University, 1948), 85–169; Josiah Quincy to Samuel Eliot, August 30, 1838, 3–4, 7, 8, HUD 3529.525, Harvard Loan Fund (1838–1959), Harvard Loan Fund Miscellaneous I, Harvard University Archives, Cambridge, MA.

32. Letter signed by Samuel A. Eliot, George Hayward, Charles P. Curtis, John A. Lowell, John G. Palfrey, William H. Gardiner, and Stephen C. Phillips, October 16, 1838, 1–2, HUD 3529.525, Harvard Loan Fund (1838–1959), Harvard Loan Fund Miscellaneous I, Harvard University Archives, Cambridge, MA.

33. Untitled history of the fund (April 1938), 2, HUD 3529.525, Harvard Loan Fund (1838–1959), Harvard Loan Fund Miscellaneous I, Harvard University Archives, Cambridge, MA. The data on scholarship endowments comes from the statistical analysis in *Endowment Funds of Harvard University*, 85–169.

34. Untitled history of the fund (April 1938), HUD 3529.525, Harvard Loan Fund (1838–1959), Harvard Loan Fund Miscellaneous I, and Proposed Press Release, "How $11,000 Grew to $2,000,000," 5, HUD 3529.525, Harvard Loan Fund (1838–1959), Harvard Loan Fund Miscellaneous II, Harvard University Archive, Cambridge, MA.

2

The Introduction of National Scholarship Programs at Private Colleges in the Northeast in the 1930s and 1940s

Thomas Adam

Philanthropy was an integral part of American higher education from its inception. And the conflict over state interference into college education in the case of Dartmouth College—a privately and state funded institution—even contributed to the legal definition of philanthropy. Philanthropic support came in many forms and in many sizes. Funds to create scholarships for students were just one of the many ways in which donors could support a college of their choice. Such donations always came with conditions about the qualifications—gender, religion, race, place of residence—of the prospective student. Such donations for scholarship funds were, thus, almost always grounded in a (discriminatory) vision of the donor about the composition of the intellectual elite.[1]

Philanthropic action created a contact zone in which the visions of the college administration that sought funds and the visions of the donors who were willing to provide funds met. The visions of college administrators and donors often but not always aligned, and donors—as in the case of the national scholarship programs at Harvard and Princeton—went along with and supported the goals of these colleges. Both Harvard and Princeton embarked on an ambitious fundraising campaign for their respective national scholarship programs that was to enlarge the geographic reach in student recruitment of both institutions. And while scholars such as Jerome Karabel have portrayed this program exclusively in the context of anti-Semitic policies, college administrators at the time presented these programs as a way to overcome the parochialism of New England's private colleges in the pursuit of achieving the status of a national university. This expansion seems to have led to the inclusion of underrepresented ethnic groups such as Hispanics. Since college administrators at Princeton and Harvard insisted that this geographic expansion should not increase the overall student population, increasing the geographic diversity came, nevertheless, at the price of decreasing the share of Jewish students. In fact, some donors supportive of the national scholarship plan suggested that Harvard had too many Jewish students. They argued that Harvard could be a national university only if the share of Jewish students was to be in line with the overall share of Jews in the American population.[2]

When in 1935 Harvard president James B. Conant spoke of his vision for Harvard to become a national university, he defined a national university by the geographic and socioeconomic diversity of its student body. Realizing that such a project could be carried out only with extensive financial support by donors, college administrators such as Conant called upon the alumni and donors to provide the funding for national scholarships, which would enable talented but poor students from throughout the country to attend an expensive East Coast college. With this call he invited donors to share his vision and to help realize it, but he also invited donors to expand the program by offering their own visions.

This chapter will explore the creation of national scholarship programs at Harvard, Princeton, and Cornell during the 1930s and 1940s. These programs were intended to attract students from across the country to these colleges and thereby enhance the geographic diversity of their student populations. The first part of this chapter will discuss the geographic origin of the students at East Coast private colleges in the nineteenth and early twentieth centuries. During that time students at colleges such as Harvard, Dartmouth, Yale, and Princeton largely came from the immediate geographic environment of these colleges. The case of Princeton further highlights the increasing number of private school graduates among the student population. East Coast colleges saw in the 1920s and 1930s a significant increase in students who came from well-off families. These families could afford to pay the skyrocketing tuition fees and living expenses that increasingly limited access to these colleges. "It has even been said," Philip Cowen, research associate at the New York State Education Department, wrote about private East Coast colleges in 1930, "that some of our institutions have assumed the exclusiveness of country clubs."[3]

The second part of this chapter will analyze the national scholarship programs developed at Harvard, Princeton, and Cornell as well as the impact of those programs on colleges such as Stanford. The attempt to enlarge the pool of applicants by Harvard and Princeton was seen as a danger to universities such as Stanford. Stanford considered itself the premier school for students from the Pacific Coast. Harvard and Princeton's attempts to cut into that pool, and the enormous financial resources of those two colleges—by comparison with Stanford's—that were applied to their national scholarship programs, put Stanford at a decisive disadvantage and caused college administrators at Stanford to develop comparable ambitions. They also induced Stanford administrators to reconsider their position with regard to scholarship support for students. Initially, Stanford had very few scholarships to offer its students. That had to change if Stanford wanted to compete with colleges such as Harvard and Princeton, which offered extensive scholarship support to their students.

The Composition of the Student Body at Private Colleges on the East Cost

Throughout the nineteenth century colleges such as Harvard served primarily the population of their immediate surroundings. More than 81 percent of all students at Harvard from 1800 to 1859 came, according to Colin B. Burke, from the region of New England. Most students came from Massachusetts (about 75 percent), with 50 percent of these in-state students coming from the immediate surroundings of Cambridge and Boston (Table 2.1).[4]

Education at Harvard became in the first half of the nineteenth century, as Ronald Story has shown, an integral part of the life experience among Boston's leading families. Even though not all wealthy Brahmin families sent their children to Harvard, those who chose Harvard for the education of their progeny did so for the "sake of its social advantages." Harvard became a social extension of Boston's Brahmin culture. An education at Harvard, to apply Pierre Bourdieu's concept of interchangeable forms of capital, helped to convert economic capital into cultural capital.[5]

The large share of students from Massachusetts gave Harvard's student population a more distinct parochial character than the student populations at other East Coast colleges had. In the case of Dartmouth,

Table 2.1. Geographic origin of students at Harvard University, 1836–1859

Class of	Total Number of Students	Born in					
		Massachusetts		Neighboring States		Other States	
		total	in percent	total	in percent	total	in percent
1836	39	30	77%	2	5%	7	18%
1837	47	36	76%	5	11%	6	13%
1838	46	33	72%	7	15%	6	13%
1839	62	40	64%	10	16%	12	20%
1840	45	33	73%	7	16%	5	11%
1841	44	33	75%	8	18%	3	7%
1842	56	44	78%	5	9%	7	13%
1843	67	56	84%	8	12%	3	4%
1844	60	44	73%	6	10%	10	17%
1845	61	42	69%	9	15%	10	16%
1846	64	51	80%	9	14%	4	6%
1847	61	41	67%	10	16%	10	17%
1848	62	47	76%	5	8%	10	16%
1849	78	57	73%	6	8%	15	19%
1850	66	51	77%	4	6%	11	17%
1851	62	45	73%	9	14%	8	13%
1852	88	66	75%	10	11%	12	14%
1853	89	72	81%	6	7%	11	12%
1854	90	58	64%	12	13%	20	23%
1855	81	56	69%	9	11%	16	20%
1856	92	61	66%	14	15%	17	19%
1857	65	49	75%	6	9%	10	16%
1858	91	72	74%	9	10%	10	16%
1859	92	68	74%	13	14%	11	12%
Total	1608	1185	74%	189	12%	234	14%

Source: Charles Warren, "An Inquiry Concerning the Vital Statistics of College Graduates," in *Circular of Information of the Bureau of Education* for March, 1872 (Washington, DC: Government Printing Office, 1872), 19.

students from the state of New Hampshire formed the largest share of that college's student population. However, at 53 percent it was significantly below the share of in-state students at Harvard (Table 2.2).

And in the case of Yale, students from the state of Connecticut made up only 32 percent of total enrollment, a much smaller fraction of that university's student population. These significant differences might at least partially be explained by the size of these states. While Massachusetts had in 1860 a population of more than 1.2 million people,

Table 2.2. Geographic origin of students at Dartmouth College, 1837–1860

Class of	Total Number of Students	Born in					
		New Hampshire		Neighboring States		Other States	
		total	in percent	total	in percent	total	in percent
1837	35	17	49%	18	51%	0	0%
1838	41	20	49%	19	46%	2	5%
1839	61	37	61%	23	38%	1	1%
1840	53	33	62%	19	36%	1	2%
1841	75	43	57%	31	41%	1	2%
1842	85	47	55%	32	38%	6	7%
1843	75	51	68%	24	32%	0	0%
1844	60	37	62%	21	35%	2	3%
1845	62	30	48%	28	45%	4	7%
1846	27	17	63%	10	37%	0	0%
1847	47	28	60%	15	32%	4	8%
1848	49	27	55%	17	35%	5	10%
1849	40	18	45%	12	30%	10	25%
1850	45	24	53%	16	36%	5	11%
1851	44	22	50%	19	43%	3	7%
1852	62	29	47%	26	42%	7	11%
1853	49	20	41%	20	41%	9	18%
1854	55	28	51%	23	42%	4	7%
1855	51	22	43%	26	51%	3	6%
1856	58	30	52%	22	38%	6	10%
1857	61	35	57%	14	23%	12	20%
1858	57	27	47%	23	40%	7	13%
1859	68	27	40%	33	48%	8	12%
1860	65	34	52%	23	35%	8	13%
Total	1325	703	53%	514	39%	108	8%

Source: Charles Warren, "An Inquiry Concerning the Vital Statistics of College Graduates," in *Circular of Information of the Bureau of Education for March, 1872* (Washington, DC: Government Printing Office, 1872), 20.

Connecticut and New Hampshire counted about 460,000 and about 326,000 inhabitants, respectively (Table 2.3).[6]

If we compare the share of students each college attracted not just from their home state but also from neighboring states, it becomes clear that these colleges drew predominantly students from East Coast states. Eighty-five percent of Harvard students came from Massachusetts and the surrounding states. In the case of Dartmouth, the share of students who came from New Hampshire and its surrounding states reached

Table 2.3. Geographic origin of students at Yale University, 1837–1860

Class of	Total Number of Students	Born in					
		Connecticut		Neighboring States		Other States	
		total	in percent	total	in percent	total	in percent
1837	102	56	55%	27	26%	19	19%
1839	91	47	52%	27	30%	17	27%
1840	99	33	33%	33	33%	33	33%
1841	78	27	35%	27	35%	24	30%
1842	98	40	41%	38	39%	20	20%
1843	94	43	46%	28	30%	23	24%
1846	80	23	29%	28	35%	29	36%
1848	86	30	35%	20	23%	36	42%
1849	91	22	24%	27	30%	42	46%
1850	78	22	28%	26	33%	30	38%
1851	92	28	30%	38	41%	26	29%
1852	93	32	34%	23	25%	38	41%
1853	100	32	32%	39	39%	29	29%
1854	99	24	24%	38	38%	37	38%
1855	91	25	27%	33	36%	33	37%
1856	97	26	27%	37	38%	34	35%
1857	107	31	29%	38	35%	38	36%
1858	102	21	21%	41	40%	40	39%
1859	105	26	25%	40	38%	39	37%
1860	108	29	27%	53	49%	26	24%
Total	1891	617	33%	661	35%	613	32%

Source: Charles Warren, "An Inquiry Concerning the Vital Statistics of College Graduates," in *Circular of Information of the Bureau of Education for March, 1872* (Washington, DC: Government Printing Office, 1872), 20.

92 percent. Yale showed 68 percent of its students coming from Connecticut and surrounding states—a much lower share than Harvard's and Dartmouth's. The share of students coming to Yale from regions outside the Northeastern states increased from 1837 to 1860. In 1837 only 19 percent of the student body came from states outside the New England region. Twenty-three years later that share had increased to 24 percent. In the 1850s the share of students from faraway states ran as high as 35 percent. Among the suppliers of students were many Southern states, such as Alabama, Georgia, and Mississippi. However, Colin B. Burke's suggestion that Yale had overcome the geographic limitation with regards to its student population does not seem to be

supported by statistical evidence.[7] From 1837 to 1860, more than two-thirds of all Yale students came from Connecticut and its bordering states.

In the aftermath of the Civil War, students' preference for local colleges continued to determine the composition of the student populations at East Coast colleges with regards to the geographic origin of its students. Only 32 percent of Harvard's student population in 1871 came from outside of Massachusetts. And Harvard was not an exception among the colleges in Massachusetts. Of the 1,186 college students enrolled at six colleges of Massachusetts, which included the College of the Holy Cross, Harvard University, Tufts College, Boston College, Amherst College, and Williams College, 656 students (55 percent) came from Massachusetts, 166 students came from New York State (14 percent), and another 103 students (9 percent) came from the other bordering states of New Hampshire (31), Vermont (33), Connecticut (29), and Rhode Island (10). Seventy-eight percent of the total college student population at these six colleges, thus, came in 1871 from either Massachusetts or its neighboring states.[8]

In general, students from Massachusetts and New England attended colleges in their home state or in a neighboring state within New England. Very few of the students enrolled at New England's colleges came from outside of that region—mainly from Michigan, Illinois, and Ohio. The share of students from states other than the East Coast and the three Midwestern states ran far below 10 percent.

Table 2.4. Geographic origin of student populations at selected eastern colleges and universities as of 1870–71

College/ University	Total Number of Students	Geographic Origin of the Student Population											
		CT	IL	ME	MA	MI	NH	NJ	NY	OH	PA	VT	Other States
Amherst College	260	20	8	10	119	1	6	1	40	7	11	11	26
Columbia College	196	0	0	0	0	2	0	21	168	0	1	0	4
Cornell University	609	10	22	5	21	17	11	15	343	37	37	9	82
Dartmouth College	381	6	10	23	44	3	139	0	22	15	0	85	34
Harvard University	658	3	9	22	423	2	20	5	65	20	23	3	63
Rutgers College	181	0	0	0	0	0	0	124	52	0	2	0	3
Yale College	645	209	19	8	40	5	4	26	156	39	54	1	84

Source: *The Harvard College National Scholarships: A Descriptive Report at the End of Six Years* (Cambridge: Harvard University, 1941), 45–50.

The report about Harvard's National Scholarship Plan published in 1941 readily admitted that "Harvard's enrollment has in the past consisted too exclusively of students from New England and the East." And the report continued: "Not only can a boy who lives in one of the New England states, or in New York, New Jersey, or Pennsylvania, come to Harvard more easily than can a boy from the South or West, but also the idea of coming to Harvard is a more familiar one to him than it is to a boy to whom Harvard is remote in every sense of the word."[9]

The overrepresentation of students from the New England and Mid-Atlantic states at East Coast colleges continued into the first half of the twentieth century. In 1944 an internal memorandum about Amherst's student body composition came to the conclusion that there were too few students at Amherst and Harvard from regions other than the Northeast. About 77 percent of Amherst's students came in the 1930s from New England and the Mid-Atlantic states. In 1934 about 29 percent came from New York State, 20 percent from Massachusetts, 13 percent from New Jersey, 9 percent from Pennsylvania, 7 percent from Connecticut, 4 percent from Ohio, 3 percent from Illinois, and 15 percent from other states. The authors of the memorandum lamented that very few students "come from west of the Mississippi River or from the middle western states; Amherst had few south of the Mason and Dixon line." Throughout the 1930s and 1940s less than 1 percent of Amherst students came in fact from Southern states and only about 5 percent from states west of the Mississippi.[10]

The situation at Princeton was not much different. A look at the composition of the classes from 1915 to 1934 at Princeton shows that students from New York and New Jersey formed consistently and continuously, with 43.1 percent in the class of 1915 and 48.2 percent in the class of 1934, the largest segment. A significant share of students also came from Pennsylvania. The latter group accounted for 24.4 percent of the class of 1915 and for 18.8 percent of the class of 1934. About two-thirds of Princeton's total undergraduate student population came, thus, from the three states of New York, New Jersey, and Pennsylvania (Table 2.5).[11]

The internal memorandum about the composition of Amherst's student body in 1944 not only showed concern for the geographic limitations of Amherst's reach across the United States, but also for the college's limitations with regard to the socioeconomic background of its

Table 2.5. Geographic origin of the Princeton undergraduate student population for the graduating classes 1915–1934

Class	1934	1933	1932	1931	1930	1929	1928	1927	1926	1925	1924	1921	1918	1915
Total Number of Students admitted	629	615	611	606	605	633	629	629	635	585	452	353	397	401
New England	23	22	25	24	27	35	29	38	25	36	20	12	25	16
New York	159	139	156	162	140	140	135	172	170	175	137	97	100	98
New Jersey	144	165	134	132	129	135	131	106	129	105	84	73	75	75
Eastern Pennsylvania	83	61	89	72	77	82	85	81	55	53	51	46	45	58
Western Pennsylvania	35	28	29	30	45	37	25	32	39	35	25	29	24	40
Potomac	36	44	32	37	39	30	40	46	34	26	25	18	22	20
Southern	15	26	20	19	18	13	15	14	25	16	11	9	9	16
Midwestern	51	48	46	39	43	52	44	46	53	49	31	24	28	23
Chicago	38	26	26	32	30	48	44	34	38	34	26	12	19	10
Northern	9	7	8	4	7	8	16	8	5	19	2	5	7	3
Saint Louis	10	19	22	28	20	23	27	20	28	10	0	6	21	17
Rocky Mountain	5	8	4	3	6	7	3	5	9	4	1	4	6	4
Northwestern	2	2	0	3	3	0	3	5	4	5	2	2	5	4
Pacific	8	2	3	5	9	8	13	7	6	8	3	2	4	5
Southwestern	5	9	6	7	8	9	8	8	8	5	23	6	3	0
Foreign	6	9	11	9	4	6	11	7	7	5	11	8	4	3

Source: Report of the Committee of Five, 52, National Alumni Association of Princeton University, The Graduate Council of Princeton University, May 15, 1931, Alumni Organization Records, Box 4, folder Graduate Council reports, 1931, Princeton University Archives, Princeton, NJ.

student population. Throughout the 1930s between 27 percent and 32 percent of Amherst students had graduated from private schools. And between 20 percent and 35 percent of the students had obtained their preparatory training at both a public high school and a private school. The number of students with public high school diplomas ran, thus, between only 33 percent and 50 percent. In 1940/41 students who had attended private schools either fully or partially accounted for 67 percent of all students admitted for that year to Amherst. Since tuition for private preparatory schools was quite significant, the college administrators reasoned that these students came from well-off families.[12]

Amherst was not the only college in New England that favored admission from private schools. And the doors to these private colleges were, as the example of Princeton shows, closing to children from public high schools. A statistical analysis of the entering classes by type of school—private or public—from the "Report of the Committee of Five" of the Graduate Council from the year of 1931 concluded that the share of graduates of private schools among the students of the entering classes increased from 69 percent in the class of 1915 to 85 percent among the students of the class of 1934.[13]

During the period from 1922 to 1933, graduates of high schools accounted for far less than a quarter of the students admitted to Princeton (Table 2.6). While the overrepresentation of private school graduates among the college student population deeply worried administrators at Amherst, Princeton administrators showed little concern. The secretary of the Admissions Committee at Princeton even wrote in a letter to Lewis N. Lukens Jr., the chairman of the Graduate Council Committee on Scholarships, in December 1933 that the committee had never concerned itself with deliberating "how many high school boys we want at Princeton." In the eyes of the secretary, attendance of a private school was commensurate with better academic preparation and higher intelligence, while attendance of a public high school was not considered sufficient for admission to a private college such as Princeton. "Obviously fewer high school boys go on to college and those that do are usually the cream of a high school class."[14]

These private school graduates came from a small number of private academies and preparatory schools in New England. In fact, the twelve schools listed in Table 2.7 supplied, of all Princeton students, between 31 percent in the class of 1915 and 44 percent in the class of 1934.[15]

Table 2.6. Source of Princeton's undergraduate population, 1922–1933

Year	Total Number of Students	Private Schools		High Schools	
		Absolute Numbers	Share of Total Student Number	Absolute Numbers	Share of Total Student Number
1922	607	492	81.1%	115	18.9%
1923	622	473	76.0%	149	24.0%
1924	620	519	83.7%	101	16.3%
1925	611	506	82.8%	105	17.2%
1926	604	508	84.1%	96	15.9%
1927	601	539	89.7%	62	10.3%
1928	602	517	85.9%	85	14.1%
1929	611	514	84.1%	97	15.9%
1930	630	536	85.1%	94	14.9%
1931	632	521	82.4%	111	17.6%
1932	632	536	84.8%	96	15.2%
1933	595	500	84.0%	95	16.0%

Source: Secretary of the Admission Committee to Lewis N. Lukens Jr., December 19, 1933, table attached to letter, Office of the Secretary Records, Box 22, folder 19, Princeton University Archives, Princeton, NJ.

The Drive Toward National Universities

Several East Coast colleges, including Harvard, Amherst, and Princeton, sought to break free from the geographic and socioeconomic limitations on their student populations and sought to establish themselves as truly national and democratic institutions of higher education in the 1930s and 1940s. Harvard president James B. Conant envisioned the transformation of Harvard from a local into a national college as a duty of a privately endowed college. In his address at the celebration of the fiftieth anniversary of Bryn Mawr College in November 1935, Conant insisted that only privately endowed colleges "have the opportunity of being national institutions in a sense which is all but impossible for the publicly supported colleges dependent on local taxes, the chief concern of which is quite rightly with the boys and girls of the city or State in which they are located." Private colleges, by contrast, were in Conant's view not bound by local or state limitations and at least in theory were open to students from all corners of the United States. Conant went a step further by suggesting that the intermingling of students from all states of the United States appeared necessary to prevent sectionalism. "In our colleges," Conant wrote, "it may be largely overcome; in our academic communities we have the

Table 2.7. Number of graduates entering Princeton from selected private schools

School/ Academy	State	Class of													
		1915	1918	1921	1924	1925	1926	1927	1928	1929	1930	1931	1932	1933	1934
Andover	MA	4	4	6	13	31	25	14	20	31	14	13	11	20	14
Choate	CT	0	2	3	3	4	11	12	14	14	7	12	13	17	20
Exeter	NH	7	13	16	17	33	32	28	44	28	36	28	28	33	34
Hill	PA	20	20	31	25	20	19	32	31	33	20	25	31	15	18
Hotchkiss	CT	1	0	15	1	14	16	15	20	22	25	21	15	19	21
Hun	NJ	0	0	1	7	7	9	6	15	18	21	28	32	24	30
Kent	CT	0	3	0	9	6	11	7	8	6	4	19	8	6	18
Lawrenceville	NJ	49	37	39	35	56	61	52	59	58	49	69	43	65	59
Mercersburg	PA	11	13	13	11	20	31	21	21	25	39	36	45	34	22
Newark	NJ	8	9	8	13	7	13	4	11	17	12	12	11	10	8
Princeton	NJ	14	18	4	15	10	17	7	15	12	16	15	12	10	17
St. Paul's	NH	12	18	12	14	9	14	19	19	9	21	17	25	13	15
Total		126	137	148	163	217	259	217	277	273	264	295	274	266	276

Source: Report of the Committee of Five, 54–55, National Alumni Association of Princeton University, The Graduate Council of Princeton University, May 15, 1931, Alumni Organization Records, Box 4, folder Graduate Council Reports, 1931, Princeton University Archives, Princeton, NJ.

privilege of accomplishing that synthesis of local tradition and pride which must be the basis for a healthy national federalism."[16]

Conant, further, identified the exclusion from college education of students from families with insufficient means as a threat to society. With the "vanishing of the frontier" and lesser opportunities for social mobility, American society was, in Conant's pessimistic prediction, "to become more highly stratified." An intermingling of students from all parts of the country had to overlap with an intermingling of students from all socioeconomic backgrounds. Conant pleaded that "unless promising talent is given every opportunity for higher education, our democracy will fail to realize the great potentialities which are inherent in our widely developed public school system." And he added: "We can not afford to let the accident of birth cripple the educational opportunities of youths of promise."[17]

Conant's call for (re)opening Harvard's doors to students from poor families is reminiscent of Charles W. Eliot's advocacy for low tuition. Eliot resisted any attempts to raise tuition during his presidency, which lasted from 1869 to 1909. And tuition was kept at $150 per year during his tenure. Eliot feared that increasing tuition would have caused able but poor students to stay away from Harvard and turn that college into a resort for the rich.[18] And his concerns appear to have been justified, as more and more Harvard students in the 1920s and 1930s came from rich families that could afford the annual tuition, which quickly increased from $150 in 1910 to $400 in 1930.

Conant's call for the geographic expansion of Harvard's pool of applicants was, by contrast, unprecedented. He wanted Harvard to become a leading national institution. And the provision of scholarships to poor but talented students from all parts of the country was the key to realizing his vision. In 1934 Harvard College began to shift existing scholarship funds toward its innovative and unprecedented National Scholarship Plan. Acknowledging that traditional scholarships with a maximum stipend of four hundred to five hundred dollars a year provided insufficient funds to support a student whose expenses for tuition alone amounted to four hundred dollars, Conant wished for the national scholarships to provide a living stipend so that the beneficiary did not feel the need to accept jobs to support his existence. And since these scholarships were to attract students from far away and from families who could not support their sons financially, Conant insisted that they run as high as one thousand dollars during the first year in college. In contrast to older scholarship funds that provided funding for just one year, these scholarships were awarded for one year and, if the student fulfilled the academic expectations of his teachers, were granted for the following three years at twelve hundred dollars each year.[19]

In the first year of the National Scholarship Plan only ten students were admitted from the six Midwestern states of Ohio, Indiana, Illinois, Michigan, Wisconsin, and Minnesota. "This group of states was selected for the experiment," the "Memorandum Concerning National Scholarships at Harvard" read, "because the money available was not sufficient to take care of candidates from an indefinite area; because these states possess good secondary schools which keep significant records of their scholars; because relatively few of their schools are already preparing the majority of their boys for Harvard and other eastern colleges; and because these states are not too remote from Cambridge." In 1935 the geographic scope of the program was expanded to include the states of Kentucky and Iowa. In 1936 students from Missouri and Tennessee became eligible to apply for one of the scholarships. In 1937 another five states in the South and along the Pacific Coast—Louisiana, New Mexico, California, Oregon, and Washington—were included in the plan. For Harvard College administrators, the National Scholarship Plan had thereby become "more truly national in scope."[20]

The slow growth of the program was due to the limited means of scholarship funds. The program was not funded from the general endowment of the university but from existing and newly created scholarship funds that were given to Harvard by donors who determined the geographic origin of potential beneficiaries. It was, therefore, not Harvard College's vision alone that drove the direction of this expansion. The donors who put up the money for the scholarships shaped the geographic reach of the National Scholarship Plan as much as Harvard administrators did. And the vision of individual donors did not always align with the visions of Harvard administrators and educators. Jerome Karabel has described the National Scholarship Plan as primarily driven to keep Jewish students out of Harvard, since the geographic diversity disadvantaged Jewish students, who derived mostly from the Northeast of the country.[21]

Even, if that were the case, the program provided at the same time opportunities for the inclusion of students from other ethnic backgrounds, such as Hispanics, as the example of the Bronson Cutting Scholarship shows. Funded by Mrs. W. Bayard Cutting, Mrs. Bayard James, and the Marchesa Iris Origo of Siena, Italy, this scholarship, created in memory of the late US senator Bronson M. Cutting, provided scholarships for students from New Mexico. The donors, further, specified that preference should be given to an applicant of Spanish-American descent. This stipulation was motivated by the interest of Bronson M. Cutting "in the Spanish-American citizens of New Mexico" and the realization that this native population possessed very limited financial means and opportunities for obtaining a college degree. The donors also asked Harvard College to overlook the differences in the "educational standards in New Mexico from those prevailing in Eastern schools" in selecting the recipient of this national scholarship. They asked that every reasonable effort be taken to "find desirable candidates from New Mexico." If a suitable candidate was not available from New Mexico, the donors allowed the college to consider applicants from Arizona, Texas, and Oklahoma.[22]

Thirty-one men received support under the National Scholarship Program from 1934 to 1937. Of these thirty-one students, five came from Ohio, four from Missouri, three from Illinois, three from Minnesota, three from California, and two each from Indiana, Michigan, New Mexico, and Oregon. The states of Wisconsin, Kentucky, Iowa, Louisiana, and Washington each sent one student to Harvard under the plan. Ten of the thirty-one students came from well-off families who could afford a private school education for their children. These students who were not in need of financial support were awarded the title of a national scholarship holder but not the full financial award. Instead, they received a nominal award of one hundred dollars. To avoid a public discrediting of these scholarships, the college administration kept the stipends awarded to individual students a secret, wrote the dean of Harvard, "because the Scholarships are awarded as prizes regardless of need, and we do not want to make a public distinction between those who are receiving help and those who are not."[23]

Of the 161 scholarship holders for the period from 1938 to 1944, all but 14 received a cash award. Of the fathers of the 147 students receiving a financial award, 50 (34 percent) had annual incomes of less than $2,000 (Table 2.8). The most often given occupations of the students' fathers were teacher (20), engineer (12), farmer (10), executive (9), merchant (8), lawyer (7), salesman (7), and clerical worker (7). There were only two truck drivers and two carpenters but no factory workers. Twelve students had already lost their father.[24]

While the distribution of the scholarship holders across income groups according to the income of their fathers seems to be quite balanced, students from families with yearly incomes below five hundred dollars were significantly underrepresented, and students from families with incomes above four thousand dollars appear to be highly overrepresented. In fact, 32.6 percent of these students came from families with incomes above four thousand dollars, while these families accounted for only 20 percent of the total population. And only 2.7 percent of students came from families with incomes below five hundred dollars, whereas these families formed 9.6 percent of the total population.

The dean of Harvard College described the National Scholarship Plan as "a valuable service to the nation by widening the opportunities for higher education." Many of the students admitted under the plan came from small towns with little opportunity for access to college. In fact, 43.5 percent of the 161 students had grown up in towns of less

Table 2.8. Income of the fathers of national scholarship holders, 1938–1944

Income of Father	Number of Fathers in This Income Group		Share of Families With That Income in the Total Population in 1944
	In Absolute Numbers	In Percentage Points	
$0–$499	4	2.7%	9.6%
$500–$999	12	8.2%	9.5%
$1,000–$1,499	13	8.8%	10.7%
$1,500–$1,999	21	14.3%	10.8%
$2,000–$2,499	17	11.6%	11.6%
$2,500–$2,999	12	8.2%	10.2%
$3,000–$3,499	11	7.5%	10.4%
$3,500–$3,999	9	6.1%	7.5%
$4,000–$4,499	18	12.2%	4.7%
$4,500–$4,999	11	7.5%	4.1%
$5,000–$5,999	7	4.8%	4.6%
$6,000–$6,999	4	2.7%	6.3%
$7,000 and over	8	5.4%	
Total	147	100.0%	100.0%

Source: *The Harvard College National Scholarships: A Descriptive Report at the End of Six Years* (Cambridge: Harvard University, 1941), 33. The information about the general income structure of American families is derived from US Department of Commerce, Current Population Reports, Consumer Income, Washington, DC, January 28, 1948, 8.

than ten thousand inhabitants. "A large number of the applications are farm boys," the dean's report reads, "whose families because of economic conditions are unable to furnish anything beyond a small sum toward their education."[25]

And yet these scholarships were considered among Harvard students who came in the 1920s and 1930s from privileged East Coast families as "badges of poverty" rather than signs of academic achievement. University administrators involved in the introduction of the National Scholarship Plan felt compelled to address the association of scholarship aid with poverty. The authors of "Memorandum Concerning National Scholarships at Harvard" (1938) freely admitted that in "most American colleges the acceptance of a scholarship by a student has been, generally speaking, tantamount to a declaration of poverty." Furthermore, scholarship holders were seen as bookworms and asocial beings, since they had to take up additional jobs to secure the funding for their education. Scholarship holders, therefore, had neither the money nor the time to engage in college athletics "or any of the pleasant social activities of the college world."[26]

Private colleges such as Harvard were in the 1930s dominated by students who came from well-off families that could afford to pay hundreds of dollars for tuition, room, and board and for the social activities increasingly associated with college life. The authors of the memorandum showed confidence that the linkage between scholarship aid and poverty could slowly be broken with programs such as the National Scholarship Plan. They even contended that there were already some signs of improvement. This "change has been accelerated by the conscious efforts of college administrators to disassociate academic honors and awards from the earlier exclusive connection with aids to the needy." A rising number of applicants for the National Scholarship Plan seemed to the authors as evidence of this change in attitude. Hundreds of students applied every year for a place in the coveted scholarship appointments. In 1936, to take just one example, 203 candidates entered the competition for seventeen scholarships.[27]

The National Scholarship Plan introduced at Harvard College in 1934 caused other colleges along the East Coast from Amherst to Princeton to introduce similar schemes. In 1944 Amherst entertained the creation of a national scholarship program along the lines of Harvard's plan. And while plans for a national scholarship program surfaced at Princeton in the aftermath of World War I, it took until 1948 before such a national scholarship program was finally introduced. In March 1919 Princeton president John Grier Hibben announced in an article published in the *New York Evening Post* that he would dedicate significant funds—about one million dollars—to give Princeton "the character and scope of a national university." Hibben was convinced that for any university to be considered a national university it must "draw from all sections of the country." To attract students from the South and the West to Princeton, Hibben revealed that Princeton University was "planning an important extension of the system of competitive regional scholarships that will direct deserving men to us from the remote sections of our country, who otherwise could not afford to pay the additional money necessary for travelling expenses."[28]

Even though this initiative failed, the Regional Scholarship Program with temporary and permanent scholarships was introduced at Princeton in 1919. The funds did not come from the university but from individual donors and alumni associations. From 1919 to 1934 a total endowment of $533,481.60 was accumulated for providing scholarships of $200 to $500 to students from selected cities and regions "who without financial assistance might not be able to secure the advantages of an education at Princeton University."[29]

By 1934 Princeton was able to provide 82 scholarships of this kind. Fifty-nine were funded by endowments and 23 by annual contributions of donors and alumni clubs (unendowed scholarships). From 1934 to 1946 the total endowment for these regional scholarships grew from $533,481.60 to $968,558.00. This endowment was projected to produce an interest of $36,320.54 in 1945/46 (Table 2.9). It permitted the university to create 102 scholarships averaging $373.73 each. These scholarships were, however, insufficient to cover even tuition charges, which ran at $450 annually. The endowments were, furthermore, very unevenly distributed across the alumni districts. The only alumni regions with substantial endowments were Pennsylvania, the District of Columbia, and Maryland-Michigan. These three regions together held 68 percent of all endowment funds as of 1945. The alumni district of Pennsylvania had, with 34 percent of the total endowment assets, by far the largest endowments.

The success of the Regional Scholarship Program was therefore rather limited in scope and geographical reach. The projected income

Table 2.9. Princeton's regional scholarship endowments

Region	Endowment as of 1934	Endowment as of 1945	Estimated Income 1945-46 (3.75%)
California, Oregon, Washington	$26,000.00	$44,508.58	$1,669.07
Colorado	$0.00	$2152.50	$80.72
Connecticut	$10,850.00	$23,350.00	$875.62
Delaware	$10,315.87	$22,352.50	$838.22
District of Columbia	$0.00	$195,418.69	$7,328.20
Georgia	$0.00	$543.14	$20.37
Illinois	$6000.00	$31,000.00	$1,162.50
Iowa	$1000.00	$2,000.00	$75.00
Kentucky	$0.00	$5,790.09	$217.13
Louisiana	$0.00	$312.00	$11.70
Maryland, Michigan	$132,847.01	$132,847.01	$4,981.76
Massachusetts	$0.00	$362.32	$13.59
Michigan	$0.00	$5,745.78	$215.47
Minnesota, North Dakota, South Dakota	$5,019.77	$5,019.77	$188.24
Missouri	$11,113.50	$46,320.12	$1,737.01
New Jersey	$35,000.00	$71,037.29	$2,663.52
New York	$0.00	$2,525.00	$94.69
Ohio	$33,397.90	$38,317.90	$1,436.92
Pennsylvania	$251,938.45	$328,955.31	$12,335.81
Texas	$10,000.00	$10,000.00	$375.00
Total	$533,481.60	$968,558.00	$36,320.54

Source: The Report of the Special Committee on Scholarships, Princeton, May 17, 1946, 29–31, Graduate Council of Princeton University, Alumni Organization Records, Box 4, folder Graduate Council Reports, 1946, Princeton University Archives, Princeton, NJ.

for 1945 from the endowment in ten of the twenty regions was far below the tuition charged at Princeton. And only eight regions—with four being in the Northeast—could provide multiple scholarships of $500. However, a scholarship of $500 was simply not sufficient to support needy students during their education at Princeton. With tuition at Princeton University rising from $250 in 1920 to $450 in 1930, and with a minimum budget in 1930 for room, board, books, and so on, of $427, these regional scholarships proved largely insufficient in attracting students from families with low incomes. It was not only the small scholarships paid out by the university but the utter lack of scholarship funds designated for students from the South and the West that stymied Princeton's plans of making its student population more inclusive in geographic terms. An undated internal memorandum from the early 1940s lamented Princeton's excruciatingly short list of scholarship funds for students from the South and the West. The report read: "In all the States south of the Mason-Dixon line and west of Pennsylvania, the number of endowed scholarships of standard size is but 39, or slightly less than 10 per year; if Maryland and the District of Columbia are excluded, there are but 25 or 6½ per year. Only 7 exist west of the Mississippi, and only 3½ east of the Mississippi and below the Mason-Dixon line."[30]

The inauguration of a national scholarship program represented a much greater challenge to Princeton than it did to Harvard because of the rather slow growth of scholarship funds at Princeton. While Harvard and Yale received their very first scholarship endowment long before 1800, the very first such endowment was given to Princeton only in 1853. From 1853 to 1858 donations for scholarship endowments poured in. Within these five years the university received 64 such endowments. Another major push for scholarship endowments occurred in the years from 1885 to 1890, when 27 scholarship endowments were donated to Princeton. By 1900 the number of scholarship endowments at Princeton University had risen to 107. However, 97 of these 107 endowments came with assets of only $1,000. The remaining 10 endowments were provided with assets ranging from $1,500 to $15,000. The total endowment capital of scholarship funds at Princeton was in 1900 only $139,000. That was significantly less than the scholarship endowment funds at Harvard, which were $1,180,896, and at Yale, $396,157, in 1900. Even Amherst, with $210,000, and Dartmouth, with $171,800, had more assets in scholarship endowments than Princeton at that time.[31]

The low endowment assets for scholarship funds at Princeton University set that university apart from other colleges and universities in New England and throughout the country. Scholarship endowments at other institutions rarely came with funds below $3,000. There was one more distinguishing mark of these scholarships. While the selection of beneficiaries at other colleges was left to scholarship committees staffed by the university, in the case of Princeton University the donors had "the privilege . . . of selecting the student who shall enjoy its income."[32]

These scholarship funds were never sufficient to award scholarships that provided a living stipend. With tuition running at $150 in 1900, these scholarship endowments gave beneficiaries stipends of approximately $50 and thereby paid for just one-third of tuition charges. Recognizing the shortcomings of the scholarship system at Princeton, the university decided to pool all scholarships with endowment assets of less than $5,000 into one fund to maximize the income from the investment of the principal. The university also embarked on several fundraising campaigns to increase the assets of scholarship endowments. A minimum of $5,000 was established for all endowments. As a result of these two measures, the total endowment of the general scholarship funds grew from $139,000 in 1900 to $680,567.96 by 1934. Even with this progress, Princeton University did not catch up with the scholarship support provided by similar colleges in New England and New York (Table 2.10).[33]

Table 2.10. A comparison of undergraduate scholarships and loans at five colleges in the Northeast, 1932/33

	Princeton	Harvard	Yale	Columbia	Cornell
Undergraduate Enrollment	2,307	3,390	3,101	1,965	4,800
Total Value of Scholarships	$113,067.00	$180,613.00	$322,178.85	$137,862.00	$203,000.00
Total Number of Scholarship Holders	345	545	680	500	800
Share of Scholarship Holders on Undergraduate Population	15%	16%	22%	25%	17%
Average Amount of Scholarship	$327	$331	$474	$275	$253
Minimum and Maximum Value of Scholarships	$30–$1,000	$100–$1,259	$32–$1,100	$250–$500	$50–$600
Total Amount of Student Loans	$56,898.89	$37,140.00	$49,000.50	$195,000.00	$74,384.00
Total Number of Loans	252	552	223	1278	642
Share of Loan Holders on Undergraduate Population	11%	16%	7%	65%	13%
Average Amount of Loan	$225	$67	$220	$152	$155
Annual Tuition Fee	$450	$400	$450	$300	$400

Source: A Comparative Study of Scholarships and Loans at Six Universities, 1932–1933, Office of the Secretary Records, Box 22, folder 18, Princeton University Archives, Princeton, NJ.

An investigation into the scholarship support for six northeastern colleges in 1932/33 showed that only 26 percent of all undergraduate students at Princeton received either scholarships or student loans. The number of students receiving financial aid at Yale stood at 29 percent, at Cornell at 30 percent, at Harvard at 32 percent, and at Columbia at a staggering 90 percent. In this group of colleges Princeton occupied last place with regard to the amount of scholarship aid and with regard to the share of the students who received such aid.

An undated memorandum concerning scholarships from Princeton University contended: "It is becoming increasingly difficult to attract students from a distance, particularly from the West. One very considerable obstacle is the rapid growth and development of the local State Universities, which offer extensive opportunities near at home at very low comparative cost." High tuition fees at Princeton of $450 (as of 1930) and the lack of sufficient scholarship support to offset the costs of an education at Princeton limited its appeal among high school graduates outside of the Northeast. Tuition-free education at state universities became a great temptation for students who pursued professional careers. But it was not only low tuition and state universities that offered competition to Princeton. Harvard and Yale sought out the best and the brightest from the same pool of applicants as Princeton did. And Harvard and Yale had more to offer than Princeton with regard to financial support. "Harvard early recognized these conditions and undertook to offset some part of the difference in cost and carfare by establishing regional scholarships. Today, Harvard has a scholarship in every State in the Union, and in some States more than one, averaging from $250 to $350 per year. Yale has been not far behind. In Cleveland, for example, Yale Alumni are maintaining four scholarships paying $400 per year." And the memorandum concluded: "With a very few local exceptions, Princeton has no scholarships of this character, and we are unquestionably at a heavy disadvantage in this respect."[34]

Princeton's progress in expanding the national scope of its student population was hampered by the comparatively small number of alumni associations and their limited participation in the recruitment of students and the endowment of scholarship funds. While the number of Princeton University's alumni association scholarships lagged far behind similar scholarships provided by their counterparts at Yale and Harvard, each network of alumni-sponsored scholarships showed significant regional limitation. Fifteen of the twenty-two alumni association scholarships at Princeton were provided by alumni associations located in the two states of New York and New Jersey (Table 2.11). In the case of Harvard, eleven out of fifty-one scholarships went to students from Massachusetts, and another eleven scholarships went to neighboring states of the Northeast. Therefore, nearly 50 percent of the Harvard alumni scholarships were given to students

Table 2.11. Geographic scope of scholarships funded by alumni associations, 1932/33

State	Princeton	Yale	Harvard
Arizona	0	0	1
California	1	2	3
Colorado	0	2	1
Connecticut	3	28	2
Delaware	0	0	1
Georgia	0	0	1
Hawaii	0	2	0
Illinois	0	13	3
Kentucky	1	0	0
Maryland	0	0	2
Massachusetts	0	4	11
Michigan	0	1	1
Minnesota	0	0	2
Missouri	0	2	2
Nebraska	1	0	1
New Hampshire	0	0	2
New Jersey	6	7	1
New York	9	18	5
Ohio	0	11	4
Oregon	0	1	0
Pennsylvania	1	8	3
Rhode Island	0	1	2
Tennessee	0	1	0
Washington	0	0	1
Washington, DC	0	1	1
Wisconsin	0	2	1
Total	22	104	51

Source: Exhibit 6, Scholarships Founded and Maintained by Alumni Associations or Clubs, Office of the Secretary Records, Box 22, folder 18, Princeton University Archives, Princeton, NJ.

from New England and New York. The distribution of Yale alumni scholarships was very similar: twenty-eight scholarships went to students from Connecticut, and another thirty scholarships went to students from New England and New York.

Thurston J. Davies, the secretary of the Graduate Council at Princeton, developed a plan for a national scholarship program based upon a network of scholarships provided by local alumni associations. Referring to an existing local scholarship endowment for students from Western Pennsylvania and the Armstrong Scholarships, which provided support for four students from Michigan and four students from Maryland, Davies conceived of this program as a donor-driven program with little financial support from the general endowment of the university. He suggested that each alumni association was to provide one scholarship of five hundred dollars for one student each year. In addition to this scholarship each association was expected to pay another five hundred dollars per year for the duration of fourteen years into an endowment fund for one endowed scholarship. With contributions of five hundred dollars each year, each alumni association would have accumulated at least seven thousand dollars in endowment assets after fourteen years. This fund would yield sufficient income to maintain one perpetual scholarship. This approach would give a substantial number of scholarship endowments to Princeton, reduce the contributions of alumni association members, since after fourteen years annual contributions would no longer be needed, and secure Princeton a wide net for attracting future students. "The permanent endowment of a number of these scholarships," Lewis N. Lukens Jr., the chairman of the Graduate Council Committee on Scholarships wrote confidently, "would do as much to insure the permanence of national enrollment as any single step that could be taken."[35]

In April 1945 Minot C. Morgan, secretary with the Bureau of Student Aid and Employment at Princeton University, submitted a draft plan for a national scholarship program similar to the one inaugurated at Harvard eleven years earlier. Since Princeton had little chance to compete for brilliant students with Harvard because of its low scholarship support of only five hundred dollars, Morgan suggested that the regional scholarships at Princeton should be raised to one thousand dollars per year. Since only one hundred thousand dollars were available for this new program, Morgan, further, insisted that no student from New England, the Middle Atlantic States, Maryland, Virginia, West Virginia, and the District of Columbia should be considered for these scholarships. For the purpose of selecting students from outside of that region, the country was to be divided into seven districts. Each district was to select one student each year who was to be sent to Princeton with the promise of four years of uninterrupted funding.[36]

As in the case of Harvard, the expansion of the scholarship program was seen as key to securing a national standing for Princeton. An internal (undated) memorandum on scholarships from the late 1930s established that about one-third of all undergraduate students at Princeton were "enabled to meet a part, and, in some cases, all of their college expenses through financial aid by the University, or through employment, or through a combination of both." And while this high degree of support seemed to be an accomplishment, the unnamed author reminded the reader that "to assure to Princeton the continuance of her position as a University, at once democratic in character and national in scope, we need an adequately endowed scholarship program."[37]

It seems that the exclusion of students from the Northeast from this program, which was after all intended to bring students from outside of the region to campus, did not fare well with the alumni association of Princeton. When the national scholarship program was finally inaugurated in fall of 1948, the program offered twenty instead of seven scholarships, and the country was for admission purposes divided into twenty districts that included all parts of the Northeast. In fact, five of the twenty scholarships went to students from the New England and Mid-Atlantic states. The scholarship amounts were set at eight hundred dollars for residents in the five northeastern districts and twelve hundred dollars for the remaining fifteen students from the rest of the United States.[38]

Enormous sums were needed to fund the Regional Scholarship Program. The full costs for each scholarship were estimated to run between twenty-five thousand and thirty-five thousand dollars depending on the geographic region. These sums were required to create endowments that could produce a sufficiently large interest each year to pay out scholarships in the range from eight hundred to twelve hundred dollars.[39]

From the beginning of the discussion about broadening the geographic scope of its student population, Princeton administrators left no doubt that the geographic expansion should not lead to an increase in the overall student population. Princeton as a privately endowed university was "under no obligation to educate the many; its special task is to educate the few and to educate them well." However, the trustees of Princeton University acknowledged that while their institution is to educate the few and not the many, access to this privileged education should "not be restricted entirely by economic circumstances." Mirroring the argument put forward by Harvard president Conant, the trustees also invoked the perceived freedom of privately endowed colleges, since they were not restrained to focus on the education of local college populations in order to receive state and local funding. In contrast to state universities, privately endowed colleges, free from such local limitations, were expected "to supply the national influences which result from the enrollment representing all sections of the country."[40]

A manual for the Princeton scholarship committees throughout the country reminded those involved in the selection process of President Harold Willis Dodd's statement in his report for 1934/35, in which he insisted "that the students on [Princeton's] campus will always represent a cross-section of the best elements in American Life." In order to accomplish this lofty goal, "adequate provision must be made for the *properly qualified* and *deserving* student whose family's financial position makes the cost of a Princeton education too great." However, even this manual that stressed the support of financially needy students on its front page went on to state that scholarships should be awarded only "to boys of fine character and of exceptional intellectual capacity and personality." Financial need of potential beneficiaries was ranked third after the donor's wishes and academic performance. "Scholarship aid is distinctly not charity," the manual stressed, "but neither is it a prize in recognition of achievement." It concluded with the statement that "scholarships are for those only who would otherwise be unable to attend Princeton."[41]

While Harvard, Princeton, and Amherst created general nationwide scholarship programs in pursuit of securing a national standing, Cornell in 1935 inaugurated, with the McMullen Regional Scholarship Plan, a nationwide scholarship program that was targeted exclusively toward students of engineering. The funds for this program came from the bequest given to Cornell in 1921 by the owner of the

Atlantic, Gulf and Pacific Dredging Company, John McMullen of Norwalk, Connecticut. McMullen had left the residue of his estate, which was valued at two million dollars, to Cornell for the purpose of training engineers. After McMullen's two nephews, Frank and James McMullen, successfully challenged his will, the inheritance was split between the family heirs and the university, giving Cornell one million dollars for the McMullen Endowment. Initially the endowment was used to annually award nine scholarships of five hundred dollars to three students in each of the three schools within the College of Engineering.[42]

In 1934 the College of Engineering decided to revamp the use of this endowment and developed the McMullen Regional Scholarship Plan. This plan was to address the decline of the attraction of Cornell's engineering program across the country. Rising tuition fees and increased competition from state universities with advanced engineering programs caused the enrollment in Cornell's engineering program to decline steadily from over 1,600 students in 1921 to 787 in 1936 (Table 2.12). The university thus lost more than half of its student population in engineering in just fifteen years. This decline had started

Table 2.12. Decline of the enrollment in Cornell's College of Engineering, 1921–1936

Year	Tuition	Number of Students				
		Civil Engineering	Mechanical Engineering	Electrical Engineering	Chemical Engineering	Total
1921/22	$250	358	940	315	0	1,613
1922/23	$250	237	800	317	0	1,444
1923/24	$250	337	667	360	0	1,364
1924/25	$300	355	536	369	0	1,260
1925/26	$300	345	477	371	0	1,193
1926/27	$300	351	434	374	0	1,159
1927/28	$300	353	448	335	0	1,136
1928/29	$350	323	449	288	0	1,060
1929/30	$400	291	457	254	0	1,002
1930/31	$400	324	493	230	0	1,047
1931/32	$400	303	558	224	0	1,085
1932/33	$400	263	458	212	3	937
1933/34	$400	218	442	195	5	860
1934/35	$400	170	452	204	1	827
1935/36	$400	153	439	188	7	787

Source: Table I attached to letter addressed to Dean D. S. Kimball, December 11, 1935, Livingston Farrand Papers, 1921–1939, Box 19, folder 29, Cornell University Archives, Cornell, NY.

in the early 1920s and predated the Great Depression, which, according to the university administrators at the time, had only a very limited impact on this development.

Declining enrollments threatened the very existence of the college that was equipped to train twelve hundred students. At the beginning of the 1930s the College of Engineering had too many faculty for the shrinking student population. To reverse this trend, the directors of the three schools within the college, Solomon C. Hollister, Herman Diederichs, and Paul M. Lincoln, called the attention of the university administration to the problem and made three suggestions. Since the rise in tuition had been identified as one of two major reasons for the decline in student population, the three directors suggested that lowering tuition from four hundred dollars to two hundred dollars would significantly increase Cornell's attraction among potential students. "Such a figure," the three directors wrote in their letter to Dean Dexter S. Kimball, "compares favorably with non-resident tuition in many state schools; and in those schools the non-resident enrollment is about 40%." However, the authors also realized that cutting tuition in half "would require double the present enrollment to yield the same income from this source." The second suggestion was to lower the entrance requirements. The directors warned, however, that such a step "would automatically require a reduction in standards for graduation. The result would be a loss of the prestige acquired over the years."[43]

The third suggestion concerned financial aid and the funds available from the McMullen Endowment. These funds were to be redirected toward a national scholarship program that was to provide scholarships of two hundred dollars each to students from throughout the nation. Offering such a scholarship, which would pay for half of the tuition charges at Cornell University, would make the university competitive again, since it would effectively lower tuition charges to two hundred dollars. It was this third suggestion that found the support of the dean of the College of Engineering and the university administration. Beginning in 1934 Cornell offered fifteen regional scholarships of two hundred dollars for a term of four years. The number of these regional scholarships quickly increased to thirty in 1940. The scholarships were to help the university in regaining ground lost in the competition with state universities and to secure for Cornell a nationwide reservoir of potential students of high academic standing in the field of engineering.[44]

American colleges did not exist in a vacuum, and decisions made at one college had an impact on other colleges. The inauguration of national scholarship programs at northeastern colleges brought them into competition with private universities such as Stanford in the West and Tulane in the South. Stanford, which considered itself the premier university for the West Coast, was affected by the national ambitions of Harvard and Princeton. With Harvard and Princeton developing national scholarship programs that were to bring more and more students from outside the Northeast to their campuses, universities such as Stanford lost out. Stanford came late to the game of providing scholarship support for students from poor families. This lack of scholarship funds was a result of the university's decision not to charge tuition to residents of California when the university was opened in 1891. In fact, Stanford provided tuition-free education to California residents for almost three decades from 1891 to 1920.

After tuition was introduced and quickly increased from an annual $120 in 1920 to $340 in 1930 and to $520 in 1940, Stanford became the target of donors who were willing to provide scholarship support for students in need. The number of undergraduate scholarship funds increased from three by 1920 to thirty by 1940. The total endowment of undergraduate scholarship funds rose from $18,000 in 1920 to $362,608 in 1940. Stanford's scholarship endowments were, however, in 1940 still just a fragment compared to the funds available at Harvard. The inauguration of national scholarship programs at northeastern colleges put Stanford at a further disadvantage. Stanford had been founded with the mission to provide a cutting-edge education tuition-free for talented young people from the Pacific Coast. Harvard and Princeton's campaigns to entice students from throughout the nation—including the Pacific Coast—to come to their campuses and their ability to offer substantial scholarships cut into Stanford's pool of students.[45]

In an internal report about scholarship support and the admissions program, Director of Admissions Rixford K. Snyder complained that too many of the young people from California preferred to go to Harvard and other East Coast colleges rather than to Stanford. As reason for this development Snyder singled out the lack of scholarship support. Snyder wrote that "studies have made it evident that Stanford is losing outstanding young men to those universities and colleges with extensive scholarship programs. The Stanford program . . . is grossly inferior to other comparable institutions. This inferiority is definitely resulting in the fact that outstanding young men are going elsewhere because of greater scholarship opportunities."[46]

Snyder compiled for his report data about the scholarship support at Stanford and at institutions he considered comparable to Stanford. Table 2.13 was the result. While Stanford had by 1952 quite an impressive endowment of nearly $40 million and scholarship endowments (for undergraduate and graduate students) of more than $3.6 million, it was unable to provide scholarship support at the level of other institutions considered for this comparison. With only 8 percent of students supported, Stanford was far behind Harvard, Princeton, and Yale.

Snyder developed in 1952 a vision for Stanford that ran along the lines of the national scholarship programs previously developed by Harvard and Princeton during the 1930s and 1940s. He suggested that Stanford should raise the share of students of each freshmen class supported by scholarships from 8 to 20 percent. And he continued: "As a long range goal, Stanford University should be on a par with Princeton, Yale, and Harvard with a program bringing twenty-five to thirty percent of the undergraduate student body to the university with scholarship assistance."[47]

Snyder's reasoning for expanding scholarship support was guided not by expanding the socioeconomic circle of potential students but by making sure that children with middle-class background could continue to obtain a college degree. For children with working-class background, a degree from a private college, Snyder freely admitted, was "completely beyond their means." But even the middle class faced increasing challenges to meet the financial costs of a college degree at a university such as Stanford. Rising tuition and living costs for students made even students from middle-class backgrounds more and more dependent on scholarship support.[48]

In a confidential communication to the Board of Governors of Stanford Associates, Snyder went even further by suggesting that "rising cost are tending to make it impossible for all but the wealthiest students to attend an independent college or university." And Snyder was not alone in his warning about the exclusion from higher education of students from poor families. The September 1951 issue of the journal *Scientific American* was dedicated to the place of higher education in American society. Several authors stressed the need for

Table 2.13. Scholarship programs of selected independent colleges and universities in 1952

Institution	Endowment	Scholarship Funds	Annual Budget	Number of Individual Awards		Average Award	Percentage of Enrollment Aided	
				Total	Freshmen		Total	Freshmen
California Institute of Technology	$23,800,000	?	?	110	46	$442	18%	23%
Claremont Men's College	$1,000,000	?	?	40	20	?	13%	21%
Dartmouth College	$28,500,000	?	$250,000	?	?	?	20%	20%
Harvard University	$241,200,000	?	$623,000	1045	306	$600	20%	24%
Mills College	$2,500,000	$674,000	$24,600	72	22	$340	10%	10%
Northwestern University	$70,000,000	?	?	780	205	?	15%	16%
Occidental College	$1,600,000	$261,000	?	180	50	?	16%	17%
Pomona College	$5,700,000	$496,000	$112,000	160	47	$700	15%	15%
Princeton University	$51,700,000	$6,000,000	?	800	250	?	26%	31%
Scripps College	$1,600,000	$312,000	$25,600	40	10	$640	18%	13%
Yale University	$141,200,000	$13,130,000	$515,000	1300	350	$700	30%	30%
Stanford University	$39,600,000	$3,665,000	$248,000	577	87	$430	8%	8%

Source: Rixford K. Snyder, "The Scholarship Problem and the Admissions Program of Stanford University," 8, Call No. SC 216, Box 54, Folder 12, Stanford University Archives, Stanford, CA.

a better education of the American work force and even predicted an increasing shortage of well-educated and skilled specialists. George D. Stoddard, president of the University of Illinois, argued in his contribution to that special issue that the country's student population should be raised from 20 to 40 percent of the people at college age. Even though "only half the present college population earns a college degree," Stoddard saw great advantages in bringing more students to college, because "the student body is not drawn entirely from the upper reaches of intelligence." In fact, "the number of youths with college ability outruns college graduation by over four to one."[49]

Dael Wolfle, a psychologist, identified in his contribution to the special issue of *Scientific American* two main reasons for the lack of popularity of college education among the general population. Too many talented students forwent applying for college for reasons of disinterest in a college education and for the lack of financial support. For many students from working-class and middle-class background, college had little attraction because their parents did not encourage them to consider college and because they settled for a vocation that did not require a college degree. Wolfle suggested that the best and brightest students should be identified by use of intelligence tests. And he insisted that those who were talented needed financial support in the form of undergraduate scholarships.[50]

Conclusion

Scholarship support and scholarship programs appeared to university administrators at private East Coast colleges, such as Princeton president John Grier Hibben, as a key to achieving the status of a national university. Hibben publicly contended in 1919 that a national university must attract students from all corners of the country.[51] Thirty years later, Princeton and Harvard still seemed to be—if one looks at the geographic diversity of their student populations—parochial schools. With more than two-thirds of the student population at Massachusetts' private colleges hailing from the Northeast, there were very few opportunities for students from other parts of the country to obtain an Ivy League education.

The national scholarship programs, which were introduced in order to overcome the geographic limitations of colleges such as Harvard, fell short of their lofty goals even before they were implemented. Initial plans of both colleges that would have provided scholarship support only to students from outside the Northeast were abandoned because of protest from both donors and alumni. Although it had been the intention of these programs—at least in the minds of college administrators—to increase the geographic diversity of the student populations at Harvard and Princeton by decreasing the number of students from the Northeast and increasing the number of students from other regions, administrators at both colleges were in the end forced to include scholarships for students from the Northeast, which were already overrepresented and should not have received any more incentives. Donors' visions and college administrators' visions were clearly not aligned. Such modifications as well as the limited financial resources contributed to the failure of these national scholarship programs, which enlarged the geographic diversity of East Coast colleges only marginally.

The national scholarship programs equally failed in expanding the socioeconomic diversity of the student population at private East Coast colleges, as the example of Harvard shows. The majority of national scholarships from 1938 to 1944 went to students from upper-class families. An astonishing share of 46.2 percent of national scholarship holders in those six years came from upper-class families with annual incomes in excess of four thousand dollars. These numbers are striking. They remind us that the student population at private colleges was more and more dominated by students from rich families. While private colleges such as Harvard had kept their doors open to poor students in the nineteenth century, these colleges saw a fundamental change in the socioeconomic composition of their student body after 1900. Increasing tuition and expenses for social activities excluded students from lower-class and even middle-class families. A private college education became a luxury for the rich.

If we apply the parameters suggested by the college presidents of Harvard and Princeton, Conant and Hibben, who defined a national university by its geographic and socioeconomic diversity, neither of the two colleges had reached that goal through their national scholarship programs. To this very day geographic proximity to Harvard is a factor in admission to that school. It is true that Harvard has become in geographic terms much more inclusive today than a hundred years ago. However, even in 2017 nearly half of all Harvard students come from the New England and Mid-Atlantic states. Forty-seven percent of

Harvard students hail from these thirteen states in the Northeast, which are the home to only 23 percent of the entire American population. The biggest source for Harvard students outside of the region is California, which supplies about 16 percent of students. Nearly two-thirds of Harvard students in 2017 thus came from just fourteen states, which represent 35 percent of the total American population. The remaining one-third of Harvard students come from the other thirty-six states, which are the home of 65 percent of the American population.[52]

These statistics point to another problem. Neither Conant nor Hibben elaborated on their definition of a national university. Stating that a national university needs to provide an education to students from the entire country instead of limiting itself to one region of that country leaves one with many questions. At what point would Harvard be considered a national university? How many students would need to come from the Northeast and how many from the South? Would there be a need for a quota system, and should the share of students from each region be correlated to the share of that region's population within the American population? And is there such a thing as "geographic discrimination or disadvantaging" in a society in which universities such as Harvard produce a significant share of the American elites?[53]

The desire of East Coast colleges to bring talented students from throughout the country to their campuses also caused significant criticism from college administrators at schools such as Stanford, as this plan seemed to be based upon the assumption that only East Coast colleges could offer the best education. While Harvard and Princeton had limited success in expanding their geographic reach, both colleges succeeded—by producing and implementing a national scholarship plan—in creating at least the image of being a national university.

Notes

1. John R. Thelin and Richard W. Trollinger, *Philanthropy and American Higher Education* (New York: Palgrave Macmillan, 2014); Mark D. McGarvie, "The Dartmouth College Case and the Legal Design of Civil Society," in *Charity, Philanthropy, and Civility in American History*, edited by Lawrence J. Friedman and Mark D. McGarvie (Cambridge: Cambridge University Press, 2003), 91–105; David C. Hammack, ed., *Making the Nonprofit Sector in the United States: A Reader* (Bloomington: Indiana University Press, 1998), 123–41.

2. Jerome Karabel, *The Chosen: The Hidden History of Admission and Exclusion at Harvard, Yale, and Princeton* (Boston: Houghton Mifflin, 2005), 175–76; Morton

Keller and Phyllis Keller, *Making Harvard Modern: The Rise of the America's University* (Oxford: Oxford University Press 2001), 49.

3. Philip A. Cowen, *College Tuition Fees*, University of the State of New York Bulletin No. 941, February 1, 1930 (Albany: University of the State of New York Press, 1930), 6.

4. Colin B. Burke, *American Collegiate Populations: A Test of the Traditional View* (New York: New York University Press, 1982), 109, 113. See, in general, Michael David Cohen, *Reconstructing the Campus: Higher Education and the American Civil War* (Charlottesville: University of Virginia Press, 2012), 129–41.

5. Pierre Bourdieu, "Ökonomisches Kapital—Kulturelles Kapital—Soziales Kapital," in *Schriften zu Politik und Kultur I: Die verborgenen Mechanismen der Macht* (Hamburg, Germany: VSA Verlag, 1992), 49–81; Ronald Story, *The Forging of an Aristocracy: Harvard and the Boston Upper Class, 1800–1870* (Middletown, CT: Wesleyan University Press 1980), 96–97.

6. Results from the 1860 Census, The Civil War Home Page, http://www.civil-war.net/pages/1860_census.html (accessed July 9, 2016).

7. Burke, *American Collegiate Populations*, 112.

8. Cohen, *Reconstructing the Campus*; Charles Warren, "Distribution of College Students in 1870–71," in *Circular of Information of the Bureau of Education for March, 1872* (Washington, DC: Government Printing Office 1872), 47–48, 57–58.

9. *The Harvard College National Scholarships: A Descriptive Report at the End of Six Years* (Cambridge, MA: Harvard University, 1941), 11.

10. "Post War Plans for Amherst College (1944)," 5, Provisional Report, Alumni Committee on Admissions and Scholarships, Alfred Sherwood Romer 1917, Box 2, folder 6, Amherst College Archives, Amherst, MA.

11. "Report of the Committee of Five," 52, Alumni Organization Records, Box 4, folder Graduate Council Reports 1931, National Alumni Association of Princeton University, Graduate Council of Princeton University, May 15, 1931, Princeton University Archives, Princeton, NJ.

12. "Post War Plans for Amherst College (1944)," 5–6.

13. "Report of the Committee of Five," 54.

14. Secretary of the Admission Committee to Lewis N. Lukens Jr., December 19, 1933, Office of the Secretary Records, Box 22, folder 19, Princeton University Archives, Princeton, NJ.

15. "Report of the Committee of Five," 54.

16. James B. Conant, "The Role of the Privately Endowed Colleges," in *Harvard Alumni Bulletin* 38, no. 7 (November 1935): 209.

17. Ibid.

18. Seymor E. Harris, *The Economics of Harvard* (New York: McGraw-Hill, 1970), 57–58, 110–11.

19. "The 300th Anniversary Fund: Statement Adopted by the President and Fellows of Harvard College," *Journal of Higher Education* 7, no. 2 (February 1936): 63–70; "The Development of the Harvard National Scholarship Plan," reprinted from Report of the Dean of Harvard College to the President of the University

for the Academic Year 1936–37, 3, Harvard University Archives, Cambridge, MA; *Harvard College National Scholarships*, 5–6; Keller and Keller, *Making Harvard Modern*, 146–47. For a very critical evaluation of this program, see Karabel, *The Chosen*, 139–40, 175–78.

20. "Memorandum Concerning National Scholarships at Harvard," 11, Harvard University Archives, Cambridge, MA; "Development of the Harvard National Scholarship Plan," 6.

21. Karabel, *The Chosen*, 175–76. See also Keller and Keller, *Making Harvard Modern*, 47–51.

22. *Endowment Funds of Harvard University, June 30, 1947* (Cambridge: Harvard University, 1948), 106–7; "Development of the Harvard National Scholarship Plan," 6.

23. "Development of the Harvard National Scholarship Plan," 13.

24. *Harvard College National Scholarships*, 31–33.

25. "Development of the Harvard National Scholarship Plan," 19, 31–33.

26. Nicholas Lemann, *The Big Test: The Secret History of The American Meritocracy* (New York: Farrar, Straus and Giroux, 1999), 27–28; "Memorandum Concerning National Scholarships at Harvard," 8; "Conant Scholars nor Book Worms Running Straight A's in Most Classes—Interested in Outside Activities," *Harvard Crimson* 106, no. 258 (December 9, 1935).

27. "Memorandum Concerning National Scholarships at Harvard," 8; "Development of the Harvard National Scholarship Plan," 5; "Post War Plans for Amherst College (1944)," 19–23.

28. John Grier Hibben, "A National University," 1, 2, John Grier Hibben Records, Box 73, folder 4, Office of the President's Records, Series 14, Princeton University Archives, Princeton, NJ (published in *New York Evening Post*, magazine section, Saturday, March 8, 1919); "The Endowment of Princeton University," *School and Society* 10, no. 237 (July 12, 1919): 46.

29. *Catalogue of Princeton University, 1919–1920* (Princeton, NJ: Published by the University, 1920), 242.

30. Philip Wallis, "Western and Southern Scholarships," 2–3, Office of the Treasurer Records, Box 11, folder Scholarships (1941), Princeton University Archives, Princeton, NJ.

31. *Catalogue of the College of New Jersey, Princeton, 1890–91* (Princeton, NJ: Published by the College, 1890), 154; *Catalogue of Princeton University, 1900–1901* (Princeton, NJ: Princeton Press, 1900), 186–89; Report on Scholarship Funds submitted by James O. Murray, John Dixon, and Wm. M. Sloane (November 14, 1895), Office of the Secretary Records, Box 22, folder 14, Princeton University Archives, Princeton, NJ.

32. *Catalogue of the Officers and Students of the College of New Jersey, for the Academic Year, 1869-'70* (Princeton, NJ: Printed at the Standard Office, 1870), 32.

33. A Report for the Scholarship Committee (December 1932), 2, Office of the Secretary Records, Box 22, folder 18, and Graduate Council of Princeton University, Report of the Special Committee on Scholarships, Princeton, May 17, 1946,

7, Alumni Organization Records, Box 4, folder Graduate Council Reports, 1946, Princeton University Archives, Princeton, NJ.

34. Memorandum re Scholarships, 1, Office of the Secretary Records, Box 22, folder 13, Princeton University Archives, Princeton, NJ.

35. Thurston J. Davies, "Report for Committee on Survey of Scholarship Situation (May 12, 1933)," 1–2, Exhibit 6, Alumni Association Scholarships, Office of the Secretary Records, Box 22, folder 18, Princeton University Archives, Princeton, NJ.

36. Minot C. Morgan Jr., Secretary, memorandum to members of the University Committee on Scholarships, Subject: $1,000 Regional Scholarship Plan (April 6, 1945), Office of the Treasurer Records, Box 19, folder Scholarships Misc., Princeton University, Bureau of Student Aid and Employment, Princeton University Archives, Princeton, NJ.

37. Scholarships, 1, Princeton University Fund Records, 1877–1972, Box 11, folder Scholarships SPIA, Princeton University Archives, Princeton, NJ.

38. Princeton University Scholarship Program, Princeton University Fund Records, 1877–1972, Box 14, folder Princeton University Scholarship Program, Princeton University Archives, Princeton, NJ, including an announcement of the Princeton University Regional Scholarships (November 15, 1947).

39. Who Goes to Princeton? Princeton University's Scholarship Program Including Plans for Eighty New Regional Scholarships, 6, Princeton University Fund Records, 1877–1972, Box 14, folder Princeton University Scholarship Program, Princeton University Archives, Princeton, NJ.

40. Scholarships in a Privately Endowed University, 1, Princeton University Fund Records, 1877–1972, Box 4, folder Syracuse Scholarship, Princeton University Archives, Princeton, NJ.

41. To Princeton Scholarship Committee throughout the Country, 1, 2, 4, Office of the Treasurer Records, Box 8, folder Scholarships, Princeton University Archives, Princeton, NJ.

42. "Large Legacy for Cornell," *New York Times*, September 8, 1921, 23; Morris Bishop, *A History of Cornell* (Ithaca, NY: Cornell University Press, 1962), 465; "$2,000,000 Will at Issue," *New York Times*, November 2, 1921, 23; *General Information Number for 1929–30* (Ithaca, NY: Published by the University, 1928), 42.

43. Letter addressed to Dean D. S. Kimball, December 11, 1935, Box 19, folder 29, Livingston Farrand Papers, 1921–1939, Cornell University Archives, Ithaca, NY.

44. *General Information Number for 1940–41* (Ithaca, NY: Cornell University, 1940), 39.

45. *Nineteenth Annual Register, 1909–10* (Stanford, CA: Published by the University, 1910), 65–66; *Twenty-Ninth Annual Register, 1919–20* (Stanford, CA: Published by the University, 1920), 77; *Fortieth Annual Register, 1930–31* (Stanford, CA: Published by the University, 1931), 137; *Fiftieth Annual Register, 1940–41* (Stanford, CA: Published by the University, 1941), 180.

46. Rixford K. Snyder, "The Scholarship Problem and the Admissions Program of Stanford University," 5, Call No. SC 216, Box 54, Folder 12, Stanford University Archives, Stanford, CA.

47. Ibid., 3.

48. Ibid., 6.

49. Rixford K. Snyder to the Board of Governors of Stanford Associates, October 15, 1951, 1, Call No. SC 216, Box 54, Folder 12, Stanford University Archives, Stanford, CA; George D. Stoddard, "Youth," *Scientific American* 185, no. 3 (September 1951): 106.

50. Dael Wolfle, "Intellectual Resources," *Scientific American* 185, no. 3 (September 1951): 44.

51. Hibben, "A National University," 2.

52. Information about the geographic diversity of Harvard students in 2017 can be found at "Harvard University Diversity: How Good Is It?" Harvard University, Student Life, https://www.collegefactual.com/colleges/harvard-university/student-life/diversity/#secGeographic (accessed September 13, 2017). Information about the population statistics of the United States can be found at http://www.enchanedlearning.com/usa/states/population.shtml (accessed September 13, 2017).

53. Joel Warner and Aaron Clauset, "The Academy's Dirty Secret," *Slate*, February 23, 2015, http://www.slate.com/articles/life/education/2015/02/university_hiring_if_you_didn_t_get_your_ph_d_at_an_elite_university_good.html (accessed September 13, 2017).

3

Bernard Daly's Promise

Lessons from America's Oldest Place-Based Scholarship

Sam Stern and Jordan Hensley

It is hard to imagine a place more remote and distant from higher education than Lake County, Oregon, in the early nineteenth century. Located in southeastern Oregon, Lake County is larger than the state of Massachusetts, yet it has a population of less than eight thousand. When the Daly Scholarship was first awarded in 1922, there were only three state colleges in Oregon (Oregon Agricultural College in Corvallis, the University of Oregon in Eugene, and Oregon Normal School in Monmouth), and the closest to Lake County was a 250-mile, three-day trip by horse, ferry, and train. Not surprisingly, only a few Lake County students went to college. In 1922 that changed forever when Bernard Daly established a scholarship fund that made it possible for Lake County students to attend college. Since then, most of the high school graduates from that remote county have gone on to college and remarkable careers. The history and impact of this scholarship fund, America's oldest place-based scholarship, can help us better understand the impact of higher education.

Bernard Daly's life was buffeted by great, often tragic, world events, yet he thrived and did much to improve the situation wherever he lived. At age five in 1864, Bernard Daly and his family emigrated from Ireland in the aftermath of the Great Famine to Selma, Alabama, just before the end of the American Civil War. Raised by his siblings after his mother died, Daly somehow found his way to Ohio, where he graduated from Ohio Normal University (today's Ohio Northern University) in 1886. According to an account in the *Ohio Northern University Herald*, Daly was an excellent student enrolled in the "scientific course" who completed his degree in three years and in his last year taught anatomy classes.[1]

He had hoped to study medicine at Ohio Normal, but since they did not have a program in medicine, he went to the nearby University of Louisville medical school. At the time, medical training was on the verge of fundamental change, transitioning from informal apprenticeship to professional university-based education. In the nineteenth century most medical instruction occurred through an apprenticeship with an experienced doctor or at a proprietary school owned by local physicians. At the time, relatively few students attended university medical programs, and those programs were highly variable in their admission requirements, curriculum, and length.[2]

In 1904 the American Medical Association created the Council on Medical Education with the objective of restructuring medical education. The council turned to the Carnegie Foundation for the Advancement of Teaching, whose president picked Abraham Flexner to lead a nationwide survey of the state of medical education. This was an unusual choice, as Flexner was not a physician, scientist, or medical educator; in fact, he had never set foot in a medical school. He did have a bachelor's degree; operated a for-profit school in Louisville, Kentucky; and, more to the point, had just written a book, *American College*, that criticized the traditional lecture approach that seemed to make up the entirety of college instruction. With astonishing energy Flexner visited all 155 medical programs in the United States and was harshly critical of almost all of them. Among Flexner's recommendations was that medical education should last six or preferably eight years and that it adhere closely to the scientific method and be thoroughly grounded in human physiology and biochemistry. Following the report more than half of all American medical schools closed or merged, and those that remained closely followed the guidelines outlined in what is commonly referred to as the Flexner Report.[3]

Meanwhile, at the University of Louisville in 1887, Bernard Daly's medical training consisted of only two semesters of classes (didactic and clinical instruction). Yet it provided more formal preparation than most doctors at the time had received. Less than a year after he graduated from Ohio Normal, Daly graduated from medical school among the top ten of his class.[4]

Following graduation, Daly headed west, first to Fort Bidwell,

California, and then on to Lakeview by horseback. He arrived in Lakeview just ten years after the small town was established. He became the town's first doctor, member and chair of the school board, banker (he established the Bank of Lakeview), rancher (his ranch became one of the largest livestock suppliers in the county), state senator, county judge, and a regent of Oregon Agricultural College (today's Oregon State University).

When Daly first came to Lakeview it was a small community with a population of about three hundred. More than 150 miles from the nearest railroad, the town residents were self-reliant in most respects but did not have a town doctor. So when Daly arrived by horseback, threadbare and practically broke, the residents were thrilled and encouraged him to stay. And stay he did. He spent the remainder of his life in Lakeview, where he had a great impact. Although he held many prominent positions, he lived modestly in a boarding house and developed a reputation for being especially frugal. According to local accounts, he seldom bought new clothing and seemed to subsist on an occasional nickel bowl of soup and a handful of crackers.[5]

Cornelia Robertson, who was among the first group of students to receive the Daly Scholarship in 1922, told a reporter from the *Oregon Journal* about how she talked with Dr. Daly at the telegraph office where she worked while he waited for the night rates to go into effect. "He was always buying and selling cattle and sheep. A lot of people didn't think he had a lick of money, I know." When asked by the doctor what she planned to do with her life, she replied, "I'd like to study medicine, but I don't think my father can afford it." Daly replied, "Don't worry. There'll be a way." Daly died a year later, and two years after that she left for college, then to medical school, and on to a career as a doctor in New York City and San Diego.[6]

Given his reputation for frugalness, the size of Daly's estate was a shock to the community and his distant relatives. When he died without heirs in 1920, his estate (about $800,000 at the time, conservatively estimated to be the equivalent of $10 million in 2017) was dedicated to funding college scholarships for Lake County high school graduates.

Place-Based "Promise" Programs

Now, almost a century after Bernard Daly's bequest, the idea of place-based scholarships has captured the nation's attention. In response to increases in the costs of college, communities large and small have created scholarships based on place, and several states have established statewide promise programs. Place-based scholarships (and state support for higher education) engender a promise: If one lives in the place covered by the scholarship (and meets other requirements), the student will receive support to attend college. As such, these scholarships are often called "promise programs."[7]

Funded by anonymous donors in 2005, the Kalamazoo Promise Program attracted national attention and led to the creation of promise programs throughout the country and the association of college funding with a promise. The Kalamazoo Promise Program differs from other scholarship programs in that it is not awarded based on merit or need, but instead is based on place. The concept of place and the funding of higher education is not new—state support of higher education is similar in that it provides a subsidy for in-state students that enables them to pay somewhat less than the actual cost of their education while out-of-state students pay somewhat more.

The Kalamazoo Promise Program is especially generous. Since 2006, when the first scholarships were awarded, every Kalamazoo public school graduate who has been enrolled in and resided in the district since kindergarten receives full funding for tuition and mandatory fees at any of Michigan's forty-four public colleges or universities. Scholarships for graduates who were not enrolled since kindergarten are prorated, with those who attended for four years receiving 65 percent of the costs.[8]

Within a year of the announcement of the Kalamazoo Promise Program, several other communities announced their own promise programs, and a movement was born (well, reborn). In 2017, about a decade since the emergence of the Kalamazoo Promise (and a century since the Daly Fund), there are more than one hundred promise programs. While they vary in some respects, they share a focus on place, providing the assurance of college funding to youth who live in a specific area. Three areas of difference have emerged: (1) whether all or only selected students are eligible; (2) what colleges the scholarship recipients may attend; and (3) how much funding is provided.[9]

Similar to the Kalamazoo program, some programs, like the El Dorado, Arkansas, program provide universal coverage to all students in the designated area. In contrast, the Denver and Pittsburgh promise programs are examples of programs that limit eligibility. While both programs require residence and high school graduation from their cities, Denver limits eligibility based on need, requiring that recipients fall within one-and-one-half times the Pell Grant limit, while Pittsburg does so on merit, requiring a 2.5 GPA and 90 percent attendance in high school to qualify for full funding of up to seventy-five hundred dollars a year for four years. Some programs limit college attendance to their state's public colleges, while others, such as the LeBron James Program, limit attendance to just one college. While there are differences among the more than one hundred promise programs that have emerged over the past decade, Michelle Miller-Adams and others argue that they should be treated as a group for two reasons: they use a place-based approach to awarding scholarships, and they have similar intent and goals. As a group, they may be the fastest growing new type of support for higher education in the United States.[10]

The Daly Scholarship Fund

The Kalamazoo Promise Program and other place-based scholarships that have been established during the past decade have not yet been operating long enough for a full analysis of their impact. The Daly Fund, however, is a remarkable century-old natural experiment; generations of Lake County students have attended and graduated from college. Though it is far older than the modern place-based scholarship programs, it shares with them the most important elements of a place-based promise program. First and foremost, the Daly Fund is based on place. Daly's instructions in his will were explicit: "It is my earnest desire to help, aid and assist worthy and ambitious young men and women of my beloved county of Lake, to acquire a good education, so that they may be the better fitted and qualified to appreciate and help to preserve the laws and constitution of this free country, defend its flag, and by their conduct as good citizens reflect honor on Lake County and the State Oregon."[11]

Throughout the history of the Daly Fund, only students who attended a Lake County high school for all four years were eligible for the scholarship. As implied in his will, Daly believed that through access to higher education Lake County youth would contribute to their county, state, and nation. Beyond the requirement of place, the criteria are quite straightforward. All eligible students complete a simple one-page application form and are then ranked by a formula that considers their standardized test scores and grade point average to derive a single number for each student. When the Daly Fund trustees meet on the third Saturday in June, they receive a list of numbers derived from the formula, without student names attached, ranked from high to low. Considering the interest on the fund principal minus the amount that is already committed to continuing students, the trustees decide how many scholarships they can award in that year. Between 1999 and 2015, over 52 percent of the applicants received scholarships. It is important to note that since there are other place-based scholarships in Lake County, many of those students receive other scholarships, and a surprising number of those who do not receive scholarship support go to college anyway.[12]

Daly Fund recipients may use the scholarship funds at any state institution in Oregon, and their scholarship is automatically renewed for up to four years if they maintain the required credit load and meet the grade point average requirements. They are required to take a full load of coursework (forty-five quarter hours per year) and maintain at least a 2.2 GPA as a freshman, 2.35 as a sophomore, and 2.5 as a junior. Students can use the funds for a maximum of four consecutive years. The only permitted break in attendance is for participation in a foreign exchange program.

In the early years, the Daly Scholarship covered all costs associated with attending college, including tuition, fees, and the cost of room and board. As more students applied for the scholarship and tuition increased, the fund moved to paying only one-third of the estimated total costs for Oregon state universities (tuition, fees, books, room, and board) which, in 2016, was $8,400 for the year.

Survey of Daly Fund Recipients

To understand the impact of the Daly Fund, a thirty-seven-question web-based survey was developed. But before the survey could be administered, contact information for the Daly Fund recipients was needed. The Lynch and Vandenberg law office, which serves as secretary for the Daly Fund trustees, provided a list of all recipients from 1922 to 2016. The list contained 1,918 names and the year of their high school graduation, but no contact information, and it was likely that many, if not most, of the women's names had changed. Over the course of several months we pursued several strategies to obtain contact information. The first was to use a short contact information survey that we emailed to those with emails we had from prior contact and had obtained from the Oregon State Foundation alumni list. We also created a Facebook page (https://www.facebook.com/DalyFund Research/) so that people who were interested in the project could share the link with others. Through a combination of the Facebook page and the cooperation of the University of Oregon Foundation, we were able to obtain 301 unique email addresses. Although there was a total of 1,918 scholarship recipients since 1922, we estimated that any recipient who graduated before 1950 was likely to be deceased, given that they would be in their eighties. After subtracting the 447 recipients who had graduated before 1950, the estimated living population of scholarship recipients was 1,471.

In the fall of 2016 we sent emails to the 301 email addresses explaining the research project, with links to both the survey and the Facebook page, and asking them to take the survey and share it with others who had received the Daly scholarship. From those emails and the snowball effect of recipients sharing the survey web link with others, we received 303 survey responses, just over 20 percent of the estimated population of living recipients.

We excluded survey responses from recipients who had completed high school after 2011, as that would not provide sufficient time for them to understand the educational and economic impact of the scholarship. Incomplete surveys or those that could not be verified as having received the scholarship were also excluded, leaving a total of 245 usable survey responses, which serve as the basis for the analysis of the impact of the Daly Fund.

When the Daly Fund began awarding scholarships in 1922, there were only three state colleges: Oregon Agricultural College (today's Oregon State University), University of Oregon, and Oregon Normal School (today's Western Oregon University). In 2017 there are seven Oregon public universities and seventeen community colleges.[13] Most of the survey respondents graduated from Oregon State University (43 percent), followed by the University of Oregon (16.8 percent), Eastern Oregon University (6.6 percent), Western Oregon University (6.6 percent), Oregon Institute of Technology (5.3 percent), and Portland

State University (1.3 percent), with 13.3 percent from other universities. Given our affiliation with Oregon State University (OSU) and our prior interactions with OSU alumni in the Lakeview area, it is not surprising that the largest number of surveys came from OSU graduates.

An especially important indicator for higher education is the six-year graduation rate. The six-year graduation rate for first-time, full-time undergraduate students who began seeking a bachelor's degree at US public four-year degree-granting institutions in fall of 2009 was 59 percent.[14] The six-year graduation rate at Oregon State University during the same time period was 61 percent, just above the national average. In sharp contrast to both the national and state average, our survey respondents' six-year graduation rate during that same time period was 94.2 percent. Even more surprisingly, 71.2 percent of the survey respondents completed their degrees in four years, more than double the national and state average of about 30 percent. To put it another way, a higher percentage of Daly Scholarship students included in our survey completed their degrees in four years than the overall percentage of US college students who completed their college education within six years.

There are many benefits associated with timely completion of a college degree. Earlier completion reduces the cost of higher education to the student, the university, and the public and also maximizes the returns. From a cost standpoint, completing a degree in six years rather than four will cost more than an additional 50 percent of the four-year cost when one considers the value of forgone income. From an educational standpoint, students who complete undergraduate degrees earlier are more likely to complete graduate and professional degrees.

While about 12 percent of the American population has a graduate degree,[15] more than three times as many (40 percent) of our survey respondents have either a master's or an advanced professional degree. The high percentage of advanced degrees is likely to have been influenced by early completion of their bachelor's degree and the fact that they graduated without debt, giving them both time and money to invest in further education. Of note is the finding that 12.7 percent of the survey respondents completed an advanced degree (PhD, MD, JD, and the like). The large number of Daly recipients who became medical doctors (as Cornelia Robertson and her sister Jocelyn did in the 1920s) seems to echo the career of Bernard Daly.

The economic impact of the Daly Fund begins with the cost of college for scholarship recipients. As described earlier, the scholarship provides about one-third of the total costs of attendance. However, when survey respondents were asked to estimate the source of their college funds, they reported that scholarships provided 51 percent; work (summer and during school), 23 percent; family, 15 percent; debt, 7 percent; and other, 4 percent. While there appears to be a discrepancy between the one-third that was provided by the Daly Scholarship and the 51 percent reported by respondents, it is likely that the scholarship recipients stretched their dollars by minimizing expenses, and some may have received more than one scholarship. It does seem that the one-third of estimated costs was a sweet spot, enough to imagine being able to pay for college through careful management of expenses supplemented by part-time work and some support from family.

With work identified as paying for just over 20 percent of their college costs, it is not surprising that a high percentage of Daly recipients worked summers and during the academic year. Almost all (98 percent) of the survey respondents worked during the summers while in college, and about three-quarters (77.8 percent) worked during the academic year. Although a similar percentage of all American college students report working during college, many of them are part-time students, while all the Daly Scholarship students were full-time students and still worked during college. It seems that the Daly Scholarship students were motivated to complete their degrees without assuming debt and also received work experience that, in some cases, advanced their career interests.

Most of the Daly Scholarship recipients (63 percent) finished college without any debt, and those that did assume debt reported small amounts. Although the number of Daly Scholarship recipients reporting debt increased over time, the percentage was still considerably less than the national average in 2015, when 68 percent of those graduating from college reported an average debt of $30,100.[16] No doubt this is influenced by the relatively high percentage of Daly Scholarship students who complete their degrees in four years instead of five or six.

Economic returns continued as Daly Scholarship recipients left college and began their careers. Almost all of the survey respondents (82 percent) reported that the Daly Fund had some or great impact on their economic circumstances. When asked about their most recent annual household income, about half (49.6 percent) reported annual incomes greater than $100,000, and a quarter (24.8 percent) reported annual incomes greater than $150,000, almost five times greater than the median annual household income in Lake County of $32,369. The high annual household incomes reported by the Daly Scholarship recipients are largely due to their high levels of education (over 90 percent have bachelor's degrees and more than 40 percent have graduate degrees) rather than any previous family wealth. When asked how their income compares to that of their parents, more than three-quarters (77.5 percent) reported that their family income was either somewhat or much more than the income of their parents when they were growing up. This strongly suggests that the Daly Fund has been providing opportunity for upward financial mobility, fulfilling the promise of the American Dream that is becoming less realistic for too many American youth.[17]

Some Lessons from the Daly Fund

> *"Because I knew I had to put myself through college, I knew I had to receive the Daly Fund or just not go, as I couldn't have afforded it otherwise. It's an incredible legacy for Lake County."*[18]
>
> LAKEVIEW HIGH SCHOOL, 1978
> SOUTHERN OREGON UNIVERSITY 1983
> (TWO DEGREES, BUSINESS AND SPANISH)

The power of a longstanding promise is strong. All Lake County students and families know about the Daly Fund and how it works, so children begin elementary school knowing that if they do well in school they are likely to receive scholarship support. Their families and the community have an especially strong commitment to supporting their schools, because they know that investment in the schools will pay off, as most students will go on to college. At a time when 40 to 60 percent of US college students begin college needing remedial education at a cost estimated to be as high as $1.3 billion,[19] Lake County students are unusually well prepared for students from a remote and rural community. The extraordinary four-year graduation rate itself as well as the high level of graduate degree attainment are indicators of the quality of their preparation for college. They are prepared and they do well. A promise makes a difference. Whether one grows up in the remote community of Lakeview, Oregon, or in Kalamazoo, Michigan, if one knows from an early age that one will be able to go to college, most students will prepare for it.

> *"Even though I had to work both during the school and in the summer, the Fund made my life MUCH easier. I worked every summer from the age of ten and saved for college."*
>
> LAKEVIEW HIGH SCHOOL, 1962
> UNIVERSITY OF OREGON, 1964
> ECOLES JACQUES LECOQ, PARIS, 1969

In 1922, when the Daly Scholarship was first awarded, Oregon State University did not charge any tuition, and the fees (registration fee, $10; incidental fees, $5.50; gymnasium fee, $1.50 for women and $2.00 for men; and diploma fee, $5) were modest.[20] The issue at the time had more to do with the opportunity cost of attending college and forgone income, not just to the student but also to their family. This was especially true in Lake County, a poor and remote community that was dependent on ranching and farming and the labor of children. In the early years of the Daly Scholarship, the fund not only paid for the total cost of college attendance (tuition, fees, room, and board), but also for trips home during the academic year. As the costs of college went up, the Daly Fund trustees faced the choice of providing full funding for fewer students or reducing the amount of funding while continuing to award scholarships to more than half of each graduating class. They chose to fund more students with a lesser amount of scholarship funds, finding that funding one-third of the total costs seemed to be the sweet spot where almost all students were able to graduate on time and without debt by supplementing the scholarship funds through part-time work and some support from their family.

This approach of providing some support, but not all, has worked well over time, even during the past several decades when the costs of college have increased at a greater percentage than inflation. By providing a sufficient portion of the total costs, but not all, students are incentivized to make up the difference through a combination of careful money management and work, both of which are good life values and likely to serve the students well in their future lives.[21]

> *"It was one of the best motivators to do well in high school and maintain that work ethic through college. Without the Daly Fund I would not have done as well, or finished as quickly."*
>
> LAKEVIEW HIGH SCHOOL, 2008
> OREGON STATE UNIVERSITY, 2012
> (ENGINEERING DEGREE IN FOUR YEARS)

A corollary to the "some but not all" approach to scholarship funding is the method by which students are selected for the Daly scholarship. It is an approach that encourages academic competition (based on overall grade point average and SAT scores), with more than half of the students receiving scholarships.[22] In describing how this works, we often ask people to consider two scenarios. In the first, students are told that they will get a scholarship if they graduate in the top 3 percent of their class. In the second scenario, students are told they will get a scholarship if they graduate in the top 60 percent. It makes a big difference. In the second scenario, most students will be able to see the possibility getting a scholarship if they work hard.

> *"Dr. Daly provided an incredible opportunity for Lake County students to pursue higher education; his impact on people in our county has been huge."*
>
> LAKEVIEW HIGH SCHOOL, 1961
> OREGON STATE UNIVERSITY, 1965
> STANFORD UNIVERSITY, 1969

The Daly Scholarship Fund is America's oldest continuously operating place-based scholarship. It has sustained itself for almost a hundred years through a combination of good beginnings (through the instructions of Bernard Daly in his will), excellent local management (with the participation of representatives from each state university in Oregon), and strong community support. The idea of place-based scholarships taps into our innate desire to help those that are closest to us. This can be seen in Bernard Daly's bequest, in the donations that have been added to the fund by former recipients, in the strong community support for education in general, and in those students who, over the years, declined the scholarship because that student's family had the resources for college; declining the scholarship would make it possible for another student from their community to go on to college. While this has happened many times in Lake County, to our knowledge, no one, no matter how wealthy, has declined the state subsidy associated with in-state tuition so that others, perhaps more needy, could have additional funds for college. Perhaps a state or the entire country is too large to trigger our generosity in the way that a somewhat smaller place can. It seems to attract the type of emotional connection that is often associated with our love for local sports teams—it is a matter of place.

> *"I probably wouldn't have gone to college without this scholarship. As the oldest of six kids, my parents didn't have the means. Once I got the scholarship, the credit load and GPA requirements kept me on track to graduate in four years."*
>
> LAKEVIEW HIGH SCHOOL, 1976
> OREGON STATE UNIVERSITY, 1980

In contrast to most scholarships, the Daly Scholarship is strategic in that it influences students while they are in college, incentivizing them to carry a full credit load and maintain a good grade point average. If the students fail to complete a full credit load during the year or fails to maintain the required grade point average, they lose their funding. The very high completion rate of our survey respondents is an indication that this method works. While it is true that the requirement is likely to limit exploring different college majors, it could be argued that it also provides more opportunity to explore different areas in graduate study as the Daly Scholarship students appeared to have done.

Conclusion

Compared with other Oregonians and, for that matter, Americans in general, Daly Fund recipients from the remote and relatively poor community of Lake County are far more likely to graduate from college on time, less likely to have debt, more likely to complete graduate degrees, and more likely to have greater annual household incomes. All of this occurred because of an immigrant who, as a boy, emigrated from one of the poorest counties in Ireland to the heart of the Confederacy at the end of the Civil War. Against all odds, he attended college, then medical school, and somehow he found his way across the country to Lakeview,

Oregon, where he became a doctor, rancher, banker, county judge, and state senator. Although he accomplished much in life, his greatest impact lives on as it helps the youth of his adopted Lake County go to college through the scholarship fund that he established in 1920.

At a time when scholarships were largely nonexistent, and very few attended college, Daly pioneered a new type of scholarship—one based on place that engenders strong community support for higher education. Now, almost a hundred years after the establishment of the Daly Fund, place-based scholarships are being created in communities throughout America. At a time when the costs of college are escalating beyond the means of many, place-based scholarships are extending a promise of college, very much like the promise that Bernard Daly made to a youth of Lake County.

Notes

The authors are deeply grateful to the Daly Fund trustees and the entire community of Lake County, who have encouraged and supported our research.

1. It is likely that Bernard Daly and his family emigrated to Selma through Mobile, Alabama, the last major Confederate port to be blockaded. At the time, poor Irish were no longer welcome in the ports of New York and Boston, where state "passenger laws" limited the growing number of Irish immigrants. As a result, many Irish entered America through Confederate ports. See Hidetaka Hirota, "'The Great Entrepot for Mendicants': Foreign Poverty and Immigration Control in New York State to 1882," *Journal of American Ethnic History* 33, no. 2 (Winter 2014): 5–33. For more about the Irish experience in the South during that period, see David T. Gleeson, *The Irish in the South, 1815–1877* (Chapel Hill: University of North Carolina Press, 2002); "Alumni News," *Ohio Normal University Herald*, March 25, 1887.

2. Andrew H. Beck, "The Flexner Report and the Standardization of American Medical Education," *Journal of the American Medical Association* 291, no. 17 (2004): 2139–40.

3. Malcolm Cox et al., "American Medical Education 100 Years after the Flexner Report," *New England Journal of Medicine* 355, no. 13 (2006): 1339–44.

4. University of Louisville, *Fifty-first Annual Announcement of the Medical Department of the University of Louisville, Session of 1887 and 1888* (Louisville, KY: John P. Morton and Co., 1887).

5. Jan Holden, "A Pioneer Doctor's Life and Legacy," *Ruralite*, December 1992.

6. Helen L. Mershon, "A Proud Legacy: Lake County Scholars," *Oregon Journal*,

October 1979. As extraordinary as it was for a young woman to go to college and become a doctor in the 1920s, both Cornelia and her younger sister, who also received the Daly Scholarship, became doctors.

7. Laura W. Perna and Elaine W. Leigh, "College Promise Programs: Designing Programs to Achieve the Promise," *Higher Education Today*, February 13, 2017, http://www.higheredtoday.org/2017/02/13/college-promise-programs-designing-programs-achieve-promise/ (accessed September 6, 2017).

8. Michelle Miller-Adams, *Promise Nation: Transforming Communities through Place-Based Scholarships* (Kalamazoo, MI: W. E. Upjohn Institute for Employment Research, 2015), http://www.upjohn.org/publications/upjohn-institute-press/promise-nation-transforming-communities-through-place-based (accessed September 6, 2017).

9. Laura W. Perna, "A Comprehensive Catalog of College Promise Programs in the United States," University of Pennsylvania Graduate School of Education, 2017, http://ahead-penn.org/creating-knowledge/college-promise (accessed September 6, 2017).

10. Michelle Miller-Adams, *What Is a Promise Scholarship Program?* (Kalamazoo, MI: W. E. Upjohn Institute for Employment Research, 2015). The LeBron James I Promise Program provides full tuition and fees at the University of Akron for students who attend middle and high school in Akron public schools. For more information, see http://lebronjamesfamilyfoundation.org/page/akronipromise.

11. Bernard Daly, Will, December 27, 1919.

12. In addition to educational and economic impacts, the Daly Fund has had considerable philanthropic impact. The Daly Fund itself, started with $700,000 in 1922, has benefited from long-term growth and bequests made by recipients, the most recent of which was a $2.3 million bequest. Furthermore, the existence of the Daly Fund led to the creation of other funds to support higher education: the Collins McDonald Fund, created in 1940 to support attendance at private and out-of-state colleges; the Burt Snyder Fund, created in 1964 for graduate programs; the Anna Jones Scholarship for Paisley graduates; and the $11.5 million Ousley Fund, established in 2012. With all of these endowed scholarships, it is not surprising that Lake County has the most endowed funds for higher education in the United States.

13. Responding to the growth of community colleges, the Daly Fund permitted recipients to attend Oregon community colleges beginning in 1970.

14. National Center for Education Statistics, "Graduation Rates," 2017, https://nces.ed.gov/fastfacts/display.asp?id=40 (accessed September 6, 2017).

15. Camille L. Ryan and Kurt Bauman, "Educational Attainment in the United States: 2015, Population Characteristics," National Center for Education Statistics, US Department of Education, 2010, 2016, P20–578.

16. Debbie Cochrane and Diane Cheng, *Student Debt and the Class of 2015* (Oakland, CA: Institute for College Access & Success, 2016), https://ticas.org/sites/default/files/pub_files/classof2015.pdf (accessed September 6, 2017).

17. US Census Bureau, *Quick Facts, Lake County, Oregon*, 2016, https://www.census.gov/quickfacts/fact/table/lakecountyoregon,OR,US/INC110215 (accessed

September 6, 2017); Suzanne Mettler, *Degrees of Inequality: How the Politics of Higher Education Sabotaged the American Dream* (New York: Basic Books 2014).

18. The quotations at the beginning of each of these sections are comments written by survey respondents in response to an open-ended question asking, "Is there anything in particular you'd like us to know about you or the impact of the Daly Fund?"

19. Laura Jimenez, Scott Sargrad, Jessica Morales, and Maggie Thompson, *Remedial Education: The Cost of Catching Up* (Washington, DC: Center for American Progress, 2016), https://cdn.americanprogress.org/content/uploads/2016/09/29120402/CostOfCatchingUp2-report.pdf (accessed September 6, 2017).

20. *Oregon Agricultural College General Catalog, 1922–1923* (Corvallis, OR: Published by the College, 1922).

21. College Board, "Trends in College Pricing," *Education*, 2015, 44, http://trends.collegeboard.org/sites/default/files/trends-college-pricing-web-final-508–2.pdf (accessed September 6, 2017).

22. With several additional scholarships available to Lake County students, another 20 to 30 percent of students are likely to receive scholarships, and there is evidence that a surprising number of Lake County students go on to complete college. It does seem that the Daly Fund has impacted more students than those who receive scholarships.

4

Financing Independence

Endowments, Philanthropic Foundations, and Higher Education in American History

David C. Hammack

Walter Prescott Webb gained a reputation for his emphasis on history that engages readers, for his commitment to getting the details of a story right, and for his enthusiasm for histories of adventures. I want here to offer another adventure story—or several stories pursuing many disparate adventures. Walter Prescott Webb told adventure stories featuring the determined and creative—and hungry—explorers and settlers who brought into the American West people whose origins were mostly to be found in Northern Europe.[1]

Here I want to take up the story of another adventure, the adventure of understanding charity. The word "charity" calls for a brief discussion of terms. We have good reason to associate endowments and foundations with wealth and stability and tradition and inequality, rather than with adventures that appeal to ambitious, even hungry, young people. But consider: under American law—and before the American Revolution under English law—charitable funds are and were for the advance of charitable purposes, defined to include not only the relief of immediate need, but also the support of religious and cultural values, perspectives, and institutions. Increasingly, in the United States that has meant for the development of ideas and the creation and sustaining of new institutions under novel, as well as venerable, faiths. A charitable fund could support a religious community, science, or literature; it could support elementary education or cutting-edge research; it could underwrite established social practices or new notions that challenge inherited ways. It can seek to relieve immediate need, or it can promote social and economic development that reduces need even if, short of utopia, it does not eliminate it. Even discussions that acknowledge the centrality of values—religious and secular—to charitable activity too often fail to consider the implications. Writing on education, for example, too often sees schooling as generic, ignoring the significance to parents, students, teachers, and supporters of the ways that schools distinguish themselves as Catholic or Protestant or Jewish or Muslim, as "traditional" or "progressive." Here, I want to argue that cultural and religious ideals, as well as the personal ambitions and material concerns of founders, donors, and students, have played large and interesting roles.[2]

Three stories about the adventurous uses of charitable funds to shape American colleges and universities will, I think, make the point. First, I want to begin with a rarely acknowledged story from the nation's colonial period: the vigorous though ultimately inadequate English efforts to use endowments, mostly provided by government, to establish the Anglican Church on this side of the Atlantic. Second, I will turn to competing nineteenth-century uses of endowments. Each of these aimed to advance a distinctive religious, social-cultural, and practical purpose. Most accounts treat Protestant college-building efforts as a single phenomenon. But considered more closely, Protestants—and their colleges—disagreed among themselves, pursuing adventures that sharply conflicted with one another. On reflection, the idea that Protestant efforts conflicted should not be seen as surprising: religious division is a continuing theme of Protestant history; Protestants dominated both sides in the Civil War; Northern and Southern Protestants found it very difficult to come together for one hundred years or more after Reconstruction. Third, the most celebrated episode in the history of American foundations is the effort from about 1900 through the 1920s to use very large industrial fortunes to create the extraordinary modern American research university. Almost always missing from discussions of this story, however, is the persisting use of foundations and endowments to underwrite a wide range of competing, often religious, initiatives. In this way, foundations and endowments have helped define America's truly exceptional congeries of distinctive, competing, nongovernmental providers of education as well as of medicine, social services, and the arts.[3]

I draw a single conclusion from these stories: American endowments and foundations have underwritten many of the nation's consequential cultural and religious initiatives—advancing causes that conflict with one another at least as often as they collaborate. In seeking to connect foundations and endowments to this set of the larger themes in American history, I am largely drawing here on the studies of others; what I offer is a reframing. Bruce Kimball, Thomas Adam, Sam Stern, and others are diving deeply into the many still unexplored details of the history of the financing of American higher education, helping us all understand much better than ever before how much it has cost to provide the services of higher education. It is my aim to call attention to the importance of distinctive values in shaping the services that colleges and universities actually provide.

Colonial College Endowments and the Church of England

Let us start with the story of endowments and the Anglican Church in the American colonies. Americans have long been accustomed to think that during the nearly two hundred years of the colonial period, the great higher education adventure had to do with the creation of independent colleges in the wilderness. These did appear, and some of them did build endowments. Harvard's founders, just six years after arriving in Boston, launched a college intending to "advance learning and perpetuate it to prosperity." By 1700 Harvard may well have been covering half its operating costs with endowment income. If we are looking backward for the first appearance of a hallowed later pattern, the focus on colonial initiative makes some sense. But the adventure that preoccupied both English authorities and many colonists at the time, and that is now ignored, was the imperial effort to use Anglican institutions to establish and expand control throughout a North Atlantic dominated, at the beginning of the eighteenth century, by Spain and France.[4]

Religion and education played key roles in this struggle. Spain and France used their established Catholic churches to support their governmental and imperial authority. By the early 1700s Britain had quelled violent conflicts within its home territory among Protestants and Catholics, Anglicans and Presbyterians and Puritans. It had done this in large part by establishing a broad-based Church of England that also supported government and empire, but in part by discouraging dissent. The king formally headed the Church of England, and the

Church carried out many of the government's functions, especially in education and the regulation of family life.[5]

Higher education was important to imperial control over the colonies first, because it produced religious officials and leaders tied to London, and second, because literate graduates who lived in the colonies but were attuned to London could be very useful to both government and commerce. Materially, college architecture replicated English design. It would be wrong to overstate England's commitments. Britain's North American colonies were small societies that had many claims on their resources. It was not easy to persuade those who controlled resources to commit them to colleges. In 1691 England's attorney general objected to the idea of an endowment for the College of William and Mary, responding to a plea for the education of ministers: "Damn your souls! Make tobacco!" In 1725 George Berkeley, the noted philosopher, secured a charter for a college in Bermuda, but as Berkeley wrote, people who held "narrow and mercantile views" objected to embracing a college on a commercial island; his project never won enough support to become a reality.[6]

English authorities did charter three Anglican-related colleges in the North American colonies and did provide them with initial endowments. These are well known: William and Mary in Virginia, King's College in New York, and the University of Pennsylvania. Respectful of Quaker opinion, the last of these combined Anglican leadership with nonsectarian official status.

And the Church of England exerted influence on other schools as well. When England asserted more direct control over Massachusetts at the time of the Glorious Revolution of 1688 and after, the Church of England gained some formal influence over a Harvard that had until then been quite independently Puritan.[7] Yale opened as a second Puritan college in 1701; within a few years its top leaders had converted to the Church of England. Elsewhere, Anglicans founded still other secondary schools that developed into colleges only after the Revolution: King William's School in Annapolis (later part of Saint John's College), Kent County Free School in Maryland (later merged into Washington College), and the College of Charleston.

The English expected college students to pay some of the costs of their education; they also expected private citizens to contribute to their endowments. Legal charters of incorporation enabled colleges to hold, invest, and manage the use of endowed funds and other assets; institutions that lacked charters could not promise to protect donated funds. Lacking a charter, an institution could find it impossible to build and hold facilities, as happened with the Presbyterian "Log College" in Neshaminy, near Philadelphia, which dissolved at the 1746 death of its founder, the revivalist William Tennent.[8]

The English Society for the Propagation of the Gospel understood the need to subsidize new churches in territory where the Anglicans wished to increase their influence, such as New England. Complaining about Anglican initiatives, Puritan preacher Jonathan Mayhew observed in 1763 that the Society for the Propagation of the Gospel was supporting thirty missionaries in New England, compared to a total of only four in Georgia and the entire West Indies. The society, he argued was using its "charitable fund" for a "crusade, or spiritual siege of our [Puritan] churches, with the hope that they will one day submit to an Episcopal sovereign."[9]

It was New York that produced some of the strongest complaints against England's use of endowments to advance the Anglican Church. In 1754 imperial and Anglican authorities in New York City launched King's College. Presbyterians and Dutch Reformed constituted by far the largest portion of the city's population, and leaders of those communities pressed for religious rights in the new college. But Anglican Trinity Church in New York City had a very large endowment of land.[10] On condition that King's College exclude all except Anglicans from its religious exercises, Trinity transferred a substantial portion of its lands to King's. Non-Anglicans protested: "Our fears are greatly increased, when we consider the Episcopal Church possessed of so immense an Estate in this City; and her members enjoying the Principal part of the wealth of the Metropolis; not that we envy either the Corporation of that Church, or any private member belonging to it, in any part of their Possessions: We only notice their superior riches, as an unfailing Source of Superior influence; an influence sufficient unless opposed by the union of all the other denominations to carry almost every Election here." The complaint went on to protest new grants "of large Tracts of Land in every new township, for a parsonage glebe, and for the Society for propagating the Gospel; while the churches of every other denomination are refused even the comparatively trifling favor of a Charter, to enable them to enjoy the benefit of private Donations."[11]

Determined to build colleges to support their preferred forms and traditions of Protestantism, the "Non-Episcopalians" founded and endowed, or began to endow, competing institutions of their own. Presbyterians started the modest Augusta Academy (later Washington and Lee University) in Virginia and the Newark, Delaware, Academy in the late 1740s, as well as Dickinson in Pennsylvania and Hampden-Sydney in Virginia in the 1770s. In the 1760s, Baptists underwrote the College of Rhode Island, later Brown, and with a charter from the governor of New Jersey, the Dutch Reformed launched Queen's College, later Rutgers. The Moravians opened schools for girls or young women in 1742 and 1772.

But the Archbishop of Canterbury, who also led the Society for the Propagation of the Gospel, successfully intervened to deny a college charter for a Georgia school sought by Methodist evangelist George Whitefield. Whitefield had antagonized the archbishop by denouncing the Society's American missionaries as "ungodly despicable Ministers" who were too often "corrupt in their principles and immoral in their practices."[12]

The story of colonial college endowments, then, is a story of efforts to advance religious communities in societies in an Atlantic world in which religion reinforced conflict between England and its colonies. To train their clergy, to rally members who valued learning, to win concessions from government, religious groups needed endowed institutions. And on the English side, the adventure—never adequately supported—was to build a church establishment capable of helping the government both provide basic services to its colonists and influence the colonists' hearts and minds. An endowment conferred material advantages. Those who opposed the religious or educational—or, broadly, political—tendencies underwritten by a particular endowment complained, sometimes vehemently. A minister sent by the Society for the Propagation of the Gospel recorded strong resistance to his effort to impose Anglican order on a small community in backwoods South Carolina in 1767: "The Captain of the Corps of Militia on this creek being a Presbyterian, order'd the company to appear as this day under arms to muster. The [Anglican] Church people refus'd. He threatn'd to fire. They defy'd him: And had he attempted it, a battle would certainly have ensu'd."[13]

By some measures, opposition to domination by the Church of England did as much to bring on the American Revolution as opposition to taxation without representation.

In the twenty years before the Revolution, American colleges raised thousands of pounds from tens of thousands of Britons. Historian Beverly McAnear concluded that "many Englishmen contributed to the colleges in order to foster imperial unity."[14] Such private donors had sought to reinforce the royal policy of endowing Anglican churches and colleges in the colonies with sufficient resources to achieve imperial missions.

Yet McAnear emphasized that the imperial effort failed in the thirteen colonies. As he wrote, and as the musical *Hamilton*'s treatment of King's College in New York City is currently reminding us, "the institutions were destined, and to a great degree by intent, to become steppingstones to American intellectual autonomy." After the Revolution, Virginians spent many years debating what to do with the lands formerly allotted as endowments to parishes of the Church of England.[15] The Anglican effort to endow and establish its church failed, but an adventure it surely was.

Nineteenth-Century Academic Endowments and Foundations: East, West, and South

In the ten turbulent decades after the American Revolution, the United States won control of land that stretched "from sea to shining sea," sent a growing population into the vast area formerly controlled by Native Americans and by European authorities, and weathered a terrible civil war. Through change and conflict, Eastern colleges grew rapidly, while white settlers from Ohio to Alabama, Minnesota to Texas, and Oregon to California established scores of new colleges and universities in the nation's new states.

The numbers of students remained small—just one or two percent of the male population—but the colleges served as rallying points for a remarkable variety of initiatives, religious, cultural, and economic. These initiatives often conflicted with one another. Endowments and funds of various kinds played significant roles in each case. I will refer briefly to examples from the major regions or sections of the nation.

The American Revolution rejected not only the Church of England but also the very idea of an established church. Within a few decades that meant, in every state, rejecting the use of tax money to support religion. And because higher education emphasized religious careers and four-fifths of all pre–Civil War colleges were church-affiliated, it broadly meant rejecting the use of tax money for colleges (although that did not prevent college leaders from seeking government subsidies). Even though a few state universities developed substantial endowments during the nineteenth century, some of them significantly helped by federal land-grant funds (Map 4.1), as a group public institutions were less well financed than, and by 1900 enrolled just half as many students as, their private counterparts.[16]

To replace government funds that were not available, Protestants created financial structures capable of underwriting both religion and education. They added to the endowments of individual churches and schools. They created new denominational and interdenominational funds to underwrite the education of clergy. They subsidized publishing houses and journals that produced not only bibles, tracts, and Sunday School readers but also learned books and articles. By the 1850s the largest of the college and denominational endowments constituted substantial foundations in the modern sense that they held and invested large funds, seeking to maintain and increase the value of those funds while also generating income for charitable purposes that changed over time. Their charitable purposes were religious as well as educational.

It is crucial to the story to recognize that college professors and presidents were most often ordained ministers who generally relied on denominational funds for pensions and medical and life insurance, for the education of their sons, and for retirement homes for their widows. As settlers moved into new territories, denominational funds subsidized their new churches and ministers as well as their new colleges. Denominational funds provided important support to college faculties. This context fostered a host of adventures.

In New England, Congregationalists and Unitarians emphasized their core colleges and universities. On losing state subsidies in 1819, Congregationalist Yale launched a wide-ranging fundraising campaign, developed an endowment of perhaps $380,000 by the 1850s, successfully recruited students from other states including the South, and added new facilities, including scientific laboratories and an art museum. Unitarian Harvard aggressively built its endowment to about $1 million by 1850, focused on its own facilities across Greater Boston and its own faculty,

United States Department of Agriculture

National Institute of Food and Agriculture

NIFA LAND-GRANT COLLEGES AND UNIVERSITIES

* Central State University (CSU), in Ohio, has been designated as an 1890 LGU. Under the law, CSU will be eligible to receive certain capacity funds in October 2014 and others in fiscal year 2016.

** College of the Muscogee Nation and Keweenaw Bay Ojibwa Community College are designated as 1994 LGUs and will be eligible to receive capacity funds in October 2014.

(On Left) Map 4.1. Land Grant Colleges, 1862, 1890, 1994. US Department of Agriculture, National Institute of Food and Agriculture, June 2014, https://nifa.usda.gov/sites/default/files/resource/lgu_map_6_25_2014_0.pdf.

and by the mid-nineteenth century was aiming to provide the best possible education to the best-prepared New England students, especially students from Boston. Boston's Lowell Institute, closely associated with Harvard and from the 1860s with the Massachusetts Institute of Technology, also operated as a substantial foundation, mounting high-quality lectures, often by significant scientists. Two Northeastern schools with ties to the Episcopal Church also held substantial endowments for their mainly regional student populations in the 1850s; these were Columbia with perhaps $700,000 and Penn with $200,000.[17]

The Northeastern schools also benefited from independent funds. From as early as 1815, as historian Natalie Naylor has shown, the interdenominational American Education Society and its predecessors—working partly like fundraisers, partly like foundations—provided scholarships to thousands of college students; in the 1830s the numbers ranged from five hundred to twelve hundred a year. The American Education Society especially aided students in New England colleges. Naylor calculates that in 1830 this one society was aiding one-sixth of the students at Yale, one-fifth of those at Amherst, more than a quarter of those at Middlebury, as well as a quarter of all students in Protestant seminaries and half at some in New England. Presbyterian funds similarly aided Princeton and its sister schools. Eastern Protestants also looked to the West. A considerable literature celebrates—and critiques—the Protestant church-related colleges built across the Old Northwest in those decades. That literature too often downplays real religious and cultural conflicts.[18]

Through an agreement known as the Plan of Union, Congregationalists cooperated with Presbyterians to build new colleges, as well as churches and academies, in the West. Their aim was to advance a well-educated evangelical Christianity in a region threatened, as they believed, by materialism, irresponsibility, Deism, and Catholicism. Conflict between Congregationalists and Presbyterians over the proper forms of church government, over religious ideas, and sometimes over social ideals soon made collaboration difficult. When some Oberlin students, who were more committed to popular evangelicalism than to the classics, burned copies of Virgil, Presbyterians seem to have taken the lead in persuading the American Education Society to end all scholarships to that college.[19]

To coordinate direct Eastern fundraising for leading Western colleges in 1843, Congregationalists persuaded some Presbyterians to join them in creating another money-raising and grantmaking fund, the Society for the Promotion of Collegiate and Theological Education at the West. In the next two decades this society aided twenty-six western colleges selected for the quality of their programs and the adequacy of their support. This society made clear choices. Its stated policy was to support just one college in each state, and in 1872 its leader argued that the society "deserves the thanks of all lovers of Christian learning for its repressive policy; for discouraging, and thereby, in many cases, destroying nascent institutions which bade fair to come up only to plague their inventors." The society's grants could easily account for more than ten percent of a school's annual income. In 1872 a Baptist leader summed up the record in admiring terms: "The net resources of all the institutions originally taken on . . . were $300,000." The society had delivered to them "$850,000, and has seen the net resources of all its beneficiaries taken together rise to about" $3 million. At that point the society reorganized more strictly within the Congregationalist denomination.[20]

Presbyterians proved to be especially thorough in placing and building colleges. Assiduously using their national Board of Education to supervise and subsidize their schools, they built more colleges than any other denomination. We have noted their determination to insist on their own religious and educational ideas and priorities. Their retirement, insurance, and education funds operated like foundations, and Presbyterians emphasized the importance of college endowments. An essay in the 1859 report of the Presbyterian Board of Education argued that an endowment was "a chief want in a college" and that "colleges cannot prosper without permanent funds." It added that "it takes a long time, commonly, to secure the funds necessary for a complete endowment," and "the endowment ought to come, as a general rule, from the region of the country where the college is located." We should also note that despite their zeal for effective organization, the Presbyterians repeatedly divided into separate groups: New School and Old School, Cumberland, and others, then after 1837, Northern and Southern.[21]

The complicated story of Southern church-related colleges in the second half of the nineteenth century is too often left out of histories of American higher education, but it also demands attention. After the Civil War the South was a section that kept to itself in many ways. During the Civil War and after, northern Protestants used their churches, denominational organizations, bequests, and foundations both to support the Union Army and to send money and hundreds of volunteer missionaries and teachers to Southern churches, schools, and colleges. The Northerners sought to bring both white and black people into their denominational communities. After the war, as is well known, Northern white Protestants set up the Peabody fund and other foundations to underwrite both college and basic education for African Americans in the South.[22]

White Southern Protestants rejected these overtures. By the end of the 1880s the leader of Southern Baptist missions insisted, "There was not a missionary to the white people of the South who did not bear a commission from either the Home Mission Board" of his denomination "or one of our State Boards." Southern philanthropy met the gifts from the North: "This could not be done without money" given to pay for more than 3,400 Sunday schools, or without the voluntary or ill-paid service of 4,500 missionaries, who in a few years raised nearly $650,000 for houses of worship and engaged more than 110,000 churches.[23] He might have made the same point about Southern colleges.

Much more than before the Civil War, Southerners organized their lives through churches and other private entities, often church-related, that worked outside government. Compared to their Northern counterparts, Southern states granted few corporate charters to charities that were not controlled by religious groups.[24] Recent histories show how Southern white churches, schools, and colleges came, despite internal opposition and some desire for racial interchange, to celebrate the Lost Cause of the Confederacy and to promote both academic arguments and a folk theology that favored white supremacy.[25]

In the 1850s some Southern colleges and universities had been better endowed than most in the North; fighting and investment in the bonds of the Confederate government destroyed many of these endowments, but Southerners quickly set to rebuilding them (Map 4.2). As in the North, Southern denominational funds helped support college faculties. In the twentieth century, foundations that helped maintain

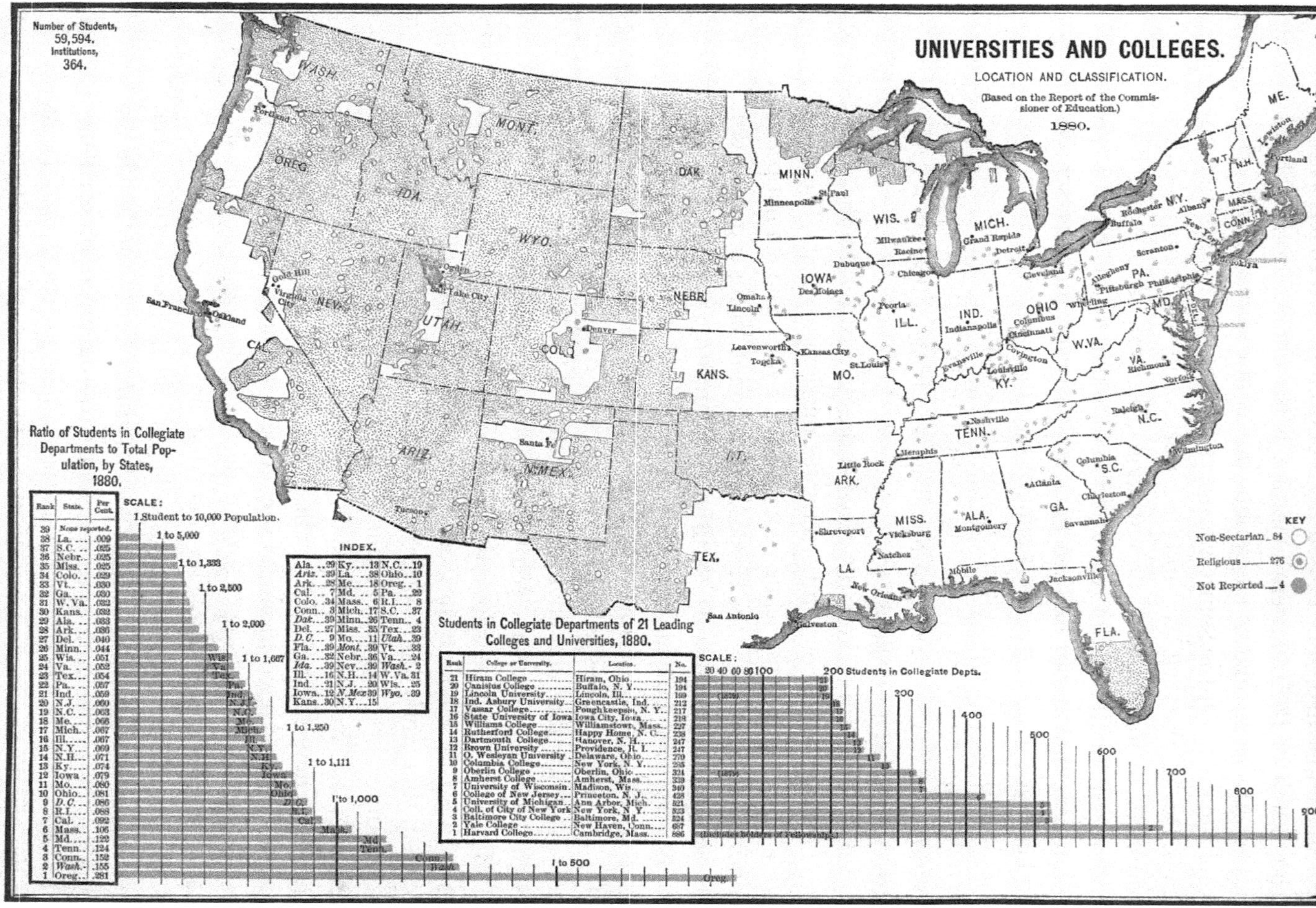

Map 4.2. Universities and Colleges in 1880, from Federal Data. By Fletcher W. Hewes and Henry Gannett, in Scribner's Statistical Atlas of the United States *(New York: Charles Scribner's Sons, 1883).*

whites-only colleges, usually church-related, also appeared in several Southern states. It was in this context that the Danforth Foundation moved in the 1950s to encourage racial integration in church-related colleges and seminaries.[26]

Through most of the nineteenth century, endowments and foundations lent their support to colleges that resembled one another regardless of region or decade. All expected students to pay tuition and to pay for room and board, and all used charitable funds to subsidize students selected for religious commitment or other qualities, as well as for general ability and need. Nearly all colleges desired endowments, though some succeeded much more than others in acquiring them (Table 4.1).[27] Very few imposed a religious test for admission, and most put some emphasis on mutual forbearance if not toleration or comity among Protestant sects. Most did discriminate against, or entirely exclude, African Americans.

Until near the very end of the century, nearly all emphasized the classical curriculum; those that demanded the most attention to classical studies generally won the highest rankings for educational quality. At the same time, nearly all earned additional income by teaching short courses outside the regular curriculum: both courses in practical applied science and accounting and training courses for teachers and ministers. Funders did not dictate these shared qualities, but they did reinforce them. Funds external to the colleges played important roles in reinforcing academic and religious standards and in connecting colleges and students to one another, to the Protestant denominations, and, especially for those outside the South, to the prominent seminaries and professional schools in the Northeast.[28]

We should add that Catholics were also building colleges as well as seminaries throughout the nineteenth century and beyond. As late as the 1930s, some Catholic leaders were expressing distress at the absence of Catholic churches and other institutions in much of the South and the West and were marking these as important areas for future development.

We can also say some very definite things about those who controlled the funds and endowments that aided these colleges. Contrary to the implications of a number of recent accounts, they did their best to use money with care and purpose.[29] They acted strategically, they explicitly thought in terms of investments, they had clear ideas about

Table 4.1. Endowments in federal table of college and university data, 1880

States and Territories	Number of Colleges	Preparatory Department		Collegiate Department		Income from productive funds in Dollars	Receipts last year from tuition in Dollars	Volumes in college libraries	Value of grounds, buildings, and apparatus in Dollars
		Number of Instructors	Number of Students	Number of Instructors	Number of Students				
Alabama	4	2	32	51	417	24,000	6,000	7,200	370,000
Arkansas	4	9	528	32	291	1,000	10,300	2,360	114,000
California	13	21	1,205	145	800	106,216	68,814	46,950	1,367,400
Colorado	3	4	239	25	57	20,518	471	9,200	190,000
Connecticut	3	—	—	73	951	126,973	102,912	147,651	472,884
Delaware	1	—	—	5	59	4,980	540	6,500	75,000
Georgia	7	10	224	45	469	35,263	12,100	31,100	966,000
Illinois	28	80	2,692	202	2,081	124,896	107,719	115,372	2,303,600
Indiana	14	32	1,376	105	1,169	64,970	29,488	56,207	1,020,000
Iowa	19	43	1,765	156	1,296	47,300	43,758	53,672	1,173,908
Kansas	8	13	772	59	323	11,800	6,450	22,175	540,000
Kentucky	15	22	692	117	1,224	32,661	56,466	39,597	773,000
Louisiana	8	30	585	38	92	15,155	15,327	50,800	418,000
Maine	3	4	70	40	431	35,700	19,251	41,771	805,000
Maryland	9	17	290	109	1,146	181,7334	13,572	42,650	520,500
Massachusetts	7	3	110	156	1,899	425,958	150,335	272,528	1,150,000
Michigan	9	22	1,121	116	1,111	78,420	81,760	56,731	1,353,442
Minnesota	6	1	471	62	351	35,834	7,265	17,441	327,650
Mississippi	4	9	683	26	284	39,443	7,100	10,700	625,000
Missouri	14	23	694	178	1,735	66,110	73,765	101,605	1,125,220
Nebraska	4	13	548	24	117	2,250	1,800	3,900	188,000
Nevada	1	1	48	—	—	—	—	—	25,000

New Hampshire	1	—	—	15	247	25,000	16,000	54,000	125,000
New Jersey	4	—	—	71	688	88,625	21,136	60,500	1,150,000
New York	29	85	3,113	439	3,512	710,164	474,229	237,224	7,266,773
North Carolina	8	10	328	70	894	10,000	27,500	29,543	539,000
Ohio	35	85	3,073	263	2,621	232,435	120,948	312,572	3,091,421
Oregon	8	18	554	37	502	21,500	15,750	9,520	255,000
Pennsylvania	27	54	1,960	300	2,454	199,368	179,932	145,266	5,135,626
Rhode Island	1	—	—	17	247	36,128	30,869	53,000	—
South Carolina	8	8	408	40	256	25,600	5,820	18,050	250,000
Tennessee	20	32	1,367	14	1,920	80,550	46,810	46,963	1,451,500
Texas	9	15	617	52	865	1,900	30,630	13,287	295,000
Vermont	2	—	—	18	102	16,368	4,990	31,552	340,000
Virginia	8	3	38	65	793	21,518	16,279	89,200	1,465,000
West Virginia	4	5	133	19	200	8,469	5,912	5,550	307,000
Wisconsin	8	6	723	95	678	52,542	62,676	48,250	798,500
District of Columbia	5	6	340	44	154	2,200	1,186	47,411	1,150,000
Utah	1	3	159	3	—	—	3,000	2,968	—
Washington Territory	2	5	83	8	117	500	2,500	1,800	100,000
Total	364	694	27,041	3,466	32,553	3,014,048	1,881,360	2,342,766	39,623,424

Source: Report of the Commissioner of Education, Table 158, Universities and Colleges in the United States in 1880, in *Index to the Executive Documents of the House of Representatives*, 47th Cong., 1st sess. (1881–82), 12:157.

cause and effect, they sought to employ leverage, they carefully monitored the uses of their grants, they emphasized data, and they paid serious attention to outcomes.

Some Concluding Thoughts on Twentieth-Century Academic Endowments and Foundations

Accounts of the adventures of American foundations generally start the story with the last couple of decades of the nineteenth century and confine their attention to nonsectarian or secular organizations.[30] So what does my emphasis on the mostly religious adventures of the Anglican Church in the colonies and of Protestant colleges in the nineteenth century have to do with the standard story?

First, we must recall that the legal definition of *charity* in the United States emphasizes religious and educational institutions. It is the legal definition that conveys corporate and tax advantages on American foundations and charitable endowments. Writers are of course free to define their subjects as they will. But for practical purposes, the legal definition matters. There are certainly various movements to exclude religious activities from a legal definition of charity, just as there are also efforts to exclude secular activities from that legal definition. It seems to me that it is important to take the entire field into account when we consider proposals to change the law. And to acknowledge that American funds, endowments, and foundations have always aimed to advance religious as well as cultural values.

It is certainly true that a remarkable group of foundations played an outsized role in the reorganization of American higher education in the early decades of the twentieth century. Johns Hopkins, Leland and Jane Stanford, and several others launched notable new institutions. The Carnegie Foundation for the Advancement of Teaching, the Carnegie Corporation, the Rockefeller Foundation, the Rockefeller-funded General Education Board, the Laura Spelman Rockefeller Memorial, the Rosenwald Fund, several Guggenheim foundations, and a number of closely associated foundations did advance a focused nonsectarian agenda. These funds did not force the separation of university and church. They did not by themselves invent the modern research university or the science-based medical research and education center. They did not dictate the adoption of the standard college-prep high school curriculum or the use of standardized college admission and placement examinations administered by the Educational Testing Service. But these funds did focus very substantial financial as well as intellectual and organizational resources on the efforts to advance these causes. In the absence of federal action in these fields before the Cold War and the Great Society, they made a significant difference.[31]

During the 1910s and 1920s conservative Christians protested their influence, largely in vain. Southern colleges and universities overwhelmingly refused to separate themselves from their sponsoring denominations and so rejected Carnegie pensions for their faculties.[32]

On their side, the great nonsectarian foundation donors and professional managers also shared a powerful set of values—that the United States should be an effective modern nation—even when Congress, divided by section, could not agree to fund the necessary education and scientific research. It should be added that most nonsectarian foundation leaders did not themselves see their work as lacking commitment to values, or indeed to religious values. F. Emerson Andrews, who played notable roles in promoting foundations both at the Russell Sage Foundation and as the long-serving founding director of the Foundation Center, wrote extensively in his autobiography of his engagement with New York City's Riverside Church. John D. Rockefeller made significant gifts to Baptist organizations and underwrote notable efforts to encourage comity among Protestant denominations. Some of the critiques of this set of foundations published during the 1930s emphasized the dominant position not only of businessmen, but also of Protestants, on their boards.[33]

But to focus only on nonsectarian and secular work of American foundations in the early decades of the twentieth century is to leave out of the account the continuing activity of religious foundations. The nineteenth-century patterns continued, even as nonsectarian private and state research universities and popular state colleges multiplied. The persistence of religion can be seen in foundations as well as colleges. The Russell Sage Foundation's very widely used 1946 list focused explicitly on foundations devoted to "social welfare" and excluded "ecclesiastical" funds, including several very large mission, educational, and retirement funds of the main Protestant denominations. Nevertheless, many of the funds it did include limited themselves to specific religious communities.

To take the example of Texas, the Russell Sage list included the

Baptist Foundation, nationally respected for the quality of its leadership and for its aid to Baylor and other denominational schools, as well as two nondenominational funds, the M. D. Anderson Foundation in Houston and the William Buchanan Foundation of Texarkana. The one Tennessee fund listed was the Board of Education of the Methodist Church. For other states the list included a Christian Foundation of Indiana; the Cardinal Mundelein Foundation, and the evangelical LeTourneau Foundation, both of Illinois (the latter fund later moved to Texas); and California's Pepperdine Foundation, devoted to the Churches of Christ.[34] Among the ten foundations reporting the largest grant expenditure in 1944, Russell Sage included the American Missionary Association. It also included the Duke Endowment for the Carolinas, which emphasized gifts to Methodist institutions, and the Danforth Foundation of Saint Louis, whose giving supported Protestant seminaries and chapels on college campuses as well as other purposes. In the past seventy years religious funds have grown in size.

Texas also provides its full share of examples of church-related colleges that thrived through the twentieth century: Abilene Christian, Southern Baptist Baylor, Southern Methodist, Southwestern Adventist, Texas Christian, Texas Lutheran, Presbyterian Trinity, several Catholic institutions, and many more. To focus only on the nonsectarian and secular foundations, colleges, and universities in telling the story of foundations and higher education in the twentieth century is to ignore a significant part of the story. The nineteenth-century American pattern of independently funded sectarian, Protestant, nongovernmental colleges persisted. Meanwhile Catholic institutions added complexity, as did smaller religious and other cultural groups.

Finally, it is important to put these stories into a realistic perspective. It would be wrong to conclude that private philanthropy, working through endowments and foundations as well as in other ways, sufficed to provide adequate support for nineteenth-century higher education, let alone to expect that private giving can support twenty-first-century American colleges and universities. The total of all private giving comes only to about 2 percent of US national income; that ratio has been studied carefully for one hundred years: it rose towards 2.5 percent only in the wake of World War II at the beginning of the Cold War, but then fell back. Total foundation income has grown a bit but remains under 0.5 percent of national income. Meanwhile, American consumer spending, including spending on higher education, continues to rise. Government spending has waxed and waned as a share of gross domestic product, but its share in the support of higher education did grow. Small numbers of foundations and universities have developed endowments of two billion dollars or more, and they are now distributed around the nation, but their assets cannot begin to support all students.

It strikes me that the nineteenth-century legacy is rather in three areas: First, in giving a multiplicity of purposes to American colleges and universities. Second, in helping to persuade reluctant state and federal legislators to provide tax funds directly to institutions (increasingly, to those controlled by the states as well as those that are private). Legislators well understand the religious and cultural conflicts that shape their constituents' views as to the kinds of education they are willing to fund. This, I think, helps us understand the third legacy: the political settlements that funnel most government funding not to institutions, but to competitive grants for scientific, medical, and defense-related research and to student entitlements to subsidies and to subsidized loans that must be repaid. Vouchers leave the selection of a college to the student, just as Medicare leaves the selection of a hospital to the patient and as Medicaid, rent supplements, and food stamps leave the selection of vendor to county officials and to aid recipients.

Charitable Endowments as Elements of Pluralism in American Society

The notion that charitable endowments support simple, undifferentiated "educational" or "medical" or "cultural" services, and that the key questions about endowments have to do with their size and their potential use in subsidizing public services, do not fit what we know about history or current realities. Although some endowments have grown to impressive size, endowments and foundations lack the resources to greatly reduce the growing inequality of American society. Moreover, the commitment of most endowments to specific religious, cultural, and other purposes is protected by law.

Considered from the perspective of constitutional guarantees of individual rights, endowments provide Americans with one of several tools for putting the First Amendment into action. Endowments underwrite freedom of religion, expression, and the press by allowing donors to provide permanent funds for the support of their preferred causes and by enabling later trustees and workers to preserve and increase the funds devoted to those causes. American nonprofit organizations can pursue causes that are widely accepted as appropriate and that appeal to minorities but that at a given time do not win support from the market or from a legislative majority.

Considered from the perspective of American society as a whole today, endowments increase the centers of autonomous initiative. Nonprofit organizations offer services and advance causes important to those who support them. In most cases nonprofits can offer only the services that win purchasers and attract gifts. In times of economic difficulty, disaster, war, or other crises, sales and donations can fall off. Governments subsidize nonprofits in many ways and provide services that many value highly. But political winds can shift in ways that cut off government subsidies. Even in hard times an endowed government service can continue to act. And an endowed foundation or nonprofit organization can act both to celebrate and uphold, and to provide, a distinctive service according to its conscience.

Notes

1. A very useful discussion of Webb is Dennis Reinhartz and Stephen E. Maizlish, *Essays on Walter Prescott Webb and the Teaching of History* (Arlington: University of Texas at Arlington, 1985). See also Walter Prescott Webb, "History as High Adventure," *American Historical Review* 64, no. 2 (January 1959): 265–81; Walter Prescott Webb, *The Great Plains* (Boston: Ginn & Co., 1931); Walter Prescott Webb, *The Texas Rangers: A Century of Frontier Defense* (Boston: Houghton Mifflin, 1935).

2. David C. Hammack and Helmut Anheier, *A Versatile American Institution: The Changing Ideals and Realities of Philanthropic Foundations* (Washington, DC: Brookings Institution Press, 2013).

3. Ibid.

4. Hugh Peter and Thomas Weld, "New England's First Fruits, 1643," in *Making the Nonprofit Sector in the United States: A Reader*, edited by David C. Hammack (Bloomington: Indiana University Press, 1998); Margery Somers Foster, *"Out of Smalle Beginnings . . ." An Economic History of Harvard College in the Puritan Period* (Cambridge, MA: Belknap Press of Harvard University Press, 1962), 155. A convenient overview of Atlantic political/economic geography is D. W. Meinig, *The Shaping of America: A Geographical Perspective on 500 Years of History*, vol. 1, *Atlantic America, 1492–1800* (New Haven: Yale University Press, 1986). A French map that illustrates the Atlantic context of Britain's American colonies at the beginning of the eighteenth century is Hubert Jaillot, *Amerique Septentrionale Divisée en Ses Principales Parties . . .* (Amsterdam, 1694), https://www.raremaps.com/gallery/

detail/14076/Amerique_Septentrionale_Divisee_en_Ses_Principales_Parties/Jaillot-Ottens.html.

5. For a widely praised recent overview, see Carla Gardina Pestana, *Protestant Empire: Religion and the Making of the British Atlantic World* (Philadelphia: University of Pennsylvania Press, 2009).

6. Herbert Baxter Adams, *The College of William and Mary: A Contribution to the History of Higher Education* (Washington, DC: Government Printing Office, 1887), 15; Robert L. McCaul, "Whitefield's Bethesda College Project and Other Attempts to Found Colonial Colleges: Part I," *Georgia Historical Quarterly* 44, no. 3 (September 1960): 265.

7. Norman Fiering, "The First American Enlightenment: Tillotson, Leverett, and Philosophical Anglicanism," *New England Quarterly* 54, no. 3 (September 1981): 307–44

8. Thomas J. Wertenbaker, "The College of New Jersey and the Presbyterians," *Journal of the Presbyterian Historical Society (1943–1961)* 36, no. 4 (December 1958): 209–16. The fullest nineteenth-century account noted that in later years "some owner of the property, never dreaming that there was any thing sacred in the logs of this humble edifice, had them carried away and applied to some ignoble purpose on the farm, where they have rotted away like common timber." Archibald Alexander, *Biographical Sketches of the Founder and Principal Alumni of the Log College: Together with an Account of the Revivals of Religion under Their Ministry* (Princeton, NJ: J. T. Robinson, 1845), 12.

9. Jonathan Mayhew, "Observations on the Conduct of the Society in Supporting Episcopal Missions and Schools in New England," Section 6 in *Observations on the Charter and Conduct of the Society for the Propagation of the Gospel in Foreign Parts* (Boston and London: n.p., 1763).

10. Elizabeth Mensch, "Religion, Revival, and the Ruling Class: A Critical History of Trinity Church." *Buffalo Law Review* 36 (1987): 427.

11. "The Society of Dissenters Founded at New York in 1769," *American Historical Review* 6 (1901): 498.

12. McCaul, "Whitefield's Bethesda College Project," quotation on 276. McCaul notes that "not one of the six colleges founded in the colonies between 1745 and 1775 had been chartered by the Crown"; their charters had been signed "by the governor, acting governor, or lieutenant governor . . . and by act of the provincial assembly" (272).

13. Charles Woodmason, *The Carolina Backcountry on the Eve of the Revolution: The Journal and Other Writings of Charles Woodmason, Anglican Itinerant* (Chapel Hill: University of North Carolina Press, 1953), 31.

14. Beverly McAnear, "The Raising of Funds by the Colonial Colleges," *Mississippi Valley Historical Review* 38, no. 4 (March 1952): 607.

15. Thomas J. Buckley, *Church and State in Revolutionary Virginia, 1776–1787* (Charlottesville: University Press of Virginia, 1977). In New York City, Trinity Church drew on its endowment to establish Episcopalian leadership among the city's Protestant churches; Kyle T. Bulthuis, *Four Steeples over the City Streets: Religion and Society in New York's Early Republic Congregations* (New York: NYU Press, 2014), 41–42.

16. Steven Brint and Charles T. Clotfelter, "US Higher Education Effectiveness," *RSF: The Russell Sage Foundation Journal of the Social Sciences* 2, no. 1 (April 2016): 2–37, https://muse.jhu.edu/article/612990/pdf.

Of about 200 colleges and universities founded before the Civil War that persisted to 1930, 166 were church related. State universities, a small handful of early polytechnics, and one or two municipal institutions constituted the only exceptions. For comprehensive lists, see Donald George Tewksbury, *The Founding of American Colleges and Universities before the Civil War: With Particular Reference to the Religious Influences Bearing upon the College Movement* (New York: Teachers College, Columbia University, 1932), and the additions and corrections offered in Colin B. Burke, *American Collegiate Populations: A Test of the Traditional View* (New York: NYU Press, 1982), appendix A. The polytechnics included Rensselaer, Cooper Union, MIT, Lehigh, and Worcester.

17. Colin B. Burke, *American Collegiate Populations: A Test of the Traditional View* (New York: NYU Press, 1982), 112; Ronald Story, *The Forging of an Aristocracy: Harvard and the Boston Upper Class, 1800–1870* (Middletown, CT: Wesleyan University Press, 1980); Margaret W. Rossiter, "Benjamin Silliman and the Lowell Institute: The Popularization of Science in Nineteenth-Century America," *New England Quarterly* 44, no. 4 (December 1971): 602–26. In *American Collegiate Populations*, 44–45, Burke provides endowment ranges by state for the 1850s.

18. Natalie A. Naylor, "'Holding High the Standard': The Influence of the American Education Society in Ante-Bellum Education," *History of Education Quarterly* 24, no. 4 (Winter 1984): 479–97.

Critiques of an overemphasis on the religious character of early western colleges include David B. Potts, "American Colleges in the Nineteenth Century: From Localism to Denominationalism," *History of Education Quarterly* 11, no. 4 (Winter 1971): 363–80; "'College Enthusiasm!' as Public Response: 1800–1860," *History of Higher Education*, 1989, 149–61; and Burke's extended critique of Tewksbury, *American Collegiate Populations*. A thoughtful review essay that critiques the critique of Walter P. Metzger's review of *American Collegiate Populations* in the *Journal of Higher Education* 55, no. 3 (May–June 1984): 419–22. An essay emphasizing the influence of Midwestern religious diversity on local colleges is Timothy L. Smith, "The Ohio Valley: Testing Ground for America's Experiment in Religious Pluralism," *Church History* 60, no. 4 (December 1991): 461–79.

19. Naylor, "Holding High the Standard," 490–91.

20. Horatio Q. Butterfield, "Policy of the Society Touching the Number of Colleges to Be Assisted in One State," in *Twenty-Ninth Report of the Society for the Promotion of Collegiate and Theological Education* (New York: The Society, 1873), 24–31; James Findlay, "The SPCTEW and Western Colleges: Religion and Higher Education in Mid-Nineteenth-Century America," *History of Education Quarterly* 17, no. 1 (Spring 1977): 57n39; Baptist leader Rev. S. S. Cutting, quoted in Horatio Q. Butterfield, *Thirtieth Report of the Society for the Promotion of Collegiate and Theological Education* (New York: The Society, 1874), 23.

21. James Findlay, "Agency, Denominations, and the Western Colleges, 1830–1860: Some Connections between Evangelicalism and American Higher Education,"

Church History 50, no. 1 (March 1981): 64–80; *Fortieth Annual Report of the Board of Education of the Presbyterian Church in the United States of America* (Philadelphia: Published by the Board, 1859), 59–60. An impressive contribution on Presbyterian zeal for building schools is a rarely cited essay by Lois W. Banner, "Presbyterians and Voluntarism in the Early Republic," *Journal of Presbyterian History* 50, no. 3 (Fall 1972): 187–205. A much-praised state study is L. C. Rudolph, *Hoosier Zion: The Presbyterians in Early Indiana* (New Haven: Yale University Press, 1963).

For a stimulating effort to place the Presbyterian divisions into the larger national worlds of antebellum benevolent institutions, see John L. Brooke, "Cultures of Nationalism, Movements of Reform, and the Composite-Federal Polity from Revolutionary Settlement to Antebellum Crisis," *Journal of the Early Republic* 29 (Spring 2009): 1–33.

22. James McPherson, *The Abolitionist Legacy: From Reconstruction to the NAACP* (Princeton, NJ: Princeton University Press, 1975); Jacqueline Jones, *Soldiers of Light and Love: Northern Teachers and Georgia Blacks, 1865–1873* (Athens: University of Georgia Press, 1992).

From the 1910s the Jewish philanthropist Julius Rosenwald also used his foundation to provide major funding for colleges as well as lower schools that served African Americans in the South; see Peter M. Ascoli, *Julius Rosenwald: The Man Who Built Sears, Roebuck and Advanced the Cause of Black Education in the American South* (Bloomington: Indiana University Press, 2006). For a range of perspectives on the work of northern foundations that supported higher education for blacks in the South, see McPherson, *Abolitionist Legacy*; James Anderson, *The Education of Blacks in the South, 1860–1935* (Chapel Hill: University of North Carolina Press, 1988); Eric A. Anderson and Alfred A. Moss Jr., *Dangerous Donations: Northern Philanthropy and Southern Black Education, 1902–1930* (Columbia: University of Missouri Press, 1999); and Joan Malczewski, *Building a New Educational State: Foundations, Schools, and the American South* (Chicago: University of Chicago Press, 2016).

23. I. T. Tichenor, "The Home Mission Board of the Southern Baptist Convention," in *A Century of Baptist Achievement*, edited by Albert Henry Newman (Philadelphia: American Baptist Publication Society, 1901), quoted in Nancy Tatom Ammerman, *Baptist Battles: Social Change and Religious Conflict in the Southern Baptist Convention* (New Brunswick, NJ: Rutgers University Press, 1990), 38.

24. Norman J. Silber, *A Corporate Form of Freedom: The Emergence of the Nonprofit Sector* (Boulder, CO: Westview, 2001); Cybelle Fox, *Three Worlds of Relief: Race, Immigration, and the American Welfare State from the Progressive Era to the New Deal* (Princeton, NJ: Princeton University Press, 2012). Consistent with these observations, nonreligious nonprofits capable of building endowments and receiving foundation grants continued through the twentieth century to be less numerous in the South than in the North. Colin B. Burke, "Nonprofit History's New Numbers (and the Need for More)," *Nonprofit and Voluntary Sector Quarterly* 30 (2001): 174–203.

25. Paul Harvey, *Redeeming the South: Religious Cultures and Racial Identities among Southern Baptists, 1865–1925* (Chapel Hill: University of North Carolina Press, 1997); Daniel W. Stowell, *Rebuilding Zion: The Religious Reconstruction of the South, 1863–1877* (New York: Oxford University Press, 1998); James B. Bennett,

Religion and the Rise of Jim Crow in New Orleans (Princeton, NJ: Princeton University Press, 2016). Alfred L. Brophy, in *University, Court, and Slave: Pro-Slavery Thought in Southern Colleges and Courts and the Coming of Civil War* (New York: Oxford University Press, 2016), describes the ways in which antebellum Southern—and Northern—colleges justified slavery.

26. Burke, *American Collegiate Populations*, 44–45. Many of the Southern foundations of the twentieth century are listed in Shelby M. Harrison and F. Emerson Andrews, *American Foundations for Social Welfare* (New York: Russell Sage Foundation, 1946). For thoughtful discussion of the encouragement of integration, see these works by Merrimon Cuninggim, a former leader of the Danforth Foundation: *Private Money and Public Service: The Role of Foundations in American Society* (New York: McGraw-Hill, 1972), and *Uneasy Partners: The College and the Church* (Nashville, TN: Abingdon Press, 1994).

27. Thus the 1881 *Statistical Abstract of the United States* (Washington, DC: Government Printing Office, 1882), 157, includes a one-page table of data about colleges and universities, by state, published in 1880 that places a column for endowments alongside columns for numbers of students and tuition income, taken from the Report of the United States Commissioner of Education (Table 4.1).

28. Horatio Q. Butterfield ("Policy of the Society," 21–24) concluded a celebratory analysis of Western college success in developing candidates for Eastern seminaries by stating that in "1871, these beneficiary colleges furnished as many graduates to our Congregational seminaries as came to them from Bowdoin, Dartmouth, Amherst, and Yale."

29. The discussion in this section documents the careful use of resources in nineteenth-century higher education. Advocates of "strategic philanthropy" too often ignore the historical evidence and repeat the complaints of Andrew Carnegie and John D. Rockefeller that too much giving was mere charity given in a thoughtlessly sentimental way. This is true even of such a thoughtful book as Peter Frumkin's *Strategic Giving: The Art and Science of Philanthropy* (Chicago: University of Chicago Press, 2008).

30. Leonard Porter Ayres, *Seven Great Foundations* (New York: Russell Sage Foundation, 1911; reprint, Cambridge, MA: Harvard University, Hauser Center for Nonprofit Organizations, 2007); Warren Weaver and George Wells Beadle, *US Philanthropic Foundations: Their History, Structure, Management, and Record* (New York: Harper & Row, 1967); Joseph C. Goulden, *The Money Givers* (New York: Random House, 1971); Waldemar A. Nielsen, *The Big Foundations* (New York: Columbia University Press, 1972); Waldemar A. Nielsen, *The Golden Donors: A New Anatomy of the Great Foundations* (New York: Truman Talley Books, 1985); Barry D. Karl and Stanley N. Katz, "The American Private Philanthropic Foundation and the Public Sphere, 1890–1930," *Minerva* 19 (1981): 236–70; Olivier Zunz, *Philanthropy in America: A History* (Princeton, NJ: Princeton University Press, 2012). A notable exception is Cuninggim, *Private Money and Public Service*.

31. Stanley Coben, "Foundation Officials and Fellowships: Innovation in the Patronage of Science," *Minerva* 14 (1976): 225–40; Ellen Condliffe Lagemann, *Private Power for the Public Good: A History of the Carnegie Foundation for the*

Advancement of Teaching (Middletown, CT: Wesleyan University Press, 1983); Ellen Condliffe Lagemann, *The Politics of Knowledge: The Carnegie Corporation, Philanthropy, and Public Policy* (Middletown, CT: Wesleyan University Press, 1989); Roger L. Geiger, *To Advance Knowledge: The Growth of American Research Universities, 1900–1940* (New York: Oxford University Press, 1986); Steven C. Wheatley, *The Politics of Philanthropy: Abraham Flexner and Medical Education* (Madison: University of Wisconsin Press, 1988); Robert E. Kohler, *Partners in Science: Foundations and Natural Scientists, 1900–1945* (Chicago: University of Chicago Press, 1991).

32. Warren Akin Candler, *Dangerous Donations and Degrading Doles: or, A Vast Scheme for Capturing and Controlling the Colleges and Universities of the Country* (Atlanta, GA: Privately printed, 1909); W. S. Plummer Bryan, *The Church, Her Colleges, and the Carnegie Foundation* (Princeton, NJ: Princeton University Press, 1911).

33. Frank Emerson Andrews, *Foundation Watcher* (Lancaster, PA: Franklin and Marshall College, 1973); Eduard Lindeman, *Wealth and Culture: A Study of One Hundred Foundations and Community Trusts and Their Operations during the Decade 1921–1930* (New York: Harcourt Brace, 1936).

34. Shelby M. Harrison and F. Emerson Andrews, *American Foundations for Social Welfare* (New York: Russell Sage Foundation, 1946).

5

The Formative Financial Era of the "Major Professional Schools"

Medicine, Law, and Business at Columbia and Harvard, 1890–1950

Bruce A. Kimball, Jeremy B. Luke, and Jamie M. Brown

During the first half of the twentieth century, universities founded many new kinds of professional schools in significant social domains. Amid this profusion, medical schools, law schools, and business schools gradually rose in prestige and influence to become what scholars have called the "major professional schools" at universities.[1] The ascendance of these three kinds, the relative standing among them, and the ranking of individual schools naturally depended on their financial resources, and these outcomes were not inevitable. The major professional schools might have included other kinds.

Theological schools were long the wealthiest professional schools. In 1899 their aggregate endowment was six times greater than that of all the schools of medicine, law, and business combined. In subsequent decades, other new kinds of professional schools might have surpassed the major professional schools. In 1920 the endowment of Harvard's new Graduate School of Education was nearly $1,250,000, compared to the $969,000 of Harvard Law School and the $476,000 of Harvard Business School. Nevertheless, these other kinds of professional schools became what scholars have called "schools of the minor professions" or the "semi-professions."[2]

Despite their importance, scholars have not studied closely the historical finances of professional schools. In fact, researchers have not even compiled detailed data. Standard histories of legal, medical, or business education provide only anecdotal data or occasional snapshots.[3] Even the institutional histories of prominent schools do not offer specific data. For example, the most recent history of Harvard Medical School neglects money matters entirely and observes that the school's accomplishments resulted from its "unusual resources, both spiritual and intellectual." Likewise, Goebel's Pulitzer-prize-winning history of Columbia University law school limits the discussion of finances to a few pages on separate incidents and lists no index entries for budget, finances, or endowment.[4]

This essay presents the first compilation and comparative analysis of financial data from schools of medicine, law, and business during the formative era between 1890 and 1950. The study focuses on the historical cases of Columbia and Harvard because these were the two leading universities in professional education at the time. On the one hand, these two were the wealthiest universities in the United States for most of this period, as seen in Table 5.1. On the other hand, Columbia and Harvard had highly ranked schools in all three domains of the major professional schools. No other university had these two attributes during these decades. Consequently, Columbia and Harvard are

Table 5.1. Largest endowments of colleges and universities, 1875–1939 (in millions of nominal dollars. Dashes indicate values that are unavailable.)

Year	Harvard	Columbia	Yale	Chicago	Stanford[a]	Cornell	Johns Hopkins	Princeton
1875	1.6	4.6	0.3	—	—	1.3	3.0	0.9
1880	4.0	4.8	1.3	—	—	1.3	3.0	1.1
1885	4.8	4.6	1.4	—	—	3.6	3.0	1.4
1890	7.0	8.1	3.1	—	—	4.9	3.0	—
1895	8.4	10.7	3.8	2.9	[18.0]	6.2	3.0	—
1900	12.6	13.3	4.9	5.7	[18.0]	6.8	3.3	2.3
1905	18.0	14.4	7.3	7.8	[30.0]	7.7	4.8	2.9
1910	22.0	25.8	12.5	14.9	24.0	8.7	4.6	—
1915	28.5	30.9	16.2	19.4	24.0	14.3	7.3	5.6
1920	44.6	39.6	24.0	28.4	33.3	16.0	9.1	10.3
1926	76.0	50.4	45.6	35.3	28.4	19.6	23.1	15.0
1930	108.1	73.4	82.9	59.6	27.8	24.7	26.8	—
1936	134.6	46.2	95.1	65.4	31.4	26.5	28.3	28.7
1939	141.3	70.7	100.4	70.9	30.5	30.9	30.4	31.5

Source: Bruce A. Kimball and Benjamin A. Johnson, "The Inception of the Meaning and Significance of Endowment in American Higher Education, 1890–1930," *Teachers College Record* 114, no. 10 (2012): 1–32.
[a]Stanford University did not own or control its endowment until after Jane Stanford died in 1905.

uniquely suited to provide a comparative analysis of the three major professional schools in this period.

Our study advances three central conclusions. First, this era was formative for the major professional schools as a group. These three schools dramatically increased their wealth faster than did the rest of their respective universities. Second, the period was also formative in establishing the financial hierarchy among these three domains. In the 1890s the endowed law schools and medical schools stood on a par in financial capital, and only one university business school existed. Over the next fifty years the financial capital of medical schools rapidly outpaced that of law schools. Meanwhile, the fledgling business schools started far behind in financial capital, as well as status and influence, but soon caught and then pulled ahead of the law schools, though not the medical schools. By 1950 the resulting and persistent order of capital wealth within the echelon was medicine, business, and law.

Finally, we identify three kinds of factors that determined these financial developments. Alumni giving was insignificant for the medical schools and the law schools, except for a few windfall bequests to the latter. And business school alumni were generally too young to contribute. Instead, the ideology of benefaction, the leadership, and the financial strategy shaped the finances of the schools.

In ideological terms, the schools responded differently to the contemporaneous shift from charity to philanthropy in Americans' understanding of benefaction. Those responses affected the amount of gifts and grants received from donors and, therefore, the wealth of the schools. Institutional leadership played a role as well, comprising the administrative and entrepreneurial work of the deans and the support from the university president and central administration. This category might therefore be framed in terms of "institutional entrepreneurs," and scholars have developed sophisticated theories in this regard.[5] Fundamentally, the questions are whether and how leaders exploit opportunities to advance their institutions in the competition for resources, prestige, and excellence. Finally, the schools adopted distinctive financial strategies that directly influenced their fortunes.

These three kinds of factors reciprocally influenced each other. For example, the deans and presidents determined the financial strategy of the school and often did so in light of the schools' prospects of attracting charity or philanthropy. Hence, these three interrelated factors determined the financial template of the major professional schools, whose contours persisted throughout the twentieth century.

Ideological Shift from Charity to Philanthropy

Between 1870 and 1920 the economy of the United States expanded enormously. In fact, this economic growth has been termed "unique in human history" by economic historian Robert Gordon.[6] The growing wealth then prompted a staggering increase in financial benefaction, most of which flowed into the endowments of colleges and universities. In the first two decades of the twentieth century, retiring industrialists established new foundations that contributed even more to higher education, including the General Education Board in 1903, the Carnegie Foundation for the Advancement of Teaching in 1905, the Carnegie Corporation of New York in 1911, and the Rockefeller Foundation in 1913.[7]

The rise in benefactions naturally influenced the finances of the major professional schools during their contemporaneous formative era. But the influence varied across the professional domains. Gifts to professional schools, like those to higher education in general, had to fit the ideology—the meaning and justification—of financial benefaction in American culture. And that meaning and justification shifted between two successive understandings during the late 1800s and early 1900s. Historians have termed these "charity" and "philanthropy."[8]

The meaning of charity in America emerged from the Protestant missionary impulse that originated in the Puritanism of colonial New England. That impulse has been attributed to the altruistic motive of compassion or, alternatively, to the wish to impose upon others the benefactor's vision of the good and proper. By either motive, charitable benefaction constitutes an individual response to personally witnessed problems of those in need. Charity means giving directly to specific individuals in order to alleviate the immediate effects of poverty, sickness, or personal distress. Thus, charitable benefactions are generally personal, small in scale, empathetic, and palliative, temporarily satisfying the needs of particular individuals known to the benefactor.

Charity also implies that the recipients relinquish their independence and humble themselves before the giver. We cannot "be charitable to our equals," observed Progressive reformer Josephine Shaw Lowell in 1879.[9] Hence, figures at colleges and universities adopted the discourse of charity when speaking about financial "embarrassment" or "begging" for money, whether metaphorical or not. In 1910 the treasurer of Yale reported with satisfaction that the university "in recent years has not borrowed in the open market any money to tide it over a temporary embarrassment." A few years later, the secretary of Yale warned that "constant personal begging on the part of a university is apt to be undignified and to lead to the public's losing confidence in that most vital of necessities—a reputation for fearless educational independence."[10] Consequently, discretion, privacy, and anonymity usually characterized charitable gifts in higher education.

While the "stigma of charity" had long been recognized as problematic, dissatisfaction with the charitable understanding of benefaction grew rapidly in industrial America.[11] During the late nineteenth century the rising authority of natural science, the increasing power of business, and the drive for systemic, administrative organization transformed many aspects of American culture, including the ideology of benefaction. A new understanding of monetary donations thus emerged, especially during the Progressive Era extending from about 1890 to 1920. Historians have termed this "philanthropy" or, sometimes, "scientific philanthropy."

The rationale of philanthropy prescribed a more scientific and businesslike approach to benefaction by emphasizing verification through reason and evidence rather than the personal, emotional response of charity. Philanthropists thus consulted scientific research and professional expertise for an assessment of social ills and sought an "*orderly* or *systematic*" strategy to curing them.[12] In particular, philanthropy relied on biological, psychological, and economic laws. Further, philanthropy intended to address "the root causes of social dysfunction" rather than the symptoms. Also, philanthropy did not foster personal relationships between donors and recipients, but established intermediary institutions, such as endowed foundations operating according to policy.[13] This philanthropic detachment necessary for the assessment and correction of social problems contrasts with the direct and often close emotional relationship between donors and recipients entailed in charity.

Finally, philanthropy prized effectiveness, economy, and efficiency. Dollars invested in benefaction had to realize a tangible return and do so efficiently. Philanthropy "depended upon the adoption of those techniques of functional specialization and centralized coordination and administration that characterized the business world."[14] In the famous phrase of John D. Rockefeller, the philanthropic "business of benevolence" required effectiveness, economy, and efficiency.[15]

Historians have generally concurred on this "much-heralded shift from charity to philanthropy" in the United States.[16] But they disagree on the timing. According to some, philanthropy began to eclipse charity in the benevolent work of Quakers in the late 1700s and then advanced in postrevolutionary New England, demonstrated by the pamphlets of the Massachusetts Society for the Suppression of Intemperance issued in the 1810s. Others see the shift occurring in the 1820s or 1830s, prompted by the new legal interpretation of corporations arising from the *Dartmouth College* case of 1819 and the emergence of "civil society" in the United States.[17]

Whatever the starting point, by 1910 contemporary figures observed that the ideology of benefaction in the United States had shifted from the palliative, personal ethic of charity to the scientific and business-like approach of philanthropy. Commensurately, the term "charity" had acquired a pejorative connotation, and its use in public discussion declined.[18] In addition, retiring industrial capitalists had begun to establish and endow new foundations dedicated to funding philanthropic approaches to social betterment.

To be sure, the traditional charitable understanding of benefaction persevered in many sectors in American culture. In fact, the two rationales were often entwined, as when the *New York Times* addressed "Charity Old and New" in 1917. But philanthropy triumphed broadly in American benefaction and higher education by the early twentieth century, when universities began to compete for funding and to focus upon amassing endowment.[19]

Major Professional Schools at Harvard and Columbia

Historical data on the finances of professional schools is difficult to obtain. The few compilations for a range of institutions, as in the reports of the US commissioner of education, are incomplete or unreliable. Collecting data on individual institutions presents significant hurdles, because many financial reports are lost or inaccessible. When available, the financial reports of most colleges and universities are fraught with "illogical classification and unsuitable terminology," according to Trevor Arnett, the leading national authority during the 1920s.[20] Analyzing the data in light of the historical context presents an additional challenge.

During the 1890s most lawyers and doctors still acquired their professional training through apprenticeship or study at an independent proprietary professional school, in which faculty profited directly from tuition. Meanwhile, degree-granting schools, whether proprietary or not, grew in number and often sought to affiliate with a college or university. In 1880 university law schools numbered 51, medical schools 100, and business schools none. In 1890 university law schools numbered 61, medical schools 133, and business schools one.[21] Thus, there were about twice as many university medical schools as law schools in the late nineteenth century. As their numbers increased, these university schools began to shift away from the proprietary model and to graduate an increasing proportion of leading professionals in their field. Like universities at the time, the schools started competing for standing and influence and realized that their financial resources determined the outcome.

In the 1890s the university law and medical schools stood on a par with each other in financial capitalization. Within each group, about 15 percent of the schools were endowed, and the financial capital of those endowed schools in each group averaged about $100,000. Also, the largest endowment in each domain was about $480,000. By comparison, the eighty-four endowed theological schools had capital funds amounting to nearly $18,000,000, averaging about $214,000 per school, in 1899.[22] Thus, the endowments of law schools and medical schools stood on a par, but far behind those of theological schools.

By the turn of the century many observers hoped that the capital funds of medical and legal education would grow to match those in theology. In 1900 the annual report of the US commissioner of education affirmed a published assessment of the same year: "Professional education in this country has not yet received, with the exception of theological education, a fitting endowment. . . . The great need of American life at the present time is better trained doctors and better trained lawyers. This need can be met only by the rich endowment of schools for the training of doctors and lawyers. . . . The next movement in the endowment of American education should be directed toward the schools of law and the schools of medicine."[23]

The call to raise endowment naturally resonated at the two wealthiest universities in the country. Columbia University had great ambitions and the largest endowment in the country as of 1873, the year that the US commissioner of education began issuing figures on college and university endowments. A decade later in *Century Magazine*, the president of Harvard observed that Columbia "is said to be the richest of our Colleges."[24] In 1910 Edwin Slosson noted in his classic *Great American Universities* that Columbia "has the best chance to become the greatest of American universities" due to its wealth and location in New York City.[25]

But the oldest university in the country, Harvard, also had ambitions. In 1884 one of the most prominent professors at Columbia, Theodore W. Burgess, observed that Boston was the only city in the nation with the means and the disposition to support a full-fledged university. Between 1885 and 1915 Harvard and Columbia jockeyed back and forth for claim to the most financial capital. Finally, in 1920 Harvard attained the leading position among university endowments that it has not relinquished. In 1930 Columbia dropped into third place, slightly behind Yale (Table 5.1).[26]

Beyond their leading financial status, Columbia and Harvard shared another significant attribute. Among the eight wealthiest universities in the nation, only Columbia and Harvard had schools in all three fields of law, medicine, and business that were considered among the best in the country. By comparison, the University of Pennsylvania was not among the wealthiest universities during those decades. At Yale, the medical school joined the leading schools early in the twentieth century, but the law school did not do so until about 1930, and the business school was not founded until after 1950. At Stanford, founded in 1893, the three professional schools did not achieve eminence until after 1945.

Founded in 1817, Harvard Law School underwent major reforms in the 1870s and 1880s, and by 1900 it was regarded both in the United States and in England as "the greatest law school in the world," in the words of Yale alumnus and future US president William H. Taft.[27] Opened in 1858, Columbia Law School emerged briefly as the most important law school due to its aspiration to upgrade legal education, but the proprietary self-interest of the faculty soon extinguished that goal. After Columbia consolidated its professional schools in 1890, successive law deans revitalized the academic standards of the school, and it remained "the nation's second best law school" until nearly 1930.[28] The academic preeminence of Columbia and Harvard law schools early in the twentieth century is shown by the percentages of college graduates among students at leading university law schools in 1905: Harvard, 99 percent; Columbia, 82 percent; Chicago, 60 percent; Yale, 35 percent; Pennsylvania, 35 percent; Northwestern, 31 percent; Michigan, 13 percent; and Cornell, 10 percent. This status led the law deans of Columbia and Harvard to consult each other more frequently than deans at other law schools in the opening decades of the twentieth century.[29]

In medicine, the school at Johns Hopkins University opened in 1893 and adopted the highest academic standards among medical schools. Some observers, such as the president of Yale, therefore associated Johns Hopkins medical school with Harvard Law School as the two standard-setting professional schools in the country. As of 1910, the second tier of medical schools comprised of Michigan and Minnesota, as well as Harvard Medical School, founded in 1783, and the medical school at Columbia, known as the College of Physicians and Surgeons, which had associated with Columbia in 1860. However, the order in financial resources was different. Harvard had the largest medical school budget, followed closely by Columbia. Third was Cornell at 80 percent of the Harvard budget, then Michigan at 60 percent, succeeded by a group of six, which included Johns Hopkins, at 40 percent or less.[30] This financial hierarchy foreshadowed Johns Hopkins's decline in academic ranking over the next decade.

Meanwhile, degree-granting business schools arose at universities. The first was founded in 1881 as the undergraduate Wharton School of Finance and Economy at the University of Pennsylvania, followed in 1898 by undergraduate programs at the University of Chicago and the University of California. In 1900 Dartmouth College established the fourth such business school, which awarded the first graduate degree in business management. In 1908 the movement accelerated after Harvard established its Graduate School of Business Administration. Apart from conferring the Harvard pedigree, this school was the first to put "business" in its name and to offer only graduate-level instruction. In 1916 the undergraduate Columbia Business School and the American Association of Collegiate Schools of Business were established, and the number of business schools then rose dramatically. By 1922 about 122 business schools were offering college degrees, and in the mid-1920s business studies became the fastest growing sector in American higher education, commensurate with the growth in the economy and managerial jobs. In 1925 Stanford founded the second exclusively graduate school of business, modeled on Harvard's.[31] Harvard and Columbia business schools thus belonged to the first generation of university business schools, and they grew rapidly.

Consequently, the two leading universities in professional education during the period between 1890 and 1950 were Columbia and Harvard. They had the largest endowments and eminent schools of law, medicine, and business. No other university had these attributes. The following acronyms for their major professional schools are employed in this essay: Columbia Law School (CLS), Columbia Business School (CBS), Columbia University College of Physicians and Surgeons (CMS), Harvard Law School (HLS), Harvard Medical School (HMS), and Harvard Graduate School of Business Administration (HBS).

Financial Strategy and Governance at Harvard and Columbia

Columbia and Harvard also had important differences that increase the significance of the commonalties between their professional schools in each domain. They differed significantly in their financial strategy and governance. Harvard had increased its financial capital without receiving enormous gifts on the scale that came to each of the seven other wealthiest universities between 1868 and 1920. Instead, Harvard built its wealth by adhering to its "free money" strategy, which gradually became the prevailing approach to building and maintaining the wealth of private universities over the course of the twentieth century. President Charles W. Eliot formulated the seven tenets of this free money strategy during his administration from 1869 to 1909.[32]

Eliot's foundational precept was that a university's academic accomplishment and reputation were determined fundamentally by its wealth. Second, Eliot narrowly defined a university's wealth to mean its endowment. Accordingly, a university must, third, refrain from depending on tuition revenue, spending its own resources on buildings, or accepting any "inexpedient" gifts that entail prohibitive expenses for the university. Fourth, a university must strive to keep its endowed funds free—unrestricted both in asset type and in purpose—although restricted gifts that are fungible, such as endowed professorships, should be strongly encouraged.

Fifth, a university must be managed like a business, operating efficiently and disclosing its finances fully and clearly so that the public appreciates its prudent management. Yet, sixth, unlike a business, a university should never carry a surplus. A university should regularly run a deficit in order to justify requests for more free money. By implication, a university's needs are, therefore, insatiable. Last, the president must assume primary responsibility for developing the wealth of the university by identifying, presenting, and justifying its needs for more free money, that is, unrestricted financial capital.

After Eliot retired in 1909, Harvard alumni conducted the first national public fundraising campaign in American higher education between 1915 and 1925. The campaign explicitly adopted Eliot's free money strategy and extended its influence.[33] Eliot's successor, A. Lawrence Lowell (1909–33), had a Brahmin's distaste for public fundraising, and his successor, chemist James B. Conant (1933–53), was neither interested nor effective in such work. Nevertheless, both Lowell and Conant followed Eliot's fundamental principle of avoiding tuition dependence and treating endowment as Harvard's "Rock of Gibraltar."[34]

At Columbia, Presidents Seth Low (1890–1901) and Nicholas M. Butler (1901–45) were more entrepreneurial than many other contemporaneous presidents in seeking funds.[35] But their financial strategy differed from Harvard's in two significant respects. First, they preferred to increase Columbia's physical plant rather than its financial capital. Butler often proclaimed that Columbia had a huge endowment, creating the impression that Columbia was "rich beyond the dreams of avarice."[36] But Butler usually included all of the university's property in what he called endowment and spent much of the $120,000,000 that he raised on buildings and land, contrary to Eliot's strategy.

Butler's focus on acquiring such property comported with Columbia's tradition of landed wealth. Most of the university's financial capital constituted New York City real estate that had been donated over the previous 250 years. As late as 1940, nearly one-third of the income of the entire university came from the rent of one eleven-acre parcel in Manhattan. Like any investment, this concentration of capital could sometimes prove advantageous, as it did during the late 1920s and 1930s. But Harvard and other universities were beginning to diversify their endowment into equities during this period, and Columbia's concentration in real estate investments proved damaging in the 1940s, 1950s, and 1960s.[37]

Butler's acquisition of land and buildings caused problems throughout his tenure. Beyond failing to diversify its capital, the university lost revenue by neglecting to channel gifts into endowment. In addition, Butler's acquisitions increased the university's expenses for operation and maintenance. Even more problematic, he accepted gifts for land and buildings that did not cover their full cost, and the university then had to borrow money in order to complete projects. The combination of foregone revenue, increased expenses, and heavy debt extended throughout Butler's presidency, forcing him to solicit gifts in order to pay for current expenses.[38] As a result, Columbia's endowment gradually fell behind that of other wealthy universities, as shown in Table 5.1.

Columbia's landed wealth mentality also detracted from public fundraising under Butler. During 1919 and 1920, as Harvard's fundraising campaign received national attention, Columbia enacted a tuition increase instead of stooping to "begging the public to provide new funds," as Butler termed it. Three years later, as the tidal wave of fundraising in higher education mounted, Butler wrote that "to throw the institution upon the mercy and pity of the public in the hope of obtaining relief [from expenses] . . . may be called the sentimental method of university administration. . . . It puts the institution in a wrong light before both itself and the public."[39] In 1927 Columbia commissioned a study to organize a campaign to raise funds for endowment, but Butler and the trustees then voted that such a campaign was "not expedient."[40]

Hence, Columbia's major gifts continued to come, as in the past, not from alumni or even trustees, but from wealthy New Yorkers not associated with the university. Finally, in 1928 Butler began to recognize that Columbia had to solicit more broadly for funds to add to the endowment. By that point, however, the large foundations were no longer giving money for university endowments, and the stock market crash in 1929 then ended the first era of higher education fundraising campaigns with Columbia sitting on the sidelines. It was not until the 1950s, after Butler retired, that the Columbia trustees reluctantly approved fundraising campaigns that the professional school deans demanded. So different from Harvard, the university's reluctance to seek money, publicly combined with its propensity "to funnel gifts . . . into acquisition of more real estate and buildings," led to the decline of its endowment to fourth place among universities by 1940 and then to sixth place by 1945 (Table 5.1).[41]

A second important difference between Columbia and Harvard was the degree of centralization in their financial governance. In the early 1800s Harvard put "each tub on its own bottom."[42] According to this policy, each Harvard school balanced its budget, retaining its own revenue and paying its own expenses. This decentralized financial governance imparted autonomy and responsibility to the units. It "allowed individual schools to keep whatever surpluses they generated. Profits from good years could be used to offset deficits from bad ones; reserves could be used to retire outstanding debts, or to finance educational experiments."[43] But the tub policy did not prohibit the central administration from assisting selected units. The Harvard presidents and the governing board—the corporation—exercised discretion over whether and how much to help a given unit, and this profoundly influenced the professional schools during the formative period.

In sharp contrast, Columbia centralized financial governance after Seth Low consolidated its disparate collection of schools under new statutes in 1890. Butler then reinforced the centralization after 1901. Under his administration the university made annual appropriations to the schools, forcing deans to plead annually to Butler about "the immediate and crying necessity, as you well know, Mr. President."[44] Centralization also meant that the university could choose to tax certain units or to assume "very large financial sacrifices" for their benefit.[45] The system led some deans to call for autonomy, hoping for "the day when the school . . . might have its own income from its own invested funds."[46] But Butler resisted decanal efforts for autonomy and remained very much in charge until 1945, despite the proliferation of layers and committees of administration at Columbia.[47]

Differences in Financial Reporting at Harvard and Columbia

Between 1890 and 1950 the length of the annual treasurer's reports grew from about 15 pages to 300 pages for Columbia and from about 75 to 450 pages for Harvard. This extensive financial reporting presents inevitable complexities and ambiguities at each institution. For example, the financial boundaries between the medical school and related units, such as the dental school, became blurred as the realm of medical education expanded. Each university also presents special problems of interpretation. Columbia initially separated "Public Law and Jurisprudence" from the law school and later combined them. Harvard in 1930 wrote up the book value of its endowed funds by 10 percent after the stock market rise of the 1920s, and then reversed course and wrote down the book value by 10 percent in 1938.[48] While such problems can be addressed individually, the difference in financial governance between Columbia and Harvard created a systemic difference in financial reporting.

Harvard's decentralized governance required the treasurer to report clearly the financial situation of each unit. Revenues, expenses, gifts, and endowment funds and their incomes were identified for each school, and annual and cumulative surpluses and deficits can therefore be identified precisely. This transparency reflects Eliot's view that "the fulness and clearness of the Treasurer's Statement" promote "public confidence in the financial administration of the University," which "is a main root of its prosperity."[49]

In contrast, the financial condition of a unit within Columbia is obscure. The reports aggregated revenues across the university, so one cannot clearly determine how much or what kind of revenue an individual unit received. Certain expenses were also aggregated across the university, and others were reported under conceptually vague and overlapping functional categories. Within some categories, expenses for a unit can be accurately identified, but the obscurity of revenues makes it impossible to determine surpluses or deficits for any department. Nor were cumulative surpluses, endowment funds, or their annual income stated for each unit, as they were for Harvard.[50] Funds given to construct buildings or purchase land are sometimes listed under permanent funds as endowment, and the actual endowment funds are not clearly linked to the income they generate, as Harvard's reports make clear. Hence, the Columbia reports exemplify the "illogical classification and unsuitable terminology" that "often characterize the financial statements" of colleges and universities during that period.[51]

As a result, Columbia treasurer's reports during the formative era make it extremely difficult to determine the financial condition not only of separate schools, but even of the whole university. In fact, these reports create the impression of a calculated effort to appear informative by providing abundant quantitative data while obscuring the salient information, such as whether units are running a surplus or a deficit. Columbia historians have suggested that Butler's administration made such a calculated effort in order to strengthen its control over financial decisions, and this explanation is consistent with Butler's preference for centralization and discreet fundraising.[52]

Despite these difficulties, it is possible to extract data from the financial reports of Columbia and Harvard that permit a comparative analysis of the financial situations and strategies of their respective law, medical, and business schools. These two universities were similarly distinctive by reason of their great wealth and the eminence of their three major professional schools. But Columbia and Harvard differed significantly in their financial strategies and their modes of governance. These differences increase the significance of the commonalities between their professional school finances during the formative period from 1890 to 1950.

In the following discussion, medical school finances are analyzed in light of the concurrent ideological shift from charity to philanthropy, the work of their institutional leaders, and their distinctive financial strategy. Next, law school finances are examined and compared to the medical schools in light of those same factors. Finally, business school finances are compared to those in law and medicine. The raw data, drawn from the financial reports of the universities, is presented in Table 5.2.

Expenses do not include construction expenses for buildings but do include maintenance and operations. Income data is not presented because it cannot be calculated from the Columbia reports, as discussed above, although income is discussed at points in the text. All dollar amounts in the text, tables, and figures are in nominal dollars, as reported in the sources, unless otherwise noted. It is not necessary to deflate the amounts to constant dollars because our purpose is to compare the schools with each other, not with an external standard such as national income or cost of living.

Medical Schools Grow Wealthy

The infusion of federal funding into medical research after 1945 is often said to have "transformed American medical schools" and established their leading financial position within universities.[53] However, that infusion simply extended the trajectory established before 1940. In the opening three decades of the twentieth century, medical schools made their greatest financial advance relative to the domains of professional education, rapidly displacing theological schools at the top of the financial hierarchy in professional education.[54]

Between 1890 and 1950, the combined endowment of Harvard and Columbia medical schools multiplied sixty-six times, compared to nearly

Table 5.2. Enrollments, endowments, annual expenses of medical, law, and business schools of Columbia and Harvard Universities, 1890–1945 (in thousands of nominal dollars)

Year	Columbia Medical School[a]	Harvard Medical School	Columbia Law School	Harvard Law School	Harvard Business School (1908)	Columbia Business School (1916)
1890						
Enrollment	215	454	212	254		
Endowment	281	240	0	185		
Expenses	NA[b]	79	35[c]	40		
1895						
Enrollment	799	454	288	404		
Endowment	300	318	0	248		
Expenses	156	120	38	56		
1900						
Enrollment	787	558[d]	380	613		
Endowment	490	958	12	361		
Expenses	134	157	37	84		
1905						
Enrollment	555	307	341	758		
Endowment	825	3,180	141	370		
Expenses	371	155[e]	45	103		
1910						
Enrollment	346	279	324	763	78	
Endowment	861	3,419	321	567	1	
Expenses	259	260	71	117	29	
1915						
Enrollment	374	321	453	730	166	
Endowment	2,419	4,197	321	735	329	
Expenses	570	370	101	155	60	
1920						
Enrollment	446	419	451	879	394	269
Endowment	4,925	7,325	488	969	476	481
Expenses	540	637	134	171	149	96[f]
1925						
Enrollment	406	506	710	1,201	614	380
Endowment	9,828	11,512	508	1,192	614	482
Expenses	868[g]	610	181	273	495	120
1930						
Enrollment	438	516	600	1,639	1,011	485
Endowment[h]	11,118	15,610	538	4,230	2,348	890
Expenses	2,542	905	303	663	1,053	180

Table 5.2. *cont.*

Year	Columbia Medical School[a]	Harvard Medical School	Columbia Law School	Harvard Law School	Harvard Business School (1908)	Columbia Business School (1916)
1935						
Enrollment	458	523	635	1,452	724	428
Endowment	12,386	17,026	605	4,776	2,516	913
Expenses	1,623	1,052	295	754	842	192
1940						
Enrollment	472	522	523	1,390	929	534
Endowment[i]	13,664	17,737	849	5,424	2,894	958
Expenses	2,157	1,312	324	697	906	210
1945						
Enrollment	506	567	218	47	57[j]	194
Endowment	13,778	18,901	871	5,365	3,774	979
Expenses	2,148	1,487	266	425	1,512	145

Sources: Columbia University, *Annual Report of the Treasurer*, *1889–90*, 14; *1894–95*, 30, 204–11; *1899–1900*, 20, 382–87; *1901–2*, 387–406; *1904–5*, 7, 277–88, 297–305; *1909–10*, 10–11, 22–36, 50–60; *1914–15*, 54, 321–40, 374–93; *1919–20*, 51, 326–50, 408–31, 488–521; *1924–25*, 59, 401–28, 488–521; *1929–30*, 10–40, 61, 106–46; *1934–35*, 10–41, 51, 122–69; *1939–40*, 10–47, 56, 131–91; *1944–45*, 10–43, 46, 131–97; Harvard University, *Annual Report of the Treasurer*, *1889–90*, 15, 30–31; *1894–95*, 15–17, 30–31, 59–71; *1899–1900*, 31–33, 52–56; *1904–5*, 35, 65–70; *1909–10*, 11, 63–70; *1914–15*, 11, 104–32; *1919–20*, 11, 130–65; *1924–25*, 10, 240–78; *1929–30*, 8, 267–311; *1934–35*, 47, 67, 73, 264–306; *1939–40*, 47, 73, 79, 241; *1944–45*, 14, 78–79.

Enrollments are calculated from *Annual Report of the President of Columbia University*, *1889–90*, 14; *1894–95*, 30; *1899–1900*, 20; *1904–5*, 7; *1909–10*, 10–11; *1914–15*, 54; *1919–20*, 51; *1924–25*, 59; *1929–30*, 61; *1934–35*, 51; *1939–40*, 56; *1944–45*, 46; *Annual Report of the President of Harvard University*, *1889–1890*, 23; *Harvard University Catalogue*, *1889–90*, 576; *1894–95*, 576; *1899–1900*, 211; *1904–5*, 230; *1909–10*, 259; *1914–15*, 249; *1919–20*, 271; *1924–25*, 357; *1929–30*, 863; *1934–35*, 928–29; *1939–40*, 928–29, 949; *1944–45*, 718.

Note: Enrollment figures do not include extension, summer, part-time, or cross-registered graduate students but do include college seniors registered as law degree candidates. Endowment includes income-producing funds and properties, but Harvard endowment totals do not include invested cash reserves. Expenses do not include construction expenses for buildings but do include maintenance and operations. Income data is not presented because it cannot be calculated from the Columbia reports, as discussed above, although income is discussed at points in the text.

[a]The reporting of expenses for the Columbia Medical School and the College of Physicians and Surgeons varies in Columbia University, *Annual Report of the Treasurer*. The figures here relate to the Medical School proper, which granted the MD degree. The medical school endowment funds do not include endowments for the teaching hospitals and clinics attached to the College of Physicians and Surgeons.

[b]Columbia assumed financial control of the College of Physicians and Surgeons in February 1891, so expenses are not listed for the years 1889/90 or 1890/91.

[c]This figure is for 1888. Columbia University, *Annual Report of the Treasurer*, *1887–88*, 7.

[d]HMS enrollment spiked to 558 in 1900 because it was the last year that students could enter without holding a bachelor's degree, and more than half of the entering class flunked out. Eliot, *Annual Report of the President of Harvard University*, *1900–1901*, 25, 49–50; Harrington, *The Harvard Medical School*, 3:1168.

[e]Harvard University, *Annual Report of the Treasurer*, *1904–05*, 35. These expenses do not include construction expenses for the new medical campus.

[f]Expenses for the business school were not identified in Columbia, *Annual Report of the Treasurer*, *1919–1920*, 319–457. This figure is for 1921–22, the first year that expenses for the business school are listed; ibid., *1921–22*, 348–74.

[g]Ibid., *1924–25*, 401–28. This figure does not include "Teacher's College Salaries," which the treasurer listed within expenses of the Medical School.

nineteen times for that of the two universities, as reported in Table 5.3.

The rapid financial ascent of the medical schools is even more impressive given that Harvard and Columbia were the wealthiest universities in the country, whose endowments grew far faster than those of the great majority of universities. Figure 5.1 depicts the rapid increase of the combined endowments of HMS and CMS, as well as their faster growth than the combined endowments of the two universities during the formative era.

How did medical schools effect this tremendous growth in financial capital? The most direct and significant cause was the great flood of grants and gifts commencing at the start of the century. Between 1902 and 1934 "nine major foundations poured $154,000,000 into medical education and research—nearly one-half of the total they contributed to all areas." Gifts from individuals were even greater. Consequently, "medicine, once the neglected stepchild . . . , became the most vigorously supported of any cultural, scientific, or humanitarian activity" by 1930, in the words of Kenneth Ludmerer, the leading historian of medical education.[55]

At Columbia, the university assumed control over the finances and operation of its College of Physicians and Surgeons in 1891. During the next two decades, the majority of gifts over $10,000 received by the university went to CMS, and several of these exceeded one million dollars.[56] As seen in Table 5.2, the sizable CMS endowment more than tripled between 1890 and 1910.

Meanwhile, in the late 1890s HMS received three endowed professorships, and its endowment, which about equaled that of CMS through 1895, catapulted to twice the CMS endowment in 1900, as shown by Table 5.2.[57] In 1901 HMS attracted commitments of more than four million dollars from several wealthy donors in order to build a new medical school campus in Boston and to endow professorships and maintenance and equipment for the buildings. In 1902 Eliot announced, "the Medical School now has a larger endowment than any other professional department of the University," whereas "thirty years ago it had the smallest endowment among the professional departments."[58] In 1906 the new medical campus opened, while the appeals for more gifts continued, and by 1910 the HMS endowment was four times as large as that of CMS.[59]

In 1910 the Carnegie Foundation published Abraham Flexner's

Table 5.3. Totals and cumulative percentage increases of combined endowments of Columbia and Harvard Universities, medical schools, law schools, and business schools, 1890–1950 (in millions of nominal dollars)

	Universities		Medical Schools		Law Schools		Business Schools
Year	Total	Cumulative Percentage Increase	Total	Cumulative Percentage Increase	Total	Cumulative Percentage Increase	Total
1890	15.2		.52		.19		NA
1895	19.1	26%	6.2	18%	.25	34%	NA
1900	25.9	71%	1.4	177%	.37	101%	NA
1905	32.4	114%	4.0	667%	.51	177%	NA
1910	47.8	216%	4.3	720%	.89	381%	NA
1915	59.4	292%	6.6	1,167%	1.1	471%	.33
1920	84.2	455%	12.3	2,247%	1.5	688%	.96
1925	119.5[a]	688%	21.3	3,988%	1.7	819%	1.1
1930	181.5	1,097%	26.7	5,020%	4.8	2,477%	3.2
1935	175.0[b]	1,055%	29.4	5,534%	5.4	2,809%	3.4
1940	209.4[c]	1,281%	31.4	5,916%	6.2	3,237%	3.9
1945	236.0[d]	1,457%	32.7	6,161%	6.3	3,271%	4.8
1950[e]	297.0[f]	1,859%	35.0[g]	6,604%	7.1[h]	3,745%	9.6[i]

Source: Data drawn from Tables 5.1 and 5.2.

[a]The Harvard University total of $69,069,909 is drawn from Harvard University, *Annual Report of the Treasurer, 1924–1925*, 240, 250. The Columbia University total endowment cannot be computed from the opaque categories in Columbia University, *Annual Report of the Treasurer, 1924–25*, 393–532. The Columbia endowment for 1925–26 of $50,389,000 is drawn from US Commissioner of Education, *Biennial Survey of Education, 1924–26*, 863–945.

[b]The Harvard University total of $128,827,068 is drawn from Harvard, *Annual Report of the Treasurer, 1934–1935*, 264, 273. The Columbia University total endowment cannot be computed from the opaque categories in Columbia, *Annual Report of the Treasurer, 1934–35*, 1–196. The Columbia endowment for 1935/36 of $46,210 is drawn from US Commissioner of Education, *Biennial Survey of Education, 1934–36*, 2:256–73.

[c]The Harvard University total of $138,701,335 is drawn from Harvard, *Annual Report of the Treasurer, 1939–1940*, 241. The Columbia University total endowment cannot be computed from the opaque categories in Columbia, *Annual Report of the Treasurer, 1939–40*, 1–221. The Columbia University endowment of $70,714 for 1939 is drawn from Clarence S. Marsh, ed., *American Universities and Colleges*, 4th ed. (Washington, DC: American Council on Education, 1940), s.v. "Columbia University." Endowment values for 1940 are not included in US Office of Education, *Statistics of Higher Education, 1939–40 and 1941–42* (Washington, DC: Government Printing Office, 1944), vol. 2.

[d]The Harvard endowment total of $156,079,410 is drawn from Harvard, *Annual Report of the Treasurer, 1944–1945*, 78–79. The Columbia endowment of $79,937,000 is extrapolated from the 1939 figure, assuming the same growth rate as Harvard's.

[e]The Harvard University amount of $196,398,000 is drawn from ibid., *1949–1950*, 92–93. The Columbia University amount of $100,596,000 is extrapolated from the 1945 figure, assuming the same growth rate as Harvard's.

[f]The Harvard amount of $196,398,000 is drawn from ibid. The Columbia amount of $100,596,000 is extrapolated from the 1945 figure, assuming the same growth rate as Harvard's.

[g]The HMS amount of $20,240,000 is drawn from ibid. The CMS amount of $14,755,000 is extrapolated from the 1945 figure, assuming the same growth rate as Harvard's.

[h]The HLS amount of $6,121,000 is drawn from ibid. The CLS amount of $993,000 is extrapolated from the 1945 figure, assuming the same growth rate as Harvard's.

[i]The HBS amount of $7,647,000 is drawn from ibid. The CBS amount of $1,984,000 is extrapolated from the 1945 figure, assuming the same growth rate as Harvard's.

famous report, which inaugurated an era of medical benefaction, when hundreds of millions of dollars flowed into medical schools from private donors and major foundations. For example, in 1918 the medical schools of Johns Hopkins, Harvard, and Columbia received together a bequest of some fifteen million dollars from Joseph DeLamar, a mine owner from Idaho who had no connection to any of the schools.[60] Such gifts contributed to increasing the CMS endowment almost sixfold between 1910 and 1920, while its budget about doubled, as seen in Table 5.2.

HMS felt slighted by the Flexner report, which recommended that

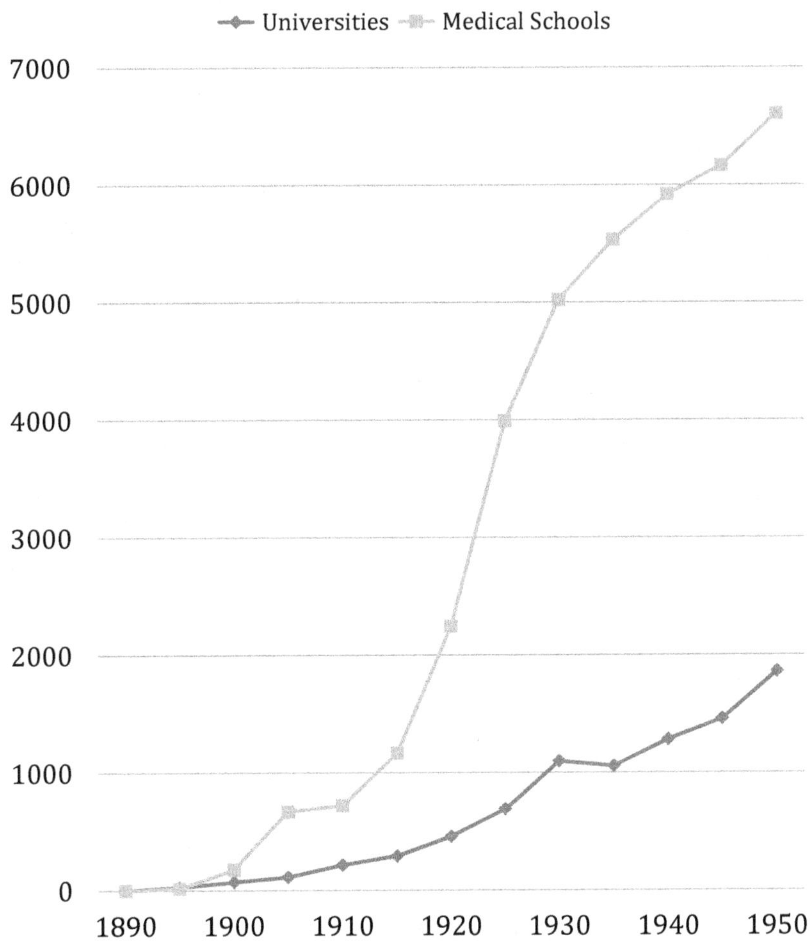

Figure 5.1. Cumulative percentage increase of university and medical school endowments at Columbia and Harvard Universities, 1890–1950.

university medical schools model themselves after Johns Hopkins by acquiring teaching hospitals. In contrast, Harvard arranged clinical teaching and research through a system of affiliated hospitals. Nevertheless, HMS continued to receive "large resources" whose prudent use justified "yet larger resources," according to the dean.[61] By the end of World War I, HMS was "the wealthiest and leading [medical] school in the country," in Ludmerer's words.[62] Moreover, it was the wealthiest and leading professional school in the country.

Columbia embraced the Johns Hopkins model that Flexner recommended. In 1919 and 1920, major foundations and donors committed some $12 million to fund the land, buildings, and endowment for a new medical center and teaching hospital for CMS.[63] These gifts contributed to increasing the CMS endowment almost sixfold between 1910 and 1920, while its budget about doubled, as seen in Table 5.2. Over the next six years, $3 million more were raised, and in 1928 the Columbia-Presbyterian Medical Center opened as "the world's first comprehensive medical center."[64] As a result, the CMS endowment more than doubled during the 1920s, when "medical schools enjoyed a golden age," according to Ludmerer.[65] Meanwhile, gifts to HMS extended its lead in financial capital, so an increasing and then predominant proportion of revenue came from endowment income and current gifts and grants.[66]

During the Depression, industrial production declined by 37 percent, prices by 33 percent, and the gross national product by 30 percent in constant dollars. Unemployment peaked at 25 percent in 1932 and stayed above 15 percent for the rest of the 1930s.[67] Faring better than many sectors, higher education generally contracted between 1932 and 1934 but then began to recover as enrollments grew after 1935, especially in public, inexpensive, and local institutions. Meanwhile, most medical schools retrenched during the 1930s. Yet medicine remained "the most generously supported area of university research" across the country.[68] At the end of World War II, Columbia and Harvard were perfectly positioned to exploit the second golden age of medical research funding, launched by the federal government.[69]

Accommodating the Shift from Charity to Philanthropy

Three kinds of factors propelled the enormous increase in the wealth of medical schools. First, they accommodated the shift in the ideology of benefaction in two respects. On the one hand, medical education and, particularly, medical research fit closely the new philanthropic rationale and attracted massive amounts of gifts and grants. On the other hand, medical schools appealed successfully on the traditional grounds of charity to solicit financial support for their students, and that support benefited the schools financially as well.

The rationale of philanthropy demanded that root causes and solutions of widespread human problems be scientifically identified and that those solutions be systematically instituted effectively, efficiently, and economically. Medical research and education fit the demand perfectly. Yet, scholars have explained this fit in different ways.

According to the structural-functionalist explanation that predominated through the 1960s, increasing therapeutic effectiveness fostered great confidence in medical expertise and research, and that confidence prompted the philanthropic donations. Some leading scholars continue to embrace this view. They argue, "The development of certain vaccines and antitoxins, the many advances in surgery, the conquest of certain nutritional and endocrine diseases, and the marked improvement in the public health" produced the "medical optimism" that attracted the munificent gifts and grants early in the twentieth century.[70] In the 1970s and 1980s, scholars proposed a different explanation. A number of critical sociologists advanced versions of a "power analysis," proposing that social power, cultural authority, and territorial competition explain much of the rising authority and status of medical expertise that attracted benefactions.[71]

The continuing scholarly debate over these two kinds of explanations and their variants cannot be resolved in this essay.[72] Our view is that different explanations fit different kinds of professional schools in different periods. And the structural-functionalist explanation fits the formative period of medical education best. Between 1890 and 1945, scientific medicine aimed primarily at acute diseases, which were easily understood by the public and did not require statistical validation. Furthermore, therapeutic effectiveness was the explanation most often cited by contemporaries. University leaders often repeated the view expressed by President Eliot in 1903: "The hope of benefic[ial] results from medical and surgical research . . . has made it easy to procure large gifts to the Medical School. Rich men . . . see that there is a fair prospect of obtaining in medical laboratories great benefactions for the human race."[73]

To be sure, donors were not solely, or even primarily, altruistic. Desire for fame, influence, social legitimation, and, perhaps, financial gain also help to explain the gifts of various donors at various times.[74] Nevertheless, medical research and education closely fit the philanthropic rationale that had emerged in the understanding of benefaction.

At the same time, medical schools appealed on the traditional grounds of charity to obtain financial support for their students, particularly endowments for scholarships. HMS and CMS made incessant requests for endowed scholarships to alleviate the burden of tuition on students. Such requests, of course, presupposed the philanthropic benefit that future physicians could provide in effectively solving widespread problems. But the requests portrayed financially strapped, hard-working, talented medical students who were deserving of short-term support until they graduated and supported themselves.[75] The many endowments received for scholarships also contributed to increasing the wealth of medical schools. In this fashion medical schools invoked traditional appeals to charity while embracing the new philanthropic rationale.

Medical Entrepreneurs

A second kind of factor contributing to the financial ascent of CMS, HMS, and other medical schools was somewhat adventitious: the support from the presidents and university leaders and the initiative and effectiveness of the dean. This support naturally depended, in part, on their response to the ideological shift.

At centrally governed Columbia, the deans prior to 1930 were not ineffective, but the presidents had the greatest influence and favored the medical school in several ways. President Low arranged the absorption of the College of Physicians and Surgeons in 1891, providing significant subsidies. During the 1910s the university covered the CMS annual deficit of about $600 per student, and "this tax on the University is borne cheerfully," reported the dean.[76] During the 1920s President Butler spearheaded the fundraising for the teaching hospital, while he and the trustees borrowed $4,750,000 and raised tuition by 25 percent across the university in order to support the loan payments.[77] The rest of the university therefore subsidized its wealthy medical center. As Butler accurately observed, "The President and Trustees have devoted a large amount of attention to the needs of the

Medical School and have done all in their power to uphold . . . the Faculty in their policies and to provide them with additional means for carrying on their work."[78]

The Harvard Corporation made its first subsidy to medical education in 1899 by committing $300,000 to support the consolidation of all the medical faculties. In the next decade President Eliot spearheaded the drive to build the new medical campus, which raised the biggest gifts that the university had received in its history.[79] Subsequently, President Lowell consistently encouraged the entrepreneurial efforts of Dean David L. Edsall, whom he appointed in 1918.

In providing this support to their medical schools, the university leaders acted as "institutional entrepreneurs" who tried to advance their institutions in the competition among universities for resources, prestige, and excellence.[80] The deans and presidents warned repeatedly that the university "must increase its expenditure for medical education or . . . fall behind . . . the other high grade medical schools in the country."[81]

Like other medical schools, CMS invoked Flexner's criticisms and recommendations in order to demonstrate the need for more funds to stay competitive. While such competitive appeals could be heard in all academic and professional fields, they resounded most loudly in medicine after 1910 because the prestige of a university and its capacity to attract philanthropy depended increasingly on the strength of its medical school.[82]

Institutional leadership also comprised the entrepreneurial initiative and administrative effectiveness of the deans. Before Edsall became dean, HMS was not fully exploiting its bountiful resources. As of 1915 the annual expenses of HMS amounted to merely 9 percent of its endowment, as compared to 24 percent at CMS. The reason for this difference, apart from hospital costs, was that other strong medical schools spent far more on research than did HMS.[83] During his tenure from 1918 to 1935, Edsall became known as the most effective medical dean in the country by increasing the productivity and resources of HMS. Focusing HMS upon research, Edsall eliminated the faculty seniority system, hired excellent young researchers, and began raising more money from major foundations and new sources. At the end of his second year he reported receiving grants of $325,000 from health companies, department stores, insurance companies, industrial corporations, and a federal agency. In 1922 Edsall also became dean of Harvard's new School of Public Health and then, additionally, dean of the dental school in 1924.[84] By the time Edsall retired in 1935, both the budget and endowment had tripled since his arrival at HMS in 1918, as indicated in Table 5.2. The dean had made the most of "academic medicine's first great bull market" and led HMS to recognized preeminence among medical schools.[85]

The endowment and expenses of CMS also about tripled between 1918 and 1935, largely due to the efforts of the university leadership. The influence of the CMS dean appeared in the 1930s and 1940s, when Dean Willard C. Rappleye (1930–58) persuaded Butler to give him more autonomy than any other dean enjoyed. The school then navigated successfully through the Depression and World War II largely due to Rappleye, who appealed to a broader range of corporate donors and to the National Research Council in the 1940s. Rappleye's entrepreneurial efforts in a stringent period allowed CMS to maintain and even improve its financial position, while the university struggled to cope with the wartime rise in wages and cost of living.[86]

Conversely, the influence of a largely ineffective dean is shown when President Conant appointed someone in his own image, who favored scientific management and did not have an entrepreneurial bent. To replace the savvy administrator Edsall in 1935, Conant therefore selected C. Sidney Burwell (1935–49), a medical scientist.[87] The HMS endowment grew merely 4 percent between 1935 and 1940, while the CMS endowment rose 10 percent. Their expenses increased by the same rates, as seen in Table 5.2. Between 1940 and 1945 HMS grew in both measures faster than CMS, but the HMS endowment rose only 6.5 percent compared to 12.5 percent for Harvard University.[88] After ten years under Burwell the school of medicine was no longer the financial pacesetter at Harvard University.

An effective, entrepreneurial dean therefore mattered, though this factor varied with the different mode of governance at the two universities. At decentralized Harvard, the dean's effectiveness was more important, although the president determined that factor by choosing the dean, as Lowell did Edsall and Conant did Burwell. At centrally governed Columbia, Presidents Low and Butler had a stronger influence than did the deans through 1930.

But exceptions occurred in the mode of governance. At Harvard,

President Eliot was a strong interventionist through his retirement in 1909. At Columbia, Dean Rappleye successfully navigated the Depression because he persuaded President Butler to give him more autonomy than any other dean enjoyed.[89] A strong, effective dean was needed in the Harvard model, unless the president intervened. A strong, effective dean helped at Columbia, if the president permitted.

Strategy: "The Most Expensive of All Forms of Education"

The strategy adopted by the medical schools contributed to their wealth, as well. Each school depressed enrollment and elevated tuition while soliciting both endowed scholarships to alleviate the burden on students and general endowment to subsidize the high cost of medical education that was partly driven by the low student/faculty ratio. Remarkably, the two schools adopted the same approach, despite the different governance models at the universities.

CMS and HMS cut their enrollment nearly in half between 1895 and 1910 as donations began to arrive and admission standards increased. They allowed it to rise in 1920 in order to accommodate returning veterans but still capped it in the 400s. Thereafter, their enrollments grew merely by one-third over the next twenty-five years, as shown by Table 5.2.[90] Columbia and Harvard were not alone in this policy. In the 1900s other leading medical schools began to limit enrollment as they shifted away from the proprietary model of profiting from tuition. After 1900, attracting philanthropic support for medical research and therapeutic advances became more important than tuition revenue. Hence, the leading schools resisted increasing their enrollments and preferred to decrease them. In 1910 Flexner reinforced this trend by recommending the extremely small enrollment of 250 students for a medical school.[91] CMS, HMS, and "most of the conspicuous medical schools" subsequently followed this policy, even in the face of strenuous opposition from their presidents.[92]

Limiting enrollment reduced tuition income but had distinct advantages in raising other kinds of revenue. The policy decreased the faculty's teaching duties and increased their opportunity to pursue research that would attract medical philanthropy. In addition, limiting enrollment made medical education more expensive by lowering the student/faculty ratio and raising the cost per student, since the school's rising expense was divided by the relatively small number of students. The effect of the policy soon became its rationale: "medical education must necessarily be the most expensive of all forms of education."[93] Between 1900 and 1945, studies by the Council on Medical Education repeatedly found that the per-student cost of medical education, excluding expenses for operating associated teaching hospitals, was about three times higher than that in law or engineering, and five or six times higher than that in business or education.[94]

The high cost per student justified raising more revenue in several respects. It provided the rationale for raising tuition, which maximized revenue from the small number of students. Both medical schools raised tuition above the norm of their universities and that of other medical schools. In the early 1910s medical schools typically charged annual tuition of $150 to $160, while CMS charged $250 and HMS $225. At the same time, the other units of Columbia University normally charged $170 and those at Harvard $150. CMS and HMS kept increasing their tuition when their universities raised the norm. In fall 1921 Harvard upped the university norm from $200 to $250, and the medical school raised its tuition to $300. In 1925 Harvard raised the university norm to $300, and the medical school tuition rose to $400 a year later.[95]

High tuition then justified charitable appeals for endowed scholarships to alleviate the burden on students.[96] CMS and HMS thus adopted a policy of small enrollment and high tuition, cushioned by scholarship funds. This was perhaps the starting point of the policy of high tuition and high student aid that proliferated in higher education after 1980.[97] Furthermore, due to the small enrollment, the revenue, even with high tuition, paid only a fraction of the cost of the medical education, it was said. The shortfall then justified appeals for general endowment and "special gifts" to make up the difference.[98] In these ways the financial strategy was crafted to suit the two poles in the ideology of benefaction.

During the stringent 1930s, gifts and investment income declined, and most medical schools increased their enrollment, while the proportion of their income derived from tuition rose from about 33 to 40 percent. Table 5.2 shows that CMS and HMS increased their number of students only modestly, and the proportion of income derived from tuition at HMS held to about 20 percent. This level persisted through 1945, as the Harvard deans reported that "tuition fees . . . play a minor role" in revenue.[99] Despite large tuition increases after 1945, the proportion of HMS income derived from tuition fell to merely 8 percent after 1950 as a result of successful fundraising and the infusion of federal funding.[100]

Law Schools Fall Behind

Law schools also significantly elevated their financial capital within the wealthy universities in the early twentieth century. Between 1890 and 1950, the combined endowment of Harvard and Columbia law schools multiplied more than thirty-seven times. This growth was nearly twice as much as that of the combined endowment of the two universities, which increased nearly nineteen times, as reported in Table 5.3. Again, this comparison is more impressive given that Harvard and Columbia were the wealthiest universities in the country. Figure 5.2 depicts the rapid increase of the combined endowments of HLS and CLS as well as their faster growth compared to the combined endowment of the two universities during the formative era.

CLS and HLS trailed far behind the medical schools, however. At the beginning of the formative period the average endowment of both

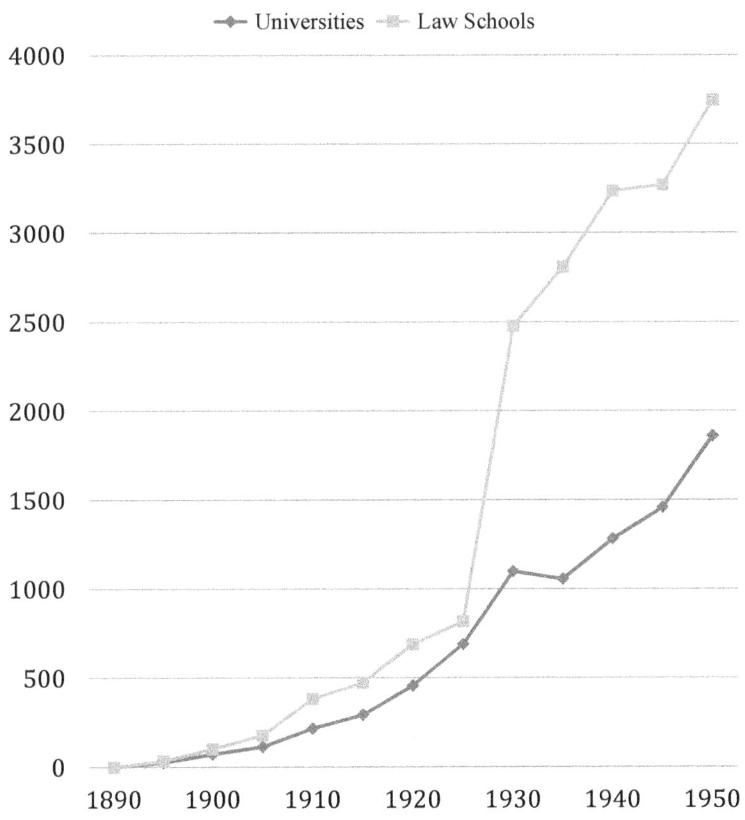

Figure 5.2. Cumulative percentage increase of university and law school endowments at Columbia and Harvard Universities, 1890–1950.

the endowed schools of law and the endowed schools of medicine was about the same: $100,000. The highest endowments in each domain also stood on a par of about $480,000. In subsequent decades the law schools rapidly fell behind the medical schools in financial capital at both Columbia and Harvard.

By the early 1930s the two medical schools' combined endowment was about five times as large as that of the two law schools. The difference in financial growth carried over to estimations of accomplishment and status, which seemed so natural and necessary that they were anachronistically projected back in time. In 1933 a Johns Hopkins professor proposed that the academic field of law had long suffered from a "lag of some three decades" behind medicine.[101] So rapidly had medicine ascended in the preceding forty years that this scholar, like many contemporary observers, did not appreciate the rough parity in financial strength, status, and accomplishment that had existed between the endowed schools of the two domains in the 1890s. The changes are illustrated in Fig. 5.3, which plots the data in Table 5.3.

Despite growing faster than the endowments of their universities, the law schools' financial capital thus fell far behind that of the medical

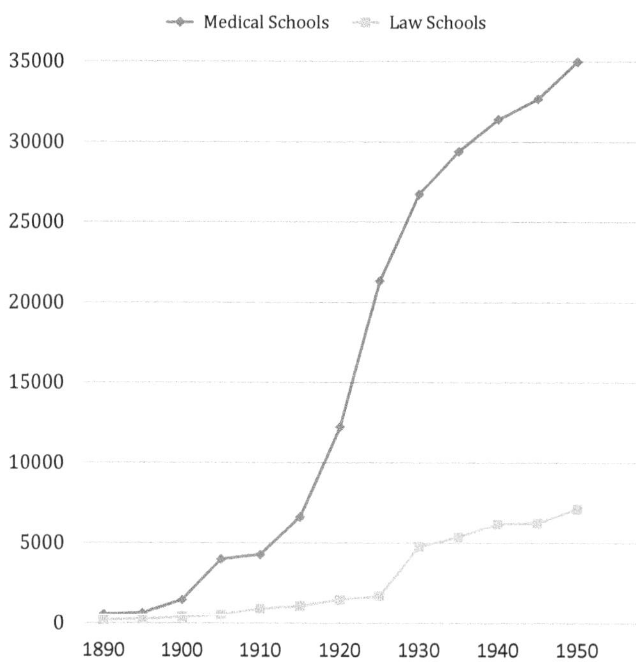

Figure 5.3. Combined endowments of medical schools vs. law schools at Columbia and Harvard Universities, 1890–1950 (in thousands of nominal dollars).

schools. This trend resulted from several factors common to both law schools. That commonality, in fact, becomes more significant given that each operated within a different model of university governance.

One factor was the law schools' counterproductive financial strategy. In addition, their leaders were generally ineffective administrators and entrepreneurs, and the presidents and university leaders did little to help their law schools. But the most significant factor was that the law schools could not negotiate the ideological shift in the understanding of benefaction. Appeals for charity did not succeed, and the schools were unable to explain how legal education or research fit the new philanthropic rationale, so they received relatively little in gifts or grants from foundations and individuals.

Failure to Attract Charity or Philanthropy

Law schools attributed their difficulty in attracting benefactions to a number of secondary causes. One was the public's longstanding "dissatisfaction with law and distrust of lawyers," as the *Centennial History of Harvard Law School* observed in 1917. President Butler made the same point at Columbia, and the chairman of the HLS centennial fundraising campaign observed with resignation: "No amount of committees or effort is going to make contributing to a law school popular."[102] But doctors were also held in low esteem throughout the nineteenth century, and the confusing plurality of medical sects persisted into the early twentieth century, detracting from physicians' status and authority.

Law schools also attributed the failure to attract benefactions to the alumni, who could not or would not organize themselves effectively to help their alma mater during the formative era. One observer of the HLS centennial campaign stated that the alumni committees "are about as capable of doing it as *a dandelion is of sustaining a boulder weighing twenty tons*." Merely 2 percent of the alumni contributed to the HLS campaign that aimed to raise $1,000,000 and yielded only $250,000 in the late 1910s.[103] CLS fared no better.[104] However, the two medical schools did not rely on alumni giving. In 1917 the treasurer of the Harvard Medical Alumni Fund complained that "there are 3,000 medical alumni and only about 10 percent contributed."[105] Similarly, alumni giving to business schools was insignificant because the business schools and their graduates were so young.[106]

Law schools received little in gifts or grants primarily because they did not successfully invoke either pole of the shifting ideology of benefaction. On the one hand, donors were not persuaded that law students deserved or needed charity. For example, in 1914 the dean of HLS asked each local chapter of the alumni association to support a scholarship for a law student. All replied negatively while repeatedly distinguishing between "law school scholarships," which they opposed, and "college scholarships," which they strongly supported. Law students, they said, did not deserve scholarship help, because such professional training served their own interests. Nor did they actually need help because they could make their own way, having already earned a bachelor's degree. Even if law students were destitute, then poor undergraduates in Harvard College ought to be helped first. In fact, discouraging destitute law students might be beneficial, because the nation has "too many lawyers."[107]

On the other hand, philanthropists did not see how legal research could benefit society. Both CLS and HLS received gifts and grants to improve the drafting of legislation, to restate the law in a clear current form, or to study social aspects of law, such as crime. But these were merely a fraction of the amount of grants to medical research, and this kind of research often required more sociology than jurisprudence.[108] HLS dean Roscoe Pound (1916–36) was the only dean at either school who wrote extensive public statements attempting to explain and justify the need for gifts to support legal research.[109] The potential for raising money for legal education depended on how well the request could be justified in terms of the philanthropic ideology, which by that point predominated in benefaction for higher education. Pound had to explain the "signal public service" that, he claimed, would issue from donations to legal education.[110]

Medical research and education were the exemplars, and Pound conjured suitable analogies. "The social hygiene involved in proper investigation in a law school is quite as important as the individual hygiene investigated in the medical school," he wrote.[111] Regarding his favorite field of criminal law, Pound suggested, "We may expect endowment of such a chair to be no less fruitful of results than the endowments of medical research which have been so conspicuously fruitful in recent years."[112] President Lowell likewise invoked the point, as did the dean of Yale Law School: "Just as the public has been ready to give necessary financial support to the improvement of medical education, the combating of disease, and the creating of better health conditions, so, we believe, will it be ready to aid efforts to improve legal education and to promote the research essential to bettering the administration of justice."[113]

But Pound appeared wary of expansive analogies to medicine. He made them only in letters and annual reports, avoiding them in his public fundraising appeals. Meanwhile, he weakened the philanthropic rationale by inadequately explaining the social benefits. He asserted that legal scholars and lawyers must assist legislatures in writing better laws and "make law-making take account of the social facts to which it must be applied, and at the same time, fit harmoniously into the legal system of which it must be a part." He also affirmed that "administration of criminal justice is admittedly the weakest point in American polity. No subject of research affords greater possibilities"[114] However, Pound did not provide details, examples, or evidence of social benefit. Above all, he neglected to address, or even acknowledge, the "widespread skepticism among a certain class of practical men, in and out of our profession" that legal research and graduate study are socially useful, as Harvard law professor James B. Thayer had warned in a famous address to the American Bar Association in 1895.[115]

Fundraising consultants hired by the law school sharply criticized Pound's statements for their ineffectiveness in attracting philanthropy:

> It serves no purpose to keep telling the average citizen what a very fine thing law research is. He wants to know what law research will do. . . . He is not interested in generalities, law books, and law libraries. He is interested in crime and crime prevention . . . [and] in the conflict and disorder whenever legislation is given an oppressive twist. . . . When we turn to the businessman, the appeal must be placed on a business basis. It is not enough to say that the science of law must keep pace with the science of business. . . . The business man is engaged in buying and selling. . . . The question that concerns him is: how does it happen that so many things get passed only to tie up in red tape? . . . The reply to this question is: things will go on that way until something is done about it, and we offer you something quite specific. . . . The purpose of this publicity is . . . to state . . . : *What Legal Research Could Accomplish*.[116]

Hence, Pound's statements actually demonstrated "the inability of the law school to tap large incomes and exploit strong civic interest in law such as prevails in health problems and roads."[117] In response, the consultants composed a long, supplementary statement trying to explain the direct causal benefit of legal research, analogous to that which motivated the philanthropic interest in medical research. But their explanations were reductionist and ineffective.[118]

All these statements intended to provide the rationale for the major fundraising campaign conducted by a law school in the second quarter of the twentieth century. Attempting to raise some $5,000,000, this new campaign by HLS in the mid-1920s yielded only about $2,250,000 in pledges, including a foundation grant of $750,000. Hence, personal donors contributed merely $1,500,000.[119] Even those amounts significantly increased the HLS endowment and contributed to the rise in the law schools' endowment during the late 1920s, as seen in Table 5.2. But raising less than half of the goal during the financial heyday of the mid-1920s was certainly disappointing.

Meanwhile, at Columbia, in the absence of a compelling philanthropic rationale for legal research, the gifts to the law school averaged about one-tenth the size of contemporaneous gifts to the medical school over the formative era. The CLS deans found themselves gratefully acknowledging donations of a few thousand, or even a few hundred, dollars. Their appeals "to do for law what generous benefaction has made it possible to do for medicine" did not move major donors.[120] Mindful of the recently completed Columbia-Presbyterian Medical Center, the CLS dean began calling in 1930 for several million dollars to build "a great law center at Columbia." But over the next fifteen years the university gave, in total, only about $15,000 and the alumni only about $10,000 for cosmetic repairs to the existing overcrowded building.[121]

Ineffective and Unsupportive Leaders

The relatively slow growth of the law schools' capital resulted also from the incapacity of the deans. At Columbia the centralized governance discouraged, even prohibited, financial initiatives by the schools, and the president eschewed public fundraising campaigns. For both reasons CLS deans in their annual reports addressed their needs and requests not to the public, but to Butler as president of the university.[122] At his discretion Butler then made public and private solicitations on behalf of the school.[123]

Some deans chafed under Butler's tight rein. After a decade of negotiating annually with Butler for appropriations, Dean Harlan F. Stone (1910–23) made the first public statement by a CLS dean requesting a large sum—half a million dollars—for the law school. In 1921 he observed that "a change of policy whereby appropriations are to be made more regularly and evenly . . . gives great advantages in planning."[124] This challenge to Butler's discretion over annual budgeting bordered on heresy, and in 1923 the president edged out Stone, who later became chief justice of the US Supreme Court.[125] Stone's resignation precipitated a period of turmoil in which four different individuals served as dean in just five years between 1923 and 1928.

Partly as a result of this decanal turmoil, the law school, like the university, did not tap into the prosperity of the 1920s. During that decade CLS received merely $75,000 in gifts to endowment, and the total of permanent funds scarcely reached $540,000 in 1930. The school lost a significant opportunity to increase its financial capital. By comparison, Yale Law School increased its endowment from $500,000 to nearly $2,087,000 during the 1920s. Meanwhile, CLS was forced to share its building, Kent Hall, with other departments and did not gain full occupancy until 1930.[126] By that point, however, CLS had outgrown Kent Hall and entered the Depression needing a new building. The school avoided a financial crisis because it received a few grants supporting research on "law as a social institution" and bequests of $300,000 for the endowment, which grew by 58 percent.[127] In 1940 the CLS financial capital totaled nearly $850,000, and it held steady through World War II, as seen in Table 5.2.

The HLS deans were scarcely more effective or entrepreneurial, though they had the opportunity and responsibility for financial initiatives in Harvard's decentralized governance. In 1906 the school was in excellent financial position, having an endowment of nearly four hundred thousand dollars plus invested cash reserves of nearly half a million dollars, which had accumulated from its annual surpluses. In total, the school owned invested funds amounting to nine times its annual expenses of $99,000 for 1905–6.[128] Thus, the wealthiest law school in the country was far better off even than appears in Table 5.2. But under Dean James Barr Ames (1895–1909), the school violated nearly every precept of Eliot's free money strategy. Without trying to raise money, HLS spent $400,000 from its invested cash reserve to build a massive new building, Langdell Hall. The result of increasing its expenses and decreasing its investment income turned an annual surplus of $49,000 in 1905–6 into an annual deficit of more than $16,000 by 1911–12.[129] Ames's successor, Dean Ezra R. Thayer (1910–15), realized the great mistake but did not have the time to correct it, because he committed suicide in 1915.

After the centennial campaign failed in the late 1910s, Dean Pound organized another campaign in the mid-1920s. Against the advice of the university administration, Pound established the extravagant goal of $5 million. Believing that his writings would persuade donors, Pound's contribution to the campaign effort consisted primarily of issuing public statements attempting to explain the need for funding legal research. Then, during the most critical nine months of the campaign, Pound absented himself by taking leave to work in Washington and deliver lectures at other universities. In the end, the mid-1920s campaign yielded less than half its goal. Pound then exacerbated that failure by borrowing nearly $1.5 million from the university to expand Langdell Hall. After Pound stepped down in 1936, President Conant appointed James M. Landis (1937–46), who favored scientific management and did not have an entrepreneurial bent. Like Burwell at the medical school, Landis took no interest in fundraising or in alumni. In 1946 his successor, Erwin N. Griswold (1946–67), found HLS to be "unbelievably poor" compared to the rest of Harvard University.[130]

Compounding the ineffectiveness of the law deans, the presidents gave little support to the law school under either governance model. They seemed to believe that law schools, like law students, were tougher, more resilient, and required less help. As President Lowell wrote in 1910, the law school was "the school that most attracts ambitious and self-reliant young men," while, among all of Harvard's schools, it "is the one that offers them the least amount of aid."[131]

The centralization at Columbia greatly benefited a school that had the president's enthusiastic backing, and Butler helped CLS initially. In 1903 the school received its first major endowment gift of $125,000 for a professorship. Over the next decade President Butler convinced the trustees to designate an unrestricted bequest of $375,000 along with two other gifts for a law building that cost $500,000. The year

1910 brought an endowment gift of $175,000 and the opening of Kent Hall, which was "an occasion for congratulation and rejoicing to the Faculty and students," who numbered 324.[132] But after 1916 Butler rarely advocated for the law school, and through 1945 the university made only a few special appropriations amounting to merely a few thousand dollars. Furthermore, what the university provided, it could take away, and CLS was forced to share its building with other departments from 1910 to 1930.[133]

At Harvard, presidential disposition also had great influence, notwithstanding the decentralized governance. The presidents and the corporation had discretion to help some "tubs" more than others, and the law school was not favored during the formative era. In 1906 Eliot urged HLS to spend its surplus to build Langdell Hall without trying to raise the money, contrary to his own free money strategy and the wishes of the faculty and dean. During the 1910s Lowell, although an alumnus of the law school himself, did little to support its centennial campaign. After that campaign ended in failure in 1917, Lowell and the corporation forced the school to delay another try until 1925, after the business school and other units had the opportunity to raise money. In 1927 the corporation did not subsidize the expansion of Langdell Hall but lent the entire cost to the school and charged a higher rate of interest than it paid on the school's endowment. As a result, HLS was the only one among the six major professional schools at Columbia and Harvard that paid to construct its major building without external aid during the formative period.

Meanwhile, the university leaders maintained that the law school did not require financial help because of its annual surpluses. Soon after Dean Griswold observed that HLS was "unbelievably poor" in 1946, President Conant omitted the law school from his public appeal for Harvard's professional schools that needed financial support. Conant wrote in his annual report that "the need for adequate endowment is particularly desperate in the School of Public Health, the School of Business Administration, the Medical School, and the School of Education."[134]

Counter-Productive Financial Strategy

Notwithstanding the two factors discussed here, the law schools might have competed with the medical schools financially if not for the law schools' counterproductive financial strategy of maintaining large enrollment, high student/faculty ratio, and low tuition. At Columbia the central administration followed this path by keeping CLS tuition the lowest at the university, while the school's student/faculty ratio inched upward from 30:1 in 1910 to 34:1 in 1921 and 47:1 in 1929.[135] At that point enrollment had grown to 600, and Kent Hall was outgrown. As a result, CLS apparently made a profit for the university, and the university administration likely found attractive the policy of large enrollment, high student/faculty ratio, and low tuition.[136] Apart from pocketing the surplus, the university benefited from the reputation of an eminent law school that presented little competition to other units for philanthropic dollars.

At Harvard the law school maintained a policy of large enrollment, high student/faculty ratio, and low tuition while raising expenses by expanding its physical plant. Between 1892 and 1911 enrollment doubled from about four hundred to over eight hundred, and the student/faculty ratio grew from 57:1 to about 80:1. Meanwhile, the school was still charging the same $150 in tuition that it had instituted thirty years earlier in 1879. The deans refused to raise the tuition out of a charitable concern about burdening their students. They did not consider that high tuition could justify appeals for more scholarships for needy students, as the medical schools were doing at the same time.[137]

HLS could have chosen a different path than constructing Langdell Hall. In 1905, if the school had raised its tuition to the medical school rate of $200 and decreased its annual surplus to the still robust $22,000, it would have needed only four hundred students to generate the necessary tuition revenue of $80,000. A student body of four hundred would have eliminated the need for a new building and lowered the student/faculty ratio to about 44:1. The annual surplus would then have supported steady growth in the faculty. Instead, building Langdell Hall led to "the hazardous dependence on necessarily fluctuating tuition fees," which the deans succeeding Ames began to lament. To escape that dependence, their only plan was to try to raise endowment in order to generate more investment income and, failing that, to expand the physical plant to house more students.[138] By 1920 the HLS enrollment reached 900, and the student/faculty ratio was 90:1. The law school tuition remained at $150, while the university had raised tuition to $200 in 1916.[139]

Apart from financial considerations, the extreme HLS policy attracted criticism on educational grounds. The CLS deans began to chide HLS, which they had long emulated. Undoubtedly referring to Harvard, Dean Stone at Columbia wrote in his annual report "that the school which permits its numbers to exceed about 700 students . . . is sacrificing educational efficiency to the necessity of mere physical growth."[140]

Finally, at the insistence of President Lowell, Dean Pound reluctantly raised tuition to $200 in 1920. But HLS still trailed the rest of Harvard, because in 1921 the university increased tuition to $250 and the medical school to $300. After five more years of urging by the president, Pound and the law faculty, despite charitable misgivings, raised tuition to $250 in 1925, at which point the rest of the university moved up to $300, the medical school to $400, and the business school to $500. As a condition of providing the loan to expand Langdell Hall, the university then required HLS to increase tuition to $400 by 1929, while other tuitions at Harvard went even higher. Over the next twenty years the HLS deans and faculty resisted raising tuition, even while paying off the burdensome mortgage on Langdell Hall.[141]

Meanwhile, Pound bemoaned the school's tuition dependence, lamenting that the law school "must live from hand to mouth."[142] But the school's only plan to escape tuition dependence was to try to raise endowment to generate more investment income and to expand the physical plant to house more students, as enrollment reached 1,200 in 1925. This campaign also fell short, and the building's expenses and mortgage consumed all the investment income from the gifts of the mid-1920s campaign plus 50 percent more. The school's balance sheet looked worse after the campaign. Like CLS, HLS escaped a financial crisis during the Depression due to a stream of small gifts for current use and significant bequests for endowment totaling nearly a million dollars. As a result, between 1930 and 1940 the endowment of HLS jumped about 28 percent, the same amount as the university's, as reported in Table 5.2.

In the late 1920s, following the strategy of the medical school would have led to a better result. Instead of expanding its building after the mid-1920s campaign, HLS could have raised tuition from $200 to the $400 charged by HMS and reduced the enrollment to 600 students, yielding the same tuition revenue of about $240,000. This approach would have decreased the student-faculty ratio to about 30:1 and opened a great deal of space in the existing HLS buildings, which accommodated eight hundred students. The elimination of both the mortgage payment and the additional expenses from the building expansion, coupled with the increase of investment income resulting from the mid-1920s campaign, would have yielded an immense annual surplus of about $160,000, more than half the annual budget.

While building a significant cash reserve, offering scholarship aid to needy students, and sharply reducing the student/faculty ratio, Dean Pound and his colleagues could still have sustained a debt-free, gradual rate of growth in both the student body and the faculty. Instead, the school stoutly resisted raising its tuition until forced to do so by the university as a condition of the loan in 1927. Through the 1930s the school struggled to pay its bills and was hit hard by declines in enrollment during World War II. The HLS endowment actually lost value between 1940 and 1945 because of wartime inflation. Only in 1948 did the school pay off the mortgage and raise its tuition.[143] Unable to attract major gifts and unwilling to raise tuition or reduce enrollment, HLS deans felt compelled to expand the physical plant to accommodate more students. But this only increased expenses and dependence on tuition drawn from large enrollment while raising the student/faculty ratio.

Criticizing the HLS strategy does not require hindsight. At the time, Columbia deans wished to follow a different course. They challenged the "obvious reasons" that legal education cost less than medical or engineering education.[144] CLS deans maintained that the cost of legal education was artificially low because of the high student/faculty ratio and that enrollment should be capped or reduced in order to provide "greater individualized instruction."[145] In the 1930s Dean Young B. Smith argued repeatedly that medical instruction was expensive primarily because of its low student/faculty ratio. Given that ratio, the law school could offer education "comparable to what is now done for the medical students."[146]

The fundamental question, wrote Smith, is "whether the proper education and training of lawyers is as important as that of doctors."[147] In effect, Butler and Columbia replied negatively, as did the presidents at Harvard. And the CLS deans did not have the discretion to choose a different course, while HLS deans did not exercise their discretion to do so. The two schools persisted in "the box office plan" of depending primarily on tuition revenue based upon large enrollment, high student/faculty ratios, and low tuition.[148]

Business Schools Rapidly Gain Ground

As their enrollments grew rapidly in the early decades of the twentieth century, the financial capital of business schools at wealthy universities rose commensurately. In the thirty-five years between 1915 and 1950, the combined endowments of Harvard and Columbia business schools multiplied more than twenty-eight times, compared to four times for the two universities, as reported in Table 5.3. Consequently, the business, law, and medical schools far outpaced their universities in expanding financial capital over that period. Between 1890 and 1950 the universities' combined endowment multiplied nearly nineteen times; the two medical schools,' sixty-six times; the two law schools,' more than thirty-seven times; and the two business schools,' more than twenty-eight times (the last in thirty-five years, between 1915 and 1950). By the end of the formative period, these three kinds of schools had established themselves as the major professional schools.

But the schools also diverged in building their financial capital. The fledgling business schools outperformed the long-standing and prestigious law schools. Between 1915 and 1950 the financial capital of the two law schools rose by nearly six times and that of the business schools by, as stated above, more than twenty-eight times. The gap would have been even greater if both CLS and HLS had not received significant bequests during the 1930s. The recently founded business schools did not, of course, have that possibility. Their different performance during the 1930s is evident in Fig. 5.4. Nevertheless, Fig. 5.4 also reveals that the combined endowment of the business schools passed that of the law schools by 1950.

The newly founded business schools did not catch the medical schools, however. Both in the absolute amount and in rate of increase, the decreasing order of financial capital by 1950 was medicine, business, and law. These trends at Harvard and Columbia are illustrated by Fig. 5.5, which relies on the data in Table 5.3. These developments were also formative because this new financial hierarchy generally persisted in the echelon of major professional schools in subsequent decades.

The proliferation of university business schools stemmed naturally from students' rising interest in business as a field of study and a career after 1900.[149] At Harvard in 1905 both the president and the law school dean observed that more Harvard College graduates were entering business careers than the law school. By 1916 some 55 percent of the graduating class entered commerce or industry, more than

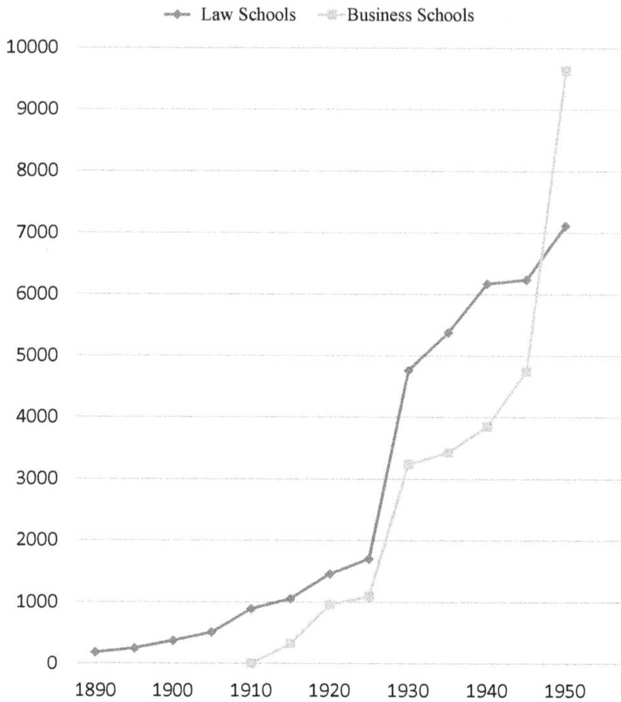

Figure 5.4. Combined endowments of law schools vs. business schools at Columbia and Harvard Universities, 1890–1950 (in thousands of nominal dollars).

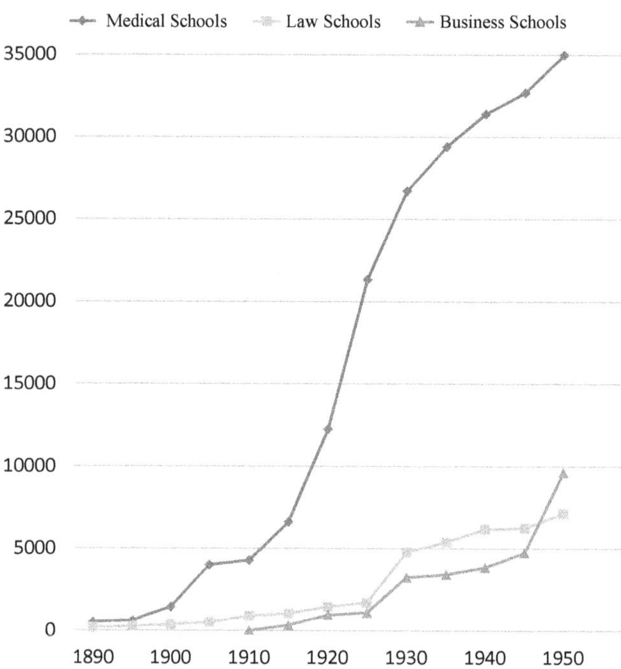

Figure 5.5. Combined endowments of medical, law, and business schools at Columbia and Harvard Universities, 1890–1950 (in thousands of nominal dollars).

the three longstanding "learned professions" of theology, medicine, and law combined.[150] Prior to the founding of HBS in 1908, many major corporations recruited their managers from HLS. When Lowell appointed Wallace B. Donham as business dean (1919–42), both intended that the business school would displace the law school as the source for the right kind of managers to lead major corporations.[151] By 1920 the HBS enrollment had grown to 394, and then by 1930 to 1,011, as indicated in Table 5.2.

At Columbia, Butler and the college faculty opposed the creation of a business school until the rising interest of undergraduates became too strong. In 1914 Butler agreed to establish "a well organized group of studies that will be as effective in the preparation for business," though he still objected to founding a business school.[152] In 1916 Columbia finally established a separate school, but with a director and administrative board rather than a dean and faculty, as the university's other professional schools had. The head of the Department of Extension Teaching, James G. Egbert (1916–32), was named director of the new school and served in both roles. Within a few months of opening, enrollment vastly exceeded expectations, and Butler could resist no longer. He and Egbert began to solicit gifts for a building. By 1920 enrollment reached 269 (Table 5.2).[153]

Also in 1916 the American Association of Collegiate Schools of Business was established, and in 1922 about 122 business schools were offering college degrees. By that time business studies were the fastest growing sector in American higher education, commensurate with the increase in managerial jobs. As of 1930 more than 3 percent of undergraduate degrees in the United States were awarded in business. Notwithstanding the financial stringency imposed by the Depression, business school enrollments grew steadily, and the proportion of undergraduate degrees awarded in business rose to 9 percent by 1940 and to 15 percent by 1950.[154]

Negotiating the Shift from Charity to Philanthropy

The capital of business schools at leading universities thus grew rapidly, although alumni giving was insignificant because the business schools and their graduates were so young.[155] Instead, three kinds of factors contributed. The business schools accommodated the ideological shift from charity to philanthropy, but differently than did the medical schools. The business schools shrewdly disavowed any claim to charity for themselves or their students while they invoked the philanthropic rationale and attracted major gifts. Yet these donations came not from foundations, but from wealthy businessmen, many of whom were not alumni or even college graduates. Consequently, the institutional interest of these donors likely played a factor as much as did the philanthropic rationales.

At Harvard, Edmund C. Converse, a New York industrialist and financier who had not attended college, gave $125,000 to endow a professorship in banking merely four years after the fledgling HBS opened. In 1914 and 1915 the friends of railroad tycoon James J. Hill, who also did not attend college, donated $250,000 in his honor to endow a professorship in transportation. During World War I, enrollment fell precipitously, but the school recovered with the help of Harvard College alumni in business, who raised money to cover the school's deficit. In 1922 and 1923 the "financial assistance and the active cooperation of business men" helped HBS rebound after the sharp recession of 1920–21, according to Dean Donham.[156]

This cooperation culminated in a fund-raising drive for the business school focused upon "men of substance who were active in business irrespective of their college affiliations." The campaign resulted in the 1924 gift of $5,000,000 from New York banker George F. Baker, who did not attend college, to build an entire campus for the school and increase the endowment. This was the largest single gift that Harvard University had received to that point in its history. When the new campus was completed in 1927, businessmen made two more endowment gifts of $1,000,000.[157] As a result, the HBS endowment in 1930 rose to almost $2,348,000, or 53 percent of the HLS endowment, the increase coming almost entirely from businessmen who were not college graduates.

Similarly, at Columbia the urging and financial assistance from A. Barton Hepburn, president of Chase National Bank, convinced Butler and the trustees to approve the creation of a business school. In the school's second year, Emerson McMillin, a New York banker and utilities developer, gave $586,500 for a new building, the largest donation made to the university during that year. In the following year CBS again received one of the largest gifts made to the university: $480,000 for endowment, donated by Hepburn.[158]

By 1920 the endowment of Columbia's business school drew even with that of the law school, as seen in Table 5.2. As at Harvard, the CBS alumni were encouraging but donated little because of their relative youth. Instead, Egbert appealed directly to the businessmen of the city.[159] Although the appeals were not immediately successful, an addition of $408,000 to the Hepburn endowment brought the total of the business school's endowment to $890,000 in 1930, surpassing the law school's endowment.[160]

The justification for these gifts to business schools was framed in the rationale of philanthropy, which required that root causes and solutions of human problems be scientifically identified and that those solutions be instituted systematically and effectively. The business problem was to expand the local and national economy, and Egbert argued that "the business men of the city . . . should supply the means whereby the School may make progress in the scientific study of business and the training of . . . the business men of the future in this great metropolis."[161] A subsequent CBS dean maintained "that philanthropy directed toward educational ends could find no more effective outlet than [business education]."[162]

Thus, business schools' solicitations and donations were fitted into the philanthropic rationale. But scholars explain that fit in different ways, which can be sorted into the two broad categories of structural-functionalist and power analyses. On the one hand, historian Alfred Chandler argued famously that the growth of industrial corporations in the late nineteenth century created many functional roles that required new expertise. The new vocation of business manager emerged between capital and labor to fill those roles, and business schools arose to provide the expertise to managers.[163] On the other hand, Rakesh Khurana has challenged the functionalist interpretation, drawing upon the power analysis of sociologists and the "new institutionalism" of other recent scholars. According to Khurana, "institutional entrepreneurs," comprising both corporate and university leaders, created business schools as a way "to legitimate and institutionalize the new occupation of management" while expanding their own enterprises, status, and influence.[164]

The continuing debate between these two interpretations cannot be resolved here. The root causes and motivations of individual wealthy donors are complicated and vary over time, location, and many other dimensions, as Francie Ostrower has analyzed in regard to late-twentieth-century New York City.[165] With respect to the structural-functionalist and power analyses, the salient point in this historical context is that few academic observers attributed the proliferation of business schools primarily to the value of their expertise. Yet many did attribute medical schools' expanding financial support to the therapeutic effectiveness of medical expertise. In fact, business schools faced persistent skepticism about the validity and utility of their courses and research. They also heard objections that the subject of business was unintellectual, concerned with profit, and therefore unsuitable to be taught at a university.[166]

Nevertheless, wealthy businessmen seemed relatively credulous that the research and instruction of the young business schools would yield a return on donations, even as those businessmen required proof about the benefit of medical and legal research. The two business schools therefore received gifts and grants far out of proportion to their academic pedigree and perceived legitimacy during the formative era. That is the key point. Business leaders believed they were making philanthropic benefactions, though their institutional interest surely played a role, as Khurana has argued. This interpretation should be distinguished from the less sophisticated view that wealthy donors gave solely or primarily to advance their self-interest, although that view may fit more recent times, as Teresa Odendahl has proposed.[167]

Entrepreneurial Leaders

The second factor contributing to the financial rise of business schools at wealthy universities was the nature of institutional leadership: the support of the central administration and the initiative and capability of the deans. At Harvard, notwithstanding the decentralized governance, Eliot and the corporation actively supported efforts during 1906 and 1907 to raise $125,000 to fund a business school for a trial period of five years. At the end of the trial, in 1912, the corporation voted to continue the school and provided an initial endowment of $25,000. During the sharp recession of 1920 and 1921, the university covered the school's deficit—"to our great relief," wrote Donham.[168]

In the mid-1920s Lowell, though he disliked fund-raising, personally organized and chaired the successful campaign that netted the business school some seven million dollars to build its new campus and endowment. While Conant initially doubted the academic merit of the study of business, he eventually became an advocate, appointed a confidant to be dean in 1942, approved a fund-raising campaign in 1945, and assigned to the business school a discretionary three-million-dollar grant from the Ford Foundation in 1950. At that point the HBS endowment stood at 125 percent of the HLS endowment due, in no small part, to the support of the Harvard presidents and central administration.[169]

Meanwhile, at centralized Columbia, the president and trustees distinctly favored CBS by cultivating the support of businessmen and financiers such as Hepburn in the late 1910s. In 1924 the one-million-dollar cost of constructing a new building for CBS ran far over budget as a result of rising construction expenses. The university covered the unfunded balance rather than saddling the school with a debt, as Harvard did to its law school three years later.[170] In addition, CBS relied directly on annual subsidies from the university during the 1920s.[171] When the Depression began in 1929, Columbia was apparently covering about 8 percent of the CBS expenses with transfers from the Extension Department.[172] During 1920s and 1930s, Butler departed from his normal policy and allowed Egbert to appeal for gifts publicly. Overall, the CBS dean had good reason to express gratitude for "the active interest of yourself and the Trustees of the University."[173]

Institutional leadership also comprised the work of the business deans. At Harvard, even before the business school opened, the first dean, Edwin F. Gay (1908–18), began making public and private appeals to businessmen and Harvard alumni for gifts. In 1919 the next dean, Donham, threw himself into the work, invoking the philanthropic rationale and spending as much as 80 percent of his time on fund-raising, he said.[174] A decade later, Donham summarized his results: "Over $1,000,000 has been spent in this research during the last six years. . . . These funds have been obtained on a temporary basis from year to year. About 27 percent . . . has been secured from various trade associations and business groups to finance studies . . . in their fields. The remaining 73 percent . . . has been obtained largely from solicited gifts and donations from business men and friends of the School."[175] In 1929 Donham tried to regularize the stream of gifts by forming the group Two Hundred Fifty Associates of the Harvard Business School, who each pledged to donate $1,000 annually, and this support helped the school significantly in the Depression.[176]

During World War II, Donham's entrepreneurial initiatives paid off again. Recognizing the nation's unpreparedness for war, he offered to provide training for military officers in 1940. No other business school in the country and no other Harvard professional school so completely abandoned its civilian degree program and contracted with the government to do military training and research. As a result, HBS flourished through WWII "in grand style, much more so than Law or Medicine" at Harvard.[177] By the academic year 1944/45 HBS revenues from military instruction and research contracts amounted to about 47 percent of the school's budget. Right after the war, the new dean, Donald K. David (1942–55), successfully petitioned Conant for permission to run an endowment campaign.[178]

At Columbia the centralized governance limited the deans' entrepreneurial activity. Nevertheless, the first CBS dean, Egbert, actively campaigned to convince university leaders "that preparation for business . . . should be on the same plane as that in other professional schools."[179] As the enrollment grew to 269 in merely four years, Egbert ceaselessly petitioned Butler for a new building. He also appealed publicly for gifts of endowment for faculty fellowships, student scholarships, and the school in general. Although Egbert did not raise much external money, his work significantly enhanced the favor of the Columbia University administration for the business school.[180]

In 1932 Roswell C. McCrea (1932–41) became dean, and he continued the entrepreneurial activity of Egbert during the Depression, encouraging alumni "to organize a campaign." In addition, McCrea formed an advisory council of businessmen to provide suggestions and financial assistance while he also appealed for grants to support research on specific areas such as industrial relations and actuarial science.[181] Nevertheless, the Depression weighed on CBS as enrollment, investment income, and expenses declined. After rising briefly in the late 1930s, annual expenses dropped again with the onset of World War II, when McCrea resigned.[182] Though not successful during the Depression, his pursuit of gifts stimulated the interest of businessmen, who increased their donations after CBS instituted the MBA degree in 1945 and then moved entirely to the graduate level in 1948.[183]

Strategy Based on "Business Principles"

Finally, business schools achieved prosperity by pursuing the strategy of "conducting the School on business principles," as Donham stated at HBS.[184] The first such principle was that business students should pay all the direct instructional costs for their education, which prepared them to earn a good living.[185] This tenet explicitly disavowed any appeal, on grounds of charity, that poor business students deserved to be subsidized. In order to provide financial aid for students of small means, HBS offered loans, "made on a strictly business basis," because the loans "lead the student to consider the business training given by the School as an investment."[186] Deans at CBS likewise appealed for gifts to endow loan funds as well as for scholarships.[187]

The second principle was to raise tuition high enough to cover the direct instructional costs, because, again, business students did not deserve charity. Even as a brand new school, HBS remarkably did not hesitate to make its tuition the highest in the university. In 1908 the new school set tuition at the university standard of $150, then raised it to $200 in 1916, $250 in 1920, $400 in 1921, $500 in 1925, and $600 in 1930, with the full support of Lowell and interested businessmen. HBS tuition remained the highest at the university through at least 1945.[188] Similarly, though less aggressively, CBS kept its fees just above the university norm and in 1935 raised them to nearly $400 in order to bring "our tuition charges more nearly into line with comparable charges by other eastern institutions."[189] Hence, the HBS tuition policy raised the bar for other university business schools.

As tuition increased, HBS expected its enrollment to stop rising, but the students kept coming. The school could have continued growing and banking more tuition revenue, as did HLS. But HBS adopted a third business principle of deliberately limiting enrollment, because "the quality of instruction which we desire can only be obtained by a reduction in the size of the teaching sections."[190] In 1930 the school capped enrollment at one thousand, "the limit of students for which [the campus] was designed."[191] This tenet not only safeguarded the educational quality but avoided the expense of constructing and maintaining more buildings.

Fourth, having stipulated that tuition should cover direct instructional costs, the school maintained that other costs—physical plant, research, service, and other activities—should legitimately be supported by other sources, such as grants and gifts. This "met with a sympathetic response from business men" and boosted fund-raising because donors and grantors did not want to subsidize business students. Hence, the fourth principle aided the dean's solicitations for these revenues.[192]

But this tenet, though helpful in fund-raising, made HBS vulnerable to the extent that it depended on annual gifts. Donham therefore adopted a fifth business principle for the school: that operating costs and research should be covered by endowment whenever possible.[193] The preference for endowment consisted entirely with Harvard's free-money strategy formulated by Eliot. In 1933 Donham argued that, relative to the rest of the university, the business school was underendowed, having 12.6 percent of the university's enrollment and 2 percent of the university's endowment.[194] Harvard presidents agreed, and Lowell and Conant supported efforts to raise endowment for the business school.

Overall, these business principles amounted to allocating different kinds of revenue to different kinds of expenses; students paid their full instructional cost via tuition, aided only by loans, while gifts, grants, and endowments were allocated to construction, research, and auxiliary functions. This strategy justified raising tuition to meet costs while obviating any charitable requests for funds to aid business students and aiming solicitations for gifts toward donors' interests. At CBS the distinctive strategy was less developed, given Columbia's centralized control over finances. But the deans followed the same general approach of raising tuition, capping enrollment, and appealing for gifts to support research and faculty.

This financial strategy helped the business schools through the tumultuous decades of the 1920s and the 1930s, as seen in Table 5.2. In the late 1920s, HBS began running an annual surplus of $90,000.[195] During the Depression, HBS enrollment rose to 1,100 in the early 1930s, but then fell to 725 by 1935. By spending reserves, cutting expenses, and obtaining current gifts totaling about $820,000, the school avoided a deficit through 1938, when enrollment recovered. The school then decreased the number of students in its course sections from 200 to 100.[196]

Meanwhile, at CBS, the total expenses had grown to $180,400 by 1930 and total revenue to $185,500, including $145,500 in tuition revenue and about $40,000 in investment income. Hence, the CBS endowment produced about 22 percent of its income, while the CLS endowment yielded merely 8 percent. Impressed by the school's solvency, the university trustees reorganized CBS along the lines of Columbia's eminent law and medical schools by replacing the Director and Administrative Board with a Dean and Faculty, as of July 1931.[197]

Merely fifteen years after it opened, CBS reached "the same plane as that in other professional schools."[198] The business principles had worked remarkably well.

Financial Template of the Major Professional Schools

This essay has presented the first compilation and analysis of the historical finances of the three major professional schools. The study focused on the two leading universities in professional education during the formative era: Columbia and Harvard. They were the two wealthiest universities between 1890 and 1950, and among the eight wealthiest universities of the period only Columbia and Harvard had schools that were considered among the best in the nation in all three fields of law, medicine, and business.

By the end of this period, a new financial template had emerged in professional education. Medicine, law, and business had become the major professional schools by increasing their wealth much faster than did the rest of the university. The template also incorporated a new financial hierarchy among those three domains. In the 1890s the endowed law schools and medical schools stood on a par in financial capital. Over the next fifty years, the financial capital of medical schools rapidly outpaced that of law schools. Meanwhile, the fledgling business schools started far behind in financial capital, as well as status, but soon caught and then pulled ahead of the law schools, though not the medical schools. By 1950 the resulting and persistent order of capital wealth within the echelon was: medicine, business, and law, as seen in Fig. 5.5. The data naturally exhibit these same trends if the figures are deflated to constant dollars, since inflation affected all the schools and universities. This is seen in Table 5.4.

Calculated in constant dollars, the compound annual growth rates for the combined endowments during the period from 1890 to 1950 were 3.40 percent for the universities, 4.56 percent for the law schools, 5.54 percent for the medical schools, and 7.43 percent for the business schools. The last figure reflects the extraordinary growth of the business schools' financial capital over the shorter period from 1915 to 1950.

The financial standing of the major professional schools within the university is seen even more clearly if the endowment totals for the schools of medicine, law, and business are subtracted from the universities' totals. In that case the compound annual growth rate for the

Table 5.4. Compound annual growth rates (CAGR) of endowments of universities and schools of medicine, law, and business, 1890–1950 (in constant dollars; 1920=1)

Type of Institution	CAGR
Universities in total	3.4%
Universities without medical, law, business schools	3.2%
Law schools	4.6%
Medical schools	5.5%
Business schools (1915–50)	7.4%

Source: The deflating factors are drawn from John J. McCusker. *How Much Is That in Real Money? A Historical Commodity Price Index for Use as a Deflator of Money Values in the Economy of the United States*, 2nd ed. (Worcester, MA: American Antiquarian Society, 2001). Note: The compound growth formula is $R = (Y/A)^{(1/X)} - 1$, where R = compound annual growth rate; Y = ending value of the variable after X periods; A = initial value of the variable; X = number of temporal periods or years.

universities' endowment drops to 3.21 percent, as compared to 4.56 percent for the law schools, 5.54 percent for the medical schools, and 7.43 percent for the business schools, calculated in constant dollars for the period from 1890 to 1950. It is important to appreciate that merely a 1 percent difference in the compound rate of annual growth produces a large absolute difference over time.

Finally, this study has addressed reasons for these trends. Three kinds of factors—ideology, leadership, and strategy—determined the new financial template of the major professional schools at wealthy universities. Their impact was complicated because the factors varied across the domains and reciprocally influenced each other.

Most significantly, the schools responded differently to the contemporary ideological shift from charity to philanthropy in Americans' understanding of benefaction. Those responses impacted the amount of gifts and grants received from donors and, therefore, the wealth of the schools. Medical schools accommodated the shift effectively by embracing both poles in the ideology of benefaction.

The business schools also effectively accommodated the shift from charity to philanthropy, but quite differently than did medical schools. The business schools shrewdly disavowed any claim to charity for themselves or their students. They then invoked the philanthropic rationale and attracted major gifts from wealthy corporations and businessmen, many of whom were not alumni or even college graduates. The paradox here is that business schools received a great deal of financial support for research to help business and the economy, despite persistent skepticism about the validity and sophistication of their expertise during the period. In fact, HBS and CBS received donations far out of proportion to the schools' academic pedigree and legitimacy. Wealthy businessmen, who scrutinized the benefit of medical and legal research, seemed willing to accept on faith the value of business education and research, so grants and gifts poured into business schools. Consequently, it appears that they were acting as institutional entrepreneurs while also responding to the philanthropic rationale.

Law schools, however, failed to accommodate either pole while the ideology of benefaction shifted from charity to philanthropy. On the one hand, the law deans claimed that "the same spirit of inquiry . . . of the Schools of Medicine and of Mines, Engineering, and Chemistry is also at work in . . . the Faculty of Law."[199] But the deans could not explain persuasively how legal research would lead directly to any significant and tangible social benefit, as medical research seemed to do. Consequently, the philanthropic gifts and grants amounted to relatively little. On the other hand, law schools occasionally made a charitable appeal for endowed scholarships to support needy law students. But few donors, even alumni, were persuaded to respond, particularly in light of the historical animus against lawyers in the United States.

The character of institutional leadership, though influenced by the ideological and strategic factors, also determined the wealth of the schools. The administrative effectiveness and entrepreneurial initiative of the deans made a significant difference, and medicine and business had striking positive examples. Law did not. At CLS, the deans were hampered by the centralized governance, which discouraged or prohibited financial initiatives. The least effective deans were those at HLS, given their opportunity and responsibility for financial initiatives in Harvard's decentralized system. Nothing is more illustrative than the contrast between Pound absenting himself to lecture at other universities during the most critical period of fund-raising for HLS in the mid-1920s, while Donham was devoting 80 percent of his time to fund-raising for HBS.

Leadership included, as well, the level of support from the university president and central administration. This varied in kind and degree. For example, Butler at Columbia wanted to maintain personal control over the deans, while Conant at Harvard preferred scientific acumen over entrepreneurial effectiveness. Despite their personal preferences, the presidents also metered the amount of their support in light of strategic opportunities. As institutional entrepreneurs, the presidents favored professional fields that seemed the most promising investment for the university.

Hence, the medical schools received unceasing encouragement throughout the formative period. After some initial skepticism, business schools received unstinting support from university leaders in the form of subventions, fund-raising assistance, and administrative facilitation. The law schools received the least help from their universities under either governance model.

In fact, the university leaders even weakened the law schools in certain respects. Columbia depressed the CLS law tuition and siphoned off the surplus revenue, while Harvard forced HLS to pay for its own buildings. HLS was the only school of the six in this study forced to do that. In effect, this amounted to siphoning off its surplus. And the presidents discriminated against the law school in public appeals. Lowell sidelined HLS in the early 1920s while personally chairing the campaign for HBS. Soon after Dean Griswold concluded that HLS was "unbelievably poor" in 1946, Conant omitted the law school from his list of Harvard's professional schools that needed financial support.[200]

The schools' financial strategies also determined their fortunes. At the turn of the century the leading medical schools deliberately began reducing their dependence on tuition revenue and seeking endowment, current gifts, and grants to support research. Their tactics included reducing enrollment, raising tuition, and soliciting endowed scholarships to alleviate students' burden. They also appealed for general endowment to subsidize the increasing per-student cost of medical education resulting from the low student/faculty ratio. The medical schools shrewdly fostered the conditions that justified the need for philanthropy.

The business schools, especially HBS, crafted a particular, highly effective financial strategy based on business principles. HBS distinguished between expenses for instruction and those for research, contract activities, and physical plant. The school then required that tuition cover instructional expenses and provided loans to allow access to students of limited means. The principle here, unlike that of the medical schools, was that business students, who will make good livings, do not deserve charity. Gifts and grants were allocated to noninstructional expenses, which would advance the study of business and not the careers of individuals. The segmentation of costs and allocation of revenues justified higher tuition in the eyes of students and more gifts in the minds of donors. Finally, the school limited its enrollment to the size of its physical plant, safeguarding educational quality while avoiding the need to construct and maintain more buildings.

The law schools' strategy was counterproductive. They were unable to attract major donors either on philanthropic grounds to support research benefiting society, as did medical schools, or due to the vested interest of institutional entrepreneurs, as did business schools. Instead, the law schools implicitly invoked charity while keeping tuition relatively low. Unlike the medical schools, they apparently did not appreciate how scholarships could selectively offset high tuition for needy students. Unlike the business schools, they did not see that the charitable impulse was misguided for professional students who could expect to earn a good living. While CLS wished to cap its enrollment but could not, HLS never seriously considered reducing or capping enrollment, as did the medical schools and business schools. HLS wished to escape tuition dependence but pursued solely the tactic of trying to raise endowment to generate more investment income. When that failed, HLS felt compelled to expand its physical plant to accommodate more students. But this only worsened its tuition dependence.

Recognizing the New Template

These ideological, strategic, and leadership factors determined the financial template of the major professional schools, illustrated by Columbia and Harvard, the leading universities in professional education at the time. During the formative era, leaders in higher education expressly began to recognize and endorse the new template.

In 1914 Yale president Arthur T. Hadley observed that leading universities throughout the country were abandoning the view that professional schools should be "supported by tuition fees alone." But Haley noted one exception: "It is frequently possible to support a first-rate law school, taught by men of real eminence, from the fees of the students. This is partly because law students see a lucrative profession not far ahead, and can therefore afford to pay high fees for good instruction; and partly because law is a subject in which large classes can be taught almost as well as small ones, so that a single efficient teacher can command the fees of a large number of interested pupils."[201] Hadley thus endorsed the exceptional model of large enrollment, high student/faculty ratio, and tuition dependence exemplified at the two leading law schools at wealthy universities during the formative era.

This exceptional and imprudent model was apparent to the deans of the other major professional schools. Initially, the business deans maintained that "the development of a School of Business . . . resembles the development of a School of Law. We have the same questions as to methods of instruction which have faced Schools of Law and the same difficulties in obtaining and retaining a satisfactory staff," as Egbert wrote at Columbia.[202] Likewise, HBS initially modeled its pedagogy on "the example of the Harvard Law School. . . . The Law School training was highly esteemed in influential business circles, and that training was effectuated by the use of the case method of instruction." Through the early 1930s successive deans "decided that instruction in the Business School should be patterned on the method used with such conspicuous success in the Law School."[203]

By the late 1930s, however, the business schools began looking to medical schools, rather than law schools, for their institutional model. The HBS dean wrote, "Quality instruction in business turns out to be much more expensive than we had assumed in the first fifteen or twenty years of our existence. In this respect it compares more nearly with medical training than it does with the work . . . in the Law School."[204] Conversely, HLS by 1950 began trying to emulate the business school's office of research and even its very different practice of case method teaching.[205] Then, by 1980, medical schools turned to the wealthy business schools for models of professional training.[206] Law schools at leading universities—though well off compared to the "minor" professional schools—were left behind, with their deans complaining about their "poverty," about living "from hand to mouth," and about being "unbelievably poor."[207]

The financial template of three major professional schools exemplified at Columbia and Harvard persisted for decades. The flood of federal funding into medical research after 1945 extended the trajectory that medical schools had already established.[208] Driven by the post-1945 boom in the US economy, the rising corporate support did the same for business schools. The prewar strategies and limitations of law schools continued after 1945 as well. In the early twenty-first century, law schools' reliance on an ever expanding pool of strong applicants collapsed.[209] The years from 1890 to 1950 therefore constitute the formative financial era of the major professional schools at leading universities.

Notes

1. Quotation is from Morton Keller and Phyllis Keller, *Making Harvard Modern: The Rise of America's University* (New York: Oxford University Press, 2001), 114. See Amitai Etzioni, ed., *The Semi-Professions in America* (New York: Free Press, 1969); Nathan Glazer, "The Schools of the Minor Professions," *Minerva* 12 (1974): 346–64.

2. Glazer, "Schools of the Minor Professions"; Etzioni, *Semi-Professions*. Figures are drawn from James R. Parsons Jr., *Professional Education* (New York: n.p. [1900]), 17; Harvard University, *Annual Report of the Treasurer, 1919–20*, 130–65 (hereafter cited as *Harvard Treasurer Report* with dates).

3. Robert Stevens, *Law School: Legal Education in America from the 1850s to the 1980s* (Chapel Hill: University of North Carolina Press, 1983); William P. LaPiana, *Logic and Experience: The Origin of Modern American Legal Education* (New York: Oxford University Press, 1994); Steve Sheppard, ed., *The History of Legal Education in the United States* (Pasadena, CA: Salem Press, 1999); Carter A. Daniel, *M.B.A.: The First Century* (Lewisberg, PA: Bucknell University Press, 1998); Rakesh Khurana, *From Higher Aims to Hired Hands: The Social Transformation of American Business Schools and the Unfulfilled Promise of Management as a Profession* (Princeton, NJ: Princeton University Press, 2007); William G. Rothstein, *American Medical Schools and the Practice of Medicine: A History* (New York: Oxford University Press, 1987). More attention to finances is found in Kenneth Ludmerer, *Learning to Heal: The Development of American Medical Education* (Baltimore: Johns Hopkins University Press, 1985); Kenneth Ludmerer, *Time to Heal: American Medical Education from the Turn of the Century to the Era of Managed Care* (New York: Oxford University Press, 1999).

4. Henry K. Beecher and Mark D. Altschule, *Medicine at Harvard: The First 300 Years* (Hanover, NH: University Press of New England, 1977), 168; Julius Goebel Jr., *A History of the School of Law: Columbia University* (New York: Columbia University Press, 1955), 95–96, 185–86, 236–37; Jeffrey L. Cruikshank, *A Delicate Experiment: The Harvard Business School, 1908–1945* (Boston: Harvard Business School Press, 1987); Thurman W. Van Metre, *A History of the Graduate School of Business, Columbia University* (New York: Columbia University Press, 1954); Arthur E. Sutherland, *The Law at Harvard: A History of Men and Ideas, 1817–1967* (Cambridge, MA: Harvard University Press, 1967); Albert R. Lamb, *The Presbyterian Hospital and the Columbia-Presbyterian Medical Center, 1868–1943* (New York: Columbia University Press, 1955); Anthony Kronman, ed., *History of the Yale Law School* (New Haven, CT: Yale University Press, 2004).

5. Khurana, *From Higher Aims*, 6. See also 18, 26–32, 44–49, 100–102, 127, 133, 150, 173.

6. Robert J. Gordon, *The Rise and Fall of American Growth: The US Standard of*

Living since the Civil War (Princeton, NJ: Princeton University Press, 2016), 285.

7. Eduard C. Lindeman, *Wealth and Culture* (New York: Harcourt, Brace, 1936); Ernest V. Hollis, *Philanthropic Foundations and Higher Education* (New York: Columbia University Press, 1938), 200; Robert Bremner, *American Philanthropy*, 2d ed. (Chicago: University of Chicago Press, 1988), 85, 106; Merle Curti and Roderick Nash, *Philanthropy in the Shaping of American Higher Education* (New Brunswick, NJ: Rutgers University Press, 1965), 41, 56, 91, 110, 164, 211.

8. The discussion of charity and philanthropy draws upon Barry D. Karl and Stanley N. Katz, "The American Private Philanthropic Foundation and the Public Sphere, 1890–1930," *Minerva* 19 (1981): 236–71; Olivier Zunz, *Philanthropy in America: A History* (Princeton, NJ: Princeton University Press, 2012), 10–18; Lawrence J. Friedman, "Philanthropy in America: Historicism and Its Discontents," 6–10, and Robert A. Gross, "Giving in America: From Charity to Philanthropy," 30–47, in *Charity, Philanthropy, and Civility in American History*, edited by Lawrence J. Friedman and Mark D. McGarvie (Cambridge, MA: Cambridge University Press, 2003); Andrea Walton, *Women and Philanthropy in Education* (Bloomington, IN: Indiana University Press, 2005), 1–35. See Scott M. Cutlip, *Fund Raising in the United States: Its Role in America's Philanthropy* (New Brunswick, NJ: Rutgers University Press, 1965), 3.

9. Josephine Shaw Lowell, *Public Relief and Private Charity* (New York: n.p., 1884), 89.

10. Quotations are from Yale University, *Annual Report of the Treasurer, 1908–9* (New Haven, CT: Yale University, 1910), 11, and *1912–13*, 45 (hereafter cited as *Yale Treasurer Report* with dates).

11. George Gordon, "A Free University," *New York Times*, July 26, 1912, 8.

12. Judith Sealander, "Curing Evils at Their Source: The Arrival of Scientific Giving," in *Charity, Philanthropy, and Civility in American History*, edited by Lawrence J. Friedman and Mark D. McGarvie (Cambridge, MA: Cambridge University Press, 2003), 218, 220–23, emphasis in the original; Karl and Katz, "American Private Philanthropic Foundation," 243–44. See also Barry D. Karl and Stanley N. Katz, "Foundations and Ruling Class Elites," *Daedalus* 116 (1987): 1, 5.

13. Karl and Katz, "The American Private," 243–4. See also Gross, "Giving in America," 31, 39, 44; Friedman, "Philanthropy in America," 7–8; Cutlip, *Fund Raising in the United States*, 3.

14. Roy Lubove, *The Professional Altruist: The Emergence of Social Work as a Career, 1880–1930* (Cambridge, MA: Harvard University Press, 1965), 6.

15. John D. Rockefeller, *Random Reminiscences of Men and Events* (New York: Doubleday & Page, 1909), 184.

16. Zunz, *Philanthropy in America*, 10.

17. Compare Sydney V. James, *A People among Peoples: Quaker Benevolence in Eighteenth-Century America* (Cambridge, MA: Harvard University Press, 1963); Conrad E. Wright, *The Transformation of Charity in Postrevolutionary New England* (Boston: Northeastern University Press, 1992); Mark D. McGarvie, "The *Dartmouth College* Case and the Legal Design of Civil Society," in *Charity, Philanthropy, and Civility in American History*, edited by Lawrence J. Friedman and Mark D. McGarvie (Cambridge, MA: Cambridge University Press, 2003), 91–105; and Gross, "Giving in

America," 29–48. Also see Kathleen A. McCarthy, *American Creed: Philanthropy and the Rise of Civil Society, 1700–1865* (Chicago: University of Chicago Press, 2003).

18. Carl Joslyn, "What Can a Man Afford?" *American Economic Review* 11, supp. no. 2 (December 1921): 118; Homer Folks, "Philanthropy, Educational Aspects of Modern," in *A Cyclopedia of Education*, edited by Paul Monroe, 5 vols. (New York: Macmillan, 1913), 4:671–74; See Cutlip, *Fund Raising in the United States*, 203–4; Karl and Katz, "American Private Philanthropic Foundation," 243–44.

19. "Charity Old and New," *New York Times*, December 11, 1917, 14. See Bruce A. Kimball and Benjamin A. Johnson, "The Inception of the Meaning and Significance of Endowment in American Higher Education, 1890–1930." *Teachers College Record* 114, no. 10 (2012): 1–32; Roger L. Geiger, *To Advance Knowledge: The Growth of American Research Universities, 1900–1940* (New York: Oxford University Press, 1986), 58–93.

20. Trevor Arnett, *College and University Finance* (New York: General Education Board, 1922), 7. See also US Commissioner of Education, *Annual Report, 1908–9* (Washington, DC: Government Printing Office, 1910), 2:1029; US Commissioner of Education, *Biennial Survey of Education, 1928–1930*, 2:526–28.

21. Alfred Z. Reed, *Training for the Public Profession of the Law* (New York: Carnegie Foundation for the Advancement of Teaching, 1921), 443; Bruce A. Kimball, *The "True Professional Ideal" in America: A History* (Oxford: Basil Blackwell, 1992), 198–300.

22. The nineteen endowed medical schools had capital funds of about $1,900,000, and the eight endowed law schools had about $850,000. The highest endowments were the $427,000 of Johns Hopkins medical school, $480,000 of Columbia medical school, and $500,000 of the law school at Harvard; Parsons, *Professional Education*, 17. The survey was conducted in 1898, before the infusion of funds to Harvard Medical School, discussed below, and counted cash balances in the endowment of HLS. The amount for law schools and for HLS includes invested cash reserves of about $130,000; *Harvard Treasurer Report, 1898–99*, 52–56.

23. US Commissioner of Education, *Annual Report, 1899–1900*, 2:1959–60.

24. Charles W. Eliot, "What Is a Liberal Education?" *Century Magazine* 28 (1884): 208. See US Commissioner, *Annual Report, 1874–75*, 2:738–47.

25. Edwin E. Slosson, *Great American Universities* (New York: Macmillan, 1910), 446.

26. John W. Burgess, *The American University: When Shall It Be? Where Shall It Be? What Shall It Be?* (Boston: Ginn, Heath, 1884), 9; Kimball and Johnson, "The Inception," 1–32.

27. William H. Taft, "Oration," in Harvard Law School Association, *Report of the Eighteenth Annual Meeting* (Boston: Harvard Law School Association, 1904), 15. See also Daniel R. Coquillette and Bruce A. Kimball, *On the Battlefield of Merit: Harvard Law School, the First Century* (Cambridge, MA: Harvard University Press, 2015).

28. Robert A. McCaughey, *Stand, Columbia: A History of Columbia University in the City of New York, 1754–2004* (New York: Columbia University Press, 2003), 231. See also Stevens, *Law School*, 23; LaPiana, *Logic and Experience*, 81, 86–88; Goebel, *History of the School of Law*, 140–46, 162–65, 182–86.

29. Charles W. Eliot, *Annual Report of the President of Harvard University*

1904–05 (Cambridge, MA: Harvard University, 1906), 39; Nicholas M. Butler, *Annual Report of the President of Columbia University 1925–26* (New York: Columbia University, 1927), 29; Young B. Smith, *Annual Report of the Dean of Columbia University School of Law 1936–37* (New York: Columbia University, 1938), 84–85. See also correspondence between CLS Dean Harlan F. Stone and HLS Dean Ezra R. Thayer in Law School Dean's Office Records, President A. Lawrence Lowell Records, Harvard University Archives, Cambridge, MA.

30. Ludmerer, *Learning to Heal*, 4, 75, 96–97, 143; Arthur T. Hadley, *Annual Report of the President of Yale University, 1901–2* (New Haven, CT: Yale University, 1903), 15; Eliot, *Annual Report, 1904–5*, 39; Henry W. Rogers, *Annual Report of the Dean of Yale Law School, 1904–5* (New Haven, CT: Yale University, 1906), 153–54; James B. Ames, *Annual Report of the Dean of Harvard Law School, 1905–6* (Cambridge, MA: Harvard University, 1907), 163.

31. R. E. Gleeson, S. Schlossman, and D. G. Allen, *The Beginnings of Graduate Management Education in the United States* (Santa Monica: Graduate Management Admission Council, 1994), 66–75; Khurana, *From Higher Aims*, 37, 67, 137–39, 144–46; Daniel, *M.B.A.*, 15–16, 39, 49, 70–71.

32. Quotation is from Eliot, *Annual Report, 1905–6*, 55–58. The following draws from Bruce A. Kimball and Benjamin A. Johnson, "The Beginning of "Free Money" Ideology in American Universities: Charles W. Eliot at Harvard, 1869–1909," *History of Education Quarterly* 52 (2012): 222–50.

33. Bruce A. Kimball, "The First Campaign and the Paradoxical Transformation of Fundraising in American Higher Education, 1915–1925," *Teachers College Record* 116, no. 7 (2014): 1–44.

34. R. Keith Kane and Dana Doten, "The Case for Endowment," *Harvard Alumni Bulletin*, November 24, 1951, 212–14. See also James B. Conant, *Annual Report of the President of Harvard University, 1950–51* (Cambridge, MA: Harvard University, 1952), 25; Cruikshank, *A Delicate Experiment*, 186; Keller and Keller, *Making Harvard*, 145–48, 179, 275, 299; Seymour E. Harris, *Economics of Harvard* (New York: McGraw-Hill, 1970), 275, 299–300.

35. Seth Low, *Annual Report of the President of Columbia University, 1889–90* (New York: Columbia University, 1891), 27–28, and *1900–1901*, 66; Butler, *Annual Report, 1901–2*, 16; *1904–5*, 36; *1915–16*, 1–2, 10; *1919–20*, 2; *1925–26*, 41–44; "The Finances of Columbia University," *School and Society* 45 (January 16, 1937): 82–83; McCaughey, *Stand, Columbia*, 301.

36. Thomas W. Lamont to Robert J Beeckman, October 15, 1919, Correspondence of Thomas W. Lamont, 1916–1921, Harvard Endowment Fund Records, box 2, Harvard University Archives, Cambridge, MA. See also Butler, *Annual Report, 1919–20*, 1–2; *1922–23*, 22.

37. John B. Pine, comp., *Columbia University . . . Gifts and Endowments, with the Names of Benefactors, 1754–1904* (New York: Columbia University, 1904); Butler, *Annual Report, 1928–29*, 5, 16–19; Horace Coon, *Columbia: Colossus on the Hudson* (New York: Dutton, 1947), 30; McCaughey, *Stand, Columbia*, 313–14, 416–17.

38. Butler, *Annual Report, 1902–3*, 12; *1906–7*, 7; *1909–10*, 3; *1913–14*, 5–6; *1919–20*, 1, 4; *1924–25*, 1–5, 54; Coon, *Columbia*, 29, 108–9; Munroe Smith,

"The Development of the University," in *A History of Columbia University, 1754–1904*, edited by Brander Matthews (New York: Columbia University Press, 1904), 265; "Finances of Columbia University," 82–83; Geiger, *To Advance Knowledge*, 52–53; McCaughey, *Stand, Columbia*, 208, 226–30, 302–15, 330, 416–18.

39. Quotations are from Butler, *Annual Report, 1919–20*, 4; *1922–23*, 20.

40. Quoted in McCaughey, *Stand, Columbia*, 309.

41. Quotation is from McCaughey, *Stand, Columbia*, 207–8; see also ibid., 231, 301, 309–16, 330, 416–418; Coon, *Columbia*, 29, 93–115; Frederick P. Keppel, *Columbia* (New York: Columbia University Press, 1914), 280–84; Geiger, *To Advance Knowledge*, 52.

42. Quotation is from George H. Williams, ed., *The Harvard Divinity School: Its Place in Harvard University and in American Culture* (Boston: Beacon Press, 1954), 174–75, 212–13. See also Conant, *Annual Report, 1949–50*, 20–21, *1951–52*, 12; Harris, *Economics*, 226–27; Keller and Keller, *Making Harvard*, 134, 184.

43. Cruikshank, *A Delicate Experiment*, 285.

44. James G. Egbert, *Annual Report of the Director of Columbia University School of Business, 1920–21* (New York: Columbia University, 1922), 209–10; *1928–29*, 345.

45. Butler, *Annual Report, 1904–5*, 35–36. See also Coon, *Columbia*, 93–115; McCaughey, *Stand, Columbia*, 301–10.

46. Samuel W. Lambert, *Annual Report of the Dean of the College of Physicians and Surgeons of Columbia University, 1909–10* (New York: Columbia University), 87–88.

47. McCaughey, *Stand, Columbia*, 309, 351; Butler, *Annual Report, 1942–43*, 22–23.

48. George W. Kirchwey, *Annual Report of the Dean of Columbia University School of Law, 1907–8* (New York: Columbia University, 1910), 71–72; *Harvard Treasurer Report, 1937–38*, 5–7.

49. Eliot, *Annual Report, 1876–77*, 39; *1904–5*, 58–59.

50. The cumulative totals of endowment for the Columbia professional schools do not appear in Columbia's financial reports, and we have calculated them as follows: Based on the lists of permanent funds with their purposes and establishment dates in the 1901–2 report, we have calculated retroactively the annual totals of endowed funds of each year prior to 1901–2. Future totals were then calculated by reviewing subsequent annual reports and adding the new gifts to the endowed funds of each school. See Columbia University, *Annual Report of the Treasurer, 1901–2* (New York: Columbia University, 1903), 387–406 (cited hereafter as *Columbia Treasurer Report* with year).

51. Arnett, *College and University*, 7.

52. Coon, *Columbia*, 31–32. See also McCaughey, *Stand, Columbia*, 302–3.

53. Roger L. Geiger, *Research and Relevant Knowledge: American Research Universities since World War II* (New York: Oxford University Press, 1993), 182.

54. Ludmerer, *Learning to Heal*, 4. See also Ludmerer, *Time to Heal*, 21, 27; Rogers, *Annual Report, 1914–15*, 320–21.

55. Quotations are from Ludmerer, *Learning to Heal*, 192. See also Rothstein, *American Medical Schools*, 150–51.

56. Low, *Annual Report, 1890–91*, 1–6; *1897–98*, 59; John G. Curtis, *Annual*

Report of the Dean of Columbia University School of Medicine, 1903–4 (New York: Columbia University, 1905), 96–97; Butler, *Annual Report, 1903–4*, 3; Lambert, *Annual Report, 1904–5*, 90; *1908–9*, 75; *1910–11*, 84.

57. Eliot, *Annual Report 1895–96*, 24–25; *1896–97*, 27; *1897–98*, 37; Thomas F. Harrington, *The Harvard Medical School: A History, Narrative and Documentary* (New York: Lewis, 1905), 3:1168.

58. Eliot, *Annual Report 1900–1901*, 49–50; see also 26, 32–37.

59. Harrington, *Harvard Medical School*, 3:1147, 1159; Eliot, *Annual Report 1906–7*, 27–29, 38–39.

60. Beecher and Altschule, *Medicine at Harvard*, 194–95; Ludmerer, *Learning to Heal*, 11, 151, 191–92; Rothstein, *American Medical Schools*, 144–49. See also Abraham Flexner, *Medical Education in the United States and Canada* (New York: Carnegie Foundation for the Advancement of Teaching, 1910); Steven C. Wheatley, *The Politics of Philanthropy: Abraham Flexner and Medical Education* (Madison: University of Wisconsin Press, 1988).

61. Henry A. Christian, *Annual Report of the Dean of Harvard Medical School, 1911–12* (Cambridge: Harvard University, 1913), 145. See also Beecher and Altschule, *Medicine at Harvard*, 168, 176–81, 188.

62. Ludmerer, *Time to Heal*, 57.

63. Lambert, *Annual Report, 1909–10*, 85, 87–88; *1910–11*, 74–75; *1918–19*, 126–27; Butler, *Annual Report, 1910–11*, 36; *1915–16*, 15; *1917–18*, 35; *1919–20*, 46; *1920–21*, 4; *1922–23*, 22; *1925–26*, 45–46; McCaughey, *Stand, Columbia*, 303, 306–7.

64. McCaughey, *Stand, Columbia*, 303. See also Lamb, *Presbyterian Hospital*, 77–79, 126–30, 162–63; William Darrach, *Annual Report of the Dean of Columbia University School of Medicine, 1925–26* (New York: Columbia University, 1927), 85–86; *1926–27*, 97; *1927–28*, 119.

65. Ludmerer, *Time to Heal*, 53.

66. David L. Edsall, *Annual Report of the Dean of Harvard Medical School 1932–33* (Cambridge: Harvard University, 1934), 220. See also 137; *1920–21*, 210; *1932–33*, 220; *1933–34*, 244–45; Beecher and Altschule, *Medicine at Harvard*, 185–86, 195, 202–7; Ludmerer, *Time to Heal*, 55–56; Rothstein, *American Medical Schools*, 235.

67. Anthony J. Badger, *The New Deal: The Depression Years, 1933–40* (New York: Hill and Wang, 1989); Robert S. McElvaine, *The Great Depression, 1929–1941*, rev. ed. (New York: Three Rivers Press, 2009).

68. Geiger, *To Advance Knowledge*, 253. See also Lamb, *Presbyterian Hospital*, 267–74, 287–92, 339; Butler, *Annual Report, 1935–36*, 7; Willard C. Rappleye, *Annual Report of the Dean of Columbia University School of Medicine, 1937–38* (New York: Columbia University, 1939), 87; *1938–39*, 111; *1939–40*, 96.

69. At Harvard, President Conant feared the entanglements of such funding. But HMS rapidly succeeded at pursuing government grants, which supplanted and then greatly surpassed the donations from foundations and individuals in earlier decades. See Conant, *Annual Report, 1947–48*, 10–11; *1948–49*, 20; Ludmerer, *Time to Heal*, 139–48; Keller and Keller, *Making Harvard*, 119; Geiger, *Research and Relevant Knowledge*, 93.

70. Quotations are respectively from Ludmerer, *Learning to Heal*, 201, and Ludmerer, *Time to Heal*, 134. The *locus classicus* of the structural-functionalist view is found in Talcott Parsons, "Professions," *International Encyclopedia of the Social Sciences*, ed. David L. Sills (New York: Macmillan, 1968), 12:536–47.

71. Paul Starr, *The Social Transformation of American Medicine* (New York: Basic Books, 1982), 143–44. See also Eliot Freidson, *Profession of Medicine: A Study of the Sociology of Applied Knowledge* (New York: Harper & Row, 1970); Magali Sarfatti Larson, *The Rise of Professionalism: A Sociological Analysis* (Berkeley: University of California, Press, 1977); Andrew Abbott, *The System of Professions: An Essay on the Division of Expert Labor* (Chicago: University of Chicago Press, 1988).

72. Eliot Freidson, *Professionalism: The Third Logic* (Chicago: University of Chicago Press, 2001).

73. Eliot, *Annual Report, 1902–3*, 22. See also Ludmerer, *Time to Heal*, 37–38; Low, *Annual Report, 1894–95*, 32–33; Butler, *Annual Report, 1911–12*, 39–40; *1928–29*, 48–49; *1933–34*, 51–52; Edsall, *Annual Report, 1918–19*, 137; *1932–33*, 220; C. Sidney Burwell, *Annual Report of the Dean of Harvard Medical School, 1946–47* (Cambridge: Harvard University, 1948), 418; Darrach, *Annual Report, 1925–26*, 121.

74. Ludmerer, *Learning to Heal*, 12.

75. Lambert, *Annual Report, 1911–12*, 86; Harris, *Economics of Harvard*, 468; Harrington, *Harvard Medical School*, 3:1147, 1159; Eliot, *Annual Report, 1906–7*, 38–39; Rappleye, *Annual Report, 1931–32*, 88; *1937–38*, 87; *1940–41*, 9; Burwell, *Annual Report, 1945–46*, 355; *1946–47*, 418.

76. Lambert, *Annual Report, 1914–15*, 85; see also *1911–12*, 86.

77. Butler, *Annual Report, 1907–8*, 33–34; *1920–21*, 2–5; *1922–23*, 22; *1924–25*, 1–5, 40–42; *1925–26*, 33, 42, 45–46; Darrach, *Annual Report, 1925–26*, 85–86; *1926–27*, 97; *1927–28*, 119.

78. Butler, *Annual Report, 1907–8*, 31–32; see also *1911–12*, 1–53; *1915–16*, 2; *1924–25*, 39; *1928–29*, 46–47; *1933–34*, 55.

79. Eliot, *Annual Report, 1900–1901*, 25–26, 32–37, 49–50; Harrington, *Harvard Medical School*, 3:1168.

80. Khurana, *From Higher Aims*, 27. See also Paul J. Dimaggio, "Interest and Agency in Institutional Theory," in *Institutional Patterns and Organizations: Culture and Environment*, edited by Lynne G. Zucker (Cambridge, MA: Ballinger, 1988), 14–15; Walter W. Powell and Paul J. Dimaggio, eds., *The New Institutionalism in Organizational Analysis* (Chicago: University of Chicago Press, 1983); Mary C. Brinton and Victor Nee, *The New Institutionalism in Sociology* (Palo Alto, CA: Stanford University Press, 2001).

81. Lambert, *Annual Report, 1918–19*, 115–16; see also ibid., 117–18; Butler, *Annual Report, 1909–10*, 31; *1924–25*, 42–43; Darrach, *Annual Report, 1925–26*, 123.

82. Ludmerer, *Time to Heal*, 12, 151, 191–92, 203, 205; Butler, *Annual Report, 1942–43*, 28; Lambert, *Annual Report, 1909–10*, 85; *1911–12*, 86; *1918–19*, 117–18. See also Wheatley, *Politics of Philanthropy*.

83. Beecher and Altschule, *Medicine at Harvard*, 194–95.

84. Edsall, *Annual Report, 1918–19*, 137; *1920–21*, 210; *1933–34*, 244–45; Rothstein, *American Medical Schools*, 235.

85. Ludmerer, *Time to Heal*, 53. See also Beecher and Altschule, *Medicine at Harvard*, 203.

86. Rappleye, *Annual Report, 1937–38*, 117; *1939–40*, 165; *1940–41*, 48. See also Ludmerer, *Time to Heal*, 54; Harry Atkins, *The Dean: Willard C. Rappleye and the Evolution of American Medical Education* (New York: Josiah Macy Jr. Foundation, 1975); McCaughey, *Stand, Columbia*, 309, 351; Lamb, *Presbyterian Hospital*, 393.

87. Keller and Keller, *Making Harvard*, 117–19, 257; Beecher and Altschule, *Medicine at Harvard*, 210–11.

88. *Harvard Treasurer Report, 1939–40*, 241; *1944–45*, 78–79.

89. Hugh Hawkins, *Between Harvard and America: The Educational Leadership of Charles W. Eliot* (Cambridge: Harvard University Press, 1972), 16–18, 72–77; Ludmerer, *Learning to Heal*, 48–53; Eliot, *Annual Report, 1900–1901*, 32–37, 49–50; McCaughey, *Stand, Columbia*, 309, 351.

90. Edsall, *Annual Report, 1919–20*, 172–73; Lambert, *Annual Report, 1918–19*, 107–8. See also Ludmerer, *Time to Heal*, 56–58. HMS enrollment spiked to 558 in 1900, the last year students could enter without holding a bachelor's degree, and more than half of the entering class flunked out. In 1901 HMS began requiring a college degree for admission, whereas only 39 percent of CMS students held college degrees. Eliot, *Annual Report, 1895–96*, 24–25; *1896–97*, 27; *1897–98*, 37; *1900–1901*, 25, 49–50; Harrington, *Harvard Medical School*, 3:1168.

91. Flexner, *Medical Education*, 133; Ludmerer, *Learning to Heal*, 141, 207; Ludmerer, *Time to Heal*, 15, 58, 62.

92. Quotation is from Edsall, *Annual Report, 1919–20*, 172–73. See also Lambert, *Annual Report, 1918–19*, 107–8; Ludmerer, *Time to Heal*, 56–58.

93. Lambert, *Annual Report 1918–19*, 115–16. See also Burwell, *Annual Report 1946–47*, 355.

94. Flexner, *Medical Education*, 133; Edsall, *Annual Report, 1932–33*, 220; Lambert, *Annual Report, 1916–17*, 90; *1918–19*, 115–16; Rothstein, *American Medical Schools*, 150–51.

95. Flexner, *Medical Education*, 129, 133; Butler, *Annual Report, 1913–14*, 7–8; *1914–15*, 7; Harvard University, *Catalogue, 1911–12* (Cambridge: Harvard University, 1911), 452, 739–40; *1915–16*, 813–14; Abbott L. Lowell, *Annual Report of the President of Harvard University, 1914–15* (Cambridge: Harvard University, 1916), 24; *1915–16*, 5–6; *1920–21*, 7; *1924–25*, 7–8; Edsall, *Annual Report, 1926–27*, 193.

96. Lambert, *Annual Report, 1911–12*, 86; Harris, *Economics of Harvard*, 468; Harrington, *Harvard Medical School*, 3:1147, 1159; Eliot, *Annual Report, 1906–7*, 38–39; Rappleye, *Annual Report, 1931–32*, 88; *1937–38*, 87; *1940–41*, 9; Burwell, *Annual Report 1945–46*, 355; *1946–47*, 418.

97. Quotation is from Roger L. Geiger, *Knowledge and Money: Research Universities and the Paradox of the Marketplace* (Palo Alto: Stanford University Press, 2004), 4.

98. Quotations are from Burwell, *Annual Report, 1945–46*, 355; *1946–47*, 418.

See also Edsall, *Annual Report, 1918–19*, 137; *1920–21*, 210; *1932–33*, 220; *1933–34*, 244–45; Beecher and Altschule, *Medicine at Harvard*, 185–86, 195, 202–7; Ludmerer, *Time to Heal*, 55–56; Rothstein, *American Medical Schools*, 235.

99. Quotation is from Edsall, *Annual Report, 1932–33*, 220. See also Burwell, *Annual Report, 1945–46*, 355; Rothstein, *American Medical Schools*, 151; *Harvard Treasurer Report, 1937–38*, 72–73. The amount of tuition revenue and overall revenue of CMS is obscure in the *Columbia Treasurer Reports*.

100. Harris, *Economics of Harvard*, 468.

101. Herman Oliphant, "Parallels in the Development of Legal and Medical Education," *Annals of the American Academy of Political and Social Science* 167 (1933): 156.

102. Quotations are from, respectively, *The Centennial History of the Harvard Law School, 1817–1917* (Cambridge, MA: Harvard Law School Association, 1918), 163; James Byrne to Abbott L. Lowell, March 3, 1917, box 84, President A. Lawrence Lowell Records, Harvard University Archives, Cambridge, MA. See also Butler, *Annual Report, 1912–13*, 41; *1936–37*, 31.

103. Quotation is from Caleb Loring to Roscoe Pound, April 17, 1916, reel 10, Roscoe Pound Papers, Microfilm Collection, Harvard Law School Library Special Collections, Cambridge, MA, emphasis in the original. See also Bruce A. Kimball, "The Disastrous First Fund-Raising Campaign in Legal Education: The Harvard Law School Centennial, 1914–1920," *Journal of the Gilded Age and Progressive Era* 12 (2013): 535–78.

104. Kirchwey, *Annual Report, 1902–3*, 97–98; *1903–4*, 94; *1909–10*, 79–80; Goebel, *History of the School of Law*, 236–37; Harlan F. Stone, *Annual Report of the Dean of Columbia University School of Law, 1913–14* (New York: Columbia University, 1915), 72; *1917–18*, 73–74; *1919–20*, 34–35; Smith, *Annual Report, 1937–38*, 83–84.

105. Malcolm Storer to Thomas W. Lamont, January 12, 1917, box 1, Correspondence of Thomas W. Lamont, 1916–1921, Harvard Endowment Fund Records, Harvard University Archives, Cambridge, MA.

106. Wallace B. Donham, *Annual Report of the Dean of Harvard Graduate School of Business Administration, 1920–21* (Cambridge: Harvard University, 1922), 129; Cruikshank, *A Delicate Experiment*, 200.

107. Quotations are from Archibald King to Joseph Sargent, March 6, 1914, box 8, Ezra R. Thayer Papers, Harvard Law School Library Special Collections, Cambridge, MA. See also Edmund K. Arnold to Ezra R. Thayer, June 20, 1914; Horace F. Baker to Joseph Sargent, March 4, 1914; Alvin A. Morris to Horace F. Baker, March 5, 1914; and Justin Bowersock to Joseph Sargent, June 17, 1914, all in ibid.

108. Butler, *Annual Report, 1915–16*, 4–5; *1916–17*, 8; *1921–22*, 5; *1928–29*, 59; *1929–30*, 46–47; Stone, *Annual Report, 1911–12*, 70–71; *1916–17*, 77; *1919–20*, 75; Smith, *Annual Report, 1927–28*, 92–93; *1928–29*, 99; *1931–32*, 7; *1933–34*, 105; *1936–37*, 89; *1937–38*, 76–77; *1939–40*, 84; *1944–45*, 11; Thomas I. Parkinson, *Annual Report of the Dean of Columbia University School of Law, 1923–24* (New York: Columbia University, 1925), 65–67; *1924–25*, 86. See also Goebel, *History of the School of Law*, 273–75, 297–305; Bruce A. Kimball,

"Charity, Philanthropy, and Law School Fundraising: The Emergence and the Failure, 1880–1930," *Journal of Legal Education* 63 (2013): 247–81.

109. Roscoe Pound, *The Harvard Law School* (New York: [Harvard Law School Association], 1919); Roscoe Pound, *The Harvard Law School: Its History, Its Development, Its Needs: A Projet* [*sic*] (New York: [Harvard Law School Association], 1925).

110. Roscoe Pound, *Annual Report of the Dean of Harvard Law School, 1923–24* (Cambridge: Harvard University, 1917), 186. See also Henry A. Yeomans, *Abbott Lawrence Lowell, 1856–1943* (Cambridge, MA: Harvard University Press, 1948), 252–53.

111. Roscoe Pound to A. L. Lowell, December 11, 1916, Harvard Law School Dean's Office Records, Records of President A. Lawrence Lowell, 1910–1933, Harvard University Archives, Cambridge, MA.

112. Pound, *Annual Report, 1926–27*, 185–86.

113. Lowell quoted in Thomas W. Swan, *Annual Report of the Dean of Yale Law School, 1923–24* (New Haven: Yale University, 1925), 124. See also Lowell, *Annual Report, 1925–26*, 23–24.

114. Pound, *Harvard Law School History*, 21–22.

115. James B. Thayer, "The Teaching of English Law at Universities," *Harvard Law Review* 9 (1895): 174.

116. Mr. Lohrke, "Memorandum Report on Developing the Human Angle of the Harvard Law School Endowment Fund" [October–November 1926], box CH, vol. 57, John Price Jones Co. Records, 1919–54, Harvard Business School Library Special Collections, Cambridge, MA, emphasis in the original.

117. Pound quoted in Harris, *Economics of Harvard*, 19.

118. *For the Safety of the Citizen and the Protection of Business, A Plan to Eliminate from the Administration of Justice in This Country Many Elements of Delay, Waste, Friction, and Uncertainty Which Are Threatening the General Security and Hampering Commerce and Industry* (New York: Harvard Law School Endowment Fund [April 1927]), box CH, vol. 57, John Price Jones Co. Records, 1919–54, Harvard Business School Library Special Collections, Cambridge, MA. The final pamphlet conflated nine separate publications that had originally been planned.

119. Kimball, "Charity, Philanthropy," 247–81.

120. Quotation is from Butler, *Annual Report, 1936–37*, 30, 31. See also Stone, *Annual Report, 1910–11*, 68; *1922–23*, 57–58; Smith, *Annual Report, 1939–40*, 84; *1940–41*, 17.

121. Quotation is from Smith, *Annual Report, 1937–38*, 76–77; see also *1930–31*, 88; *1933–34*, 101–2; *1935–36*, 82–83; *1936–37*, 96–97; *1938–39*, 78; *1939–40*, 84; *1944–45*, 11; Butler, *Annual Report, 1930–31*, 41.

122. William J. Keener, *Annual Report of the Dean of Columbia University School of Law, 1900–1* (New York: Columbia University, 1902), 98; Kirchwey, *Annual Report, 1901–2*, 130; *1905–6*, 104; Stone, *Annual Report, 1910–11*, 66; *1914–15*, 82; *1915–16*, 63; *1919–20*, 74–77; *1920–21*, 82–84; *1921–22*, 83; Smith, *Annual Report, 1933–34*, 107–8; *1936–37*, 96–97; *1937–38*, 76–77; *1944–45*, 11–13.

123. Butler, *Annual Report, 1919–20*, 34; *1936–37*, 31, 30; Stone, *Annual Report 1916–17*, 76; *1917–18*, 70.

124. Stone, *Annual Report, 1921–22*, 83. See also Goebel, *History of the School of Law*, 273.

125. McCaughey, *Stand, Columbia*, 309. See also Goebel, *History of the School of Law*, 273–74. Stone's departure has been attributed to his failure to support a reform movement at the school and his frustration with "the petty details of law school administration." Laura Kalman, *Legal Realism at Yale, 1927–1960* (Chapel Hill: University of North Carolina Press, 1986), 69. But the fundamental reason appears to be his frustration with Butler's autocratic rule and resistance to any challenge.

126. *Columbia Treasurer Report, 1924–25*, 488–521; *1929–30*, 106–46; *Yale Treasurer Report, 1919–20*, 16, 96; *1930–31*, 109–10, 190–91; Butler, *Annual Report, 1929–30*, 46–47.

127. Smith, *Annual Report, 1936–37*, 89.

128. Ames, *Annual Report, 1905–6*, 163; *Harvard Treasurer Report, 1905–6*, 67, 102–3.

129. Kimball, "Disastrous First Fund-Raising Campaign," 535–78.

130. Erwin N. Griswold to Nathan M. Pusey, September 4, 1968, box 12, Law School Dean's Office Papers, Nathan M. Pusey Presidential Records, Harvard University Archives, Cambridge, MA. See also Bruce A. Kimball and Daniel R. Coquillette, *The Intellectual Sword: Harvard Law School, the Twentieth Century* (Cambridge: Harvard University Press, forthcoming).

131. Lowell, *Annual Report, 1908–9*, 21.

132. Kirchwey, *Annual Report, 1909–10*, 79–80. See also Stone, *Annual Report, 1910–11*, 66–67; *Columbia Treasurer Report, 1909–10*, 50–60; Butler, *Annual Report, 1901–2*, 8; *1902–3*, 10, 41–42; *1903–4*, 13; *1904–5*, 3–4, 10; *1906–7*, 47; *1907–8*, 1–2; *1909–10*, 30; *1912–13*, 42; *1915–16*, 4–5; Goebel, *History of the School of Law*, 185–86.

133. Butler, *Annual Report 1911–12*, 1–53; *1915–16*, 2; *1924–25*, 1–5, 39; *1933–34*, 55; Stone, *Annual Report 1918–19*, 104; *1920–21*, 82–83; Smith, *Annual Report, 1933–34*, 105; *1934–35*, 88; *1937–38*, 80; *1938–39*, 76; *1939–40*, 84.

134. Conant, *Annual Report, 1947–48*, 11–12; see also *1944–45*, 15–16; Kimball, "Charity, Philanthropy, and Law School Fundraising," 247–81.

135. Butler, *Annual Report, 1913–14*, 7–8; *1915–16*, 4–5; Rappleye, *Annual Report, 1940–41*, 4; Smith, *Annual Report, 1940–41*, 15; Goebel, *History of the School of Law*, 233, 311, 345, 348, 473, 490.

136. This point is difficult to validate due to the murkiness of Columbia's financial reports, discussed above. But Butler indicated in 1914 that CLS, although charging $180 in tuition, was not subsidized, while Columbia's other schools, charging $250 in tuition, were heavily subsidized. In 1915 Columbia raised tuition across the board but exempted the law school, which apparently was running a surplus. At that point the 453 law students generated just over $86,000 in tuition, and the CLS endowment of $321,250 produced nearly $15,000 in income. Together, these revenues about equaled the school's expenses of $101,279. Because the law school also received some current gifts and grants, CLS must have run a surplus that the university retained in 1915. Butler, *Annual Report, 1913–14*, 7–8; *1914–15*, 7; *1932–33*, 6. These calculations do not appear anywhere in the financial reports, and the deans,

treasurer, and president did not discuss deficits or surpluses, as their counterparts did routinely in their annual reports at Harvard.

137. Pound, *Annual Report, 1915–16*, 146.

138. Quotation is from Austin W. Scott, *Annual Report of the Dean of Harvard Law School, 1909–10* (Cambridge: Harvard University, 1911), 149. See also Ezra R. Thayer, *Annual Report of the Dean of Harvard Law School, 1912–13* (Cambridge: Harvard University, 1914), 127; Lowell, *Annual Report, 1914–15*, 19; *1923–24*, 15–16; *Centennial History*, 170–73; Pound, *Annual Report, 1915–16*, 145; *1923–24*, 185; *1924–25*, 180; Pound, *Harvard Law School* (1925), 23.

139. Pound, *Annual Report, 1915–16*, 146; *1919–20*, 58; *1925–26*, 186; Lowell, *Annual Report, 1914–15*, 24; *1915–16*, 5–6; *1920–21*, 7–8.

140. Stone, *Annual Report, 1920–21*, 74. See also Smith, *Annual Report, 1935–36*, 80.

141. Pound, *Annual Report, 1925–26*, 186; Lowell, *Annual Report, 1923–24*, 16; *1924–25*, 7–8; *1926–27*, 6; Erwin N. Griswold, *Annual Report of the Dean of Harvard Law School, 1947–48* (Cambridge, MA: Harvard University, 1949), 379; Edsall, *Annual Report, 1926–27*, 193.

142. Pound, *Harvard Law School* (1919), 16. See also Kimball, "Charity, Philanthropy, and Law School Fundraising," 247–81.

143. Griswold, *Annual Report, 1947–48*, 390; James N. Landis, *Annual Report of the Dean of Harvard Law School, 1939–40* (Cambridge: Harvard University, 1941), 235–36; *1944–45*, 171.

144. Butler, *Annual Report, 1915–16*, 4–5; see also *1913–14*, 7–8.

145. Smith, *Annual Report, 1935–36*, 80. See also Stone, *Annual Report, 1920–21*, 74.

146. Quotations are from Smith, *Annual Report, 1933–34*, 100; see also *1934–35*, 79; *1935–36*, 80; *Centennial History*, 170–73.

147. Smith, *Annual Report, 1933–34*, 100.

148. Roscoe Pound to Frank W. Grinnell, April 13, 1916, box 84, Law School Dean's Office Records, President A. Lawrence Lowell Records, Harvard University Archives, Cambridge, MA.

149. June O'Neill, *Resource Use in Higher Education: Trends in Outputs and Inputs, 1930 to 1967* (Berkeley: Carnegie Foundation for the Advancement of Teaching, 1971), 50; Khurana, *From Higher Aims*, 47, 111, 125–26.

150. Kimball, *"True Professional Ideal" in America*, 99–102, 295–97, 302–3.

151. Bruce A. Kimball interviews with John C. Baker, October 19–20, 1995, Essex Falls, New Jersey, and Deane W. Malott, December 12, 1995, Ithaca, New York, who served as assistant deans of HBS during the 1920s, transcripts on file with the authors. See also Eliot, *Annual Report, 1905–6*, 27; *1906–7*, 12; *1907–8*, 26; Ames, *Annual Report, 1905–6*, 166; *1907–8*, 167; Yeomans, *Abbott Lawrence Lowell*, 232.

152. Butler, *Annual Report, 1913–14*, 25; Khurana, *From Higher Aims*, 125.

153. Butler, *Annual Report, 1915–16*, 17–20; *1916–17*, 7–8; *1918–19*, 61, 73; *1921–22*, 6; Egbert, *Annual Report, 1916–17*, 193–94; *1917–18*, 196–97; Van Metre, *History*, 32; Khurana, *From Higher Aims*, 127.

154. Daniel, *M.B.A.*, 39, 70–71, 116, 125, 144; Cruikshank, *Delicate Experiment*, 50; Khurana, *From Higher Aims*, 67, 137–39, 144–46; Schlossman et al., *Beginnings*, 66–75.

155. Donham, *Annual Report*, *1920–21*, 129; Cruikshank, *Delicate Experiment*, 200.

156. Donham, *Annual Report*, *1922–23*, 142; see also ibid., *1919–20*, 111; Edwin F. Gay, *Annual Report of the Dean of Harvard Graduate School of Business Administration*, *1911–12* (Cambridge: Harvard University, 1913), 125; *1912–13*, 112; *1914–15*, 124–25; *1915–16*, 114–15; *Harvard Treasurer Report*, *1912–13*, 82; L. F. Schaub, *Annual Report of the Dean of Harvard Graduate School of Business Administration*, *1917–18* (Cambridge: Harvard University, 1913), 97; Cruikshank, *Delicate Experiment*, 91–92.

157. Quotation is from Donham, *Annual Report*, *1923–24*, 119. See also Yeomans, *Abbott Lawrence Lowell*, 230–31; Cruikshank, *Delicate Experiment*, 99–112; Donham, *Annual Report*, *1926–27*, 120.

158. Egbert, *Annual Report*, *1916–17*, 193–94; *1917–18*, 196–97. See also Butler, *Annual Report*, *1915–16*, 17–20; *1916–17*, 7–8; *1918–19*, 61, 73; *1921–22*, 6; Van Metre, *History*, 32; Khurana, *From Higher Aims*, 127.

159. Egbert, *Annual Report 1928–29*, 345. See also *1923–24*, 227–28; *1925–26*, 250; *1926–27*, 268; *1927–28*, 291; *1928–29*, 346–47; *1929–30*, 380, 382; *1930–31*, 360–61.

160. Ibid., *1931–32*, 236; *Columbia Treasurer Report*, *1930–31*, 10–40; *1931–32*, 10–43.

161. Quotation is from Egbert, *Annual Report 1928–29*, 345; see also *1923–24*, 227–28; *1925–26*, 250; *1926–27*, 268; *1927–28*, 291; *1928–29*, 346–47; *1929–30*, 380, 382; *1930–31*, 360–61.

162. Roswell C. McCrea, *Annual Report of the Dean of Columbia University School of Business*, *1933–34* (New York: Columbia University, 1935), 347–48; see also *1935–36*, 262–63; *1936–37*, 345; *1937–38*, 255–56.

163. The contrast is well described in Khurana, *From Higher Aims*, 1–2, 24–25, 32–33. See also Alfred D. Chandler Jr., *The Visible Hand: The Managerial Revolution in American Business* (Cambridge: Harvard University Press, 1976).

164. Khurana, *From Higher Aims*, 6; see also 18, 26–32, 44–49, 100–102, 127, 133, 150, 173; Schlossman et al., *Beginnings*.

165. Francie Ostrower, *Why the Wealthy Give: The Culture of Elite Philanthropy* (Princeton: Princeton University Press, 1955).

166. Abraham Flexner, *Universities, American, English, German* (New York: Oxford University Press, 1930), 166–69; Daniel, *M.B.A.*, 27–29, 159; Khurana, *From Higher Aims*, 91–100, 120, 127–32, 140–41, 154–76, 185; Cruikshank, *Delicate Experiment*, 54, 60–61.

167. Teresa Odendahl, *Charity Begins at Home: Generosity and Self-Interest among the Philanthropic Elite* (New York: Basic Books, 1991).

168. Donham, *Annual Report*, *1921–22*, 84. See also Eliot, *Annual Report*, *1907–8*, 32–33; Gay, *Annual Report*, *1911–12*, 125; *1912–13*, 112.

169. Donham, *Annual Report, 1923–24*, 119; Yeomans, *Abbott Lawrence Lowell*, 230–35; Cruikshank, *Delicate Experiment*, 49, 93, 99–112, 124, 196; Keller and Keller, *Making Harvard*, 119–20, 149, 197; *Harvard Treasurer Report, 1949–50*, 92–93.

170. Butler, *Annual Report, 1921–22*, 6; Egbert, *Annual Report, 1917–18*, 201; *1923–24*, 223, 226–27; *1924–25*, 244–45; *1926–27*, 268–69; *1927–28*, 291; *1929–30*, 385; Van Metre, *History*, 37, 70.

171. This reliance of CBS on annual subsidies is shown by the consistent levels of expenses year after year: $97,500 in the early 1920s and $119,000 in the mid-1920s after the new building opened, then increases in the late 1920s due to new faculty hires that Egbert requested from the trustees. *Columbia Treasurer Report, 1921–22*, 348–74; *1922–23*, 382–408; *1923–24*, 365–92; *1924–25*, 401–28; *1925–26*, 401–28; *1925–26*, 401–428; *1926–27*, 9–35; *1927–28*, 10–37; *1928–29*, 10–39; *1929–30*, 10–40; Egbert, *Annual Report, 1916–17*, 191; *1917–18*, 201; *1926–27*, 267–68; *1927–28*, 277; Van Metre, *A History*, 28–29.

172. In 1929–30 total expenses for CBS were $180,638, and total revenue likely amounted to about $166,000, including about $22,000 of investment income (4.5 percent of $482,000) and about $144,000 in tuition revenue (480 students at $300). Current gifts and sundry income were apparently negligible. Consequently, the school was running a significant deficit of more than $14,000 on a budget of $180,000, and this apparently was covered by transfers from the Extension Department that otherwise would have gone to the university. In fact, CBS courses were cross-listed in the Extension Department catalog, and faculty taught in both areas "so that Extension acted as a floor to provide work for the Business faculty in case not enough students showed up." Van Metre, *A History*, 28–29. See also *Columbia Treasurer Report, 1929–30*, 10–40; Egbert, *Annual Report, 1916–17*, 191; *1917–18*, 201.

173. Egbert, *Annual Report, 1920–21*, 209–10; *1928–29*, 345.

174. Gay, *Annual Report, 1910–11*, 121; Donham, *Annual Report, 1919–20*, 115–17; *1921–22*, 89; *1922–23*, 142; *1927–28*, 131; Cruikshank, *Delicate Experiment*, 203.

175. Donham, *Annual Report, 1928–29*, 125–26.

176. Ibid., *1929–30*, 137.

177. Keller and Keller, *Making Harvard*, 120. See also Daniel, *M.B.A.*, 133; Cruikshank, *Delicate Experiment*, 209–75.

178. Donald K. David, *Annual Report of the Dean of Harvard Graduate School of Business Administration, 1944–45* (Cambridge: Harvard University, 1946), 220–21; Cruikshank, *Delicate Experiment*, 203, 213, 235; Keller and Keller, *Making Harvard*, 120; Daniel, *M.B.A.*, 137.

179. Egbert, *Annual Report, 1917–18*, 196–97. See also Butler, *Annual Report, 1915–16*, 17–18; Khurana, *From Higher Aims*, 127.

180. Butler, *Annual Report 1921–22*, 6; Egbert, *Annual Report, 1917–18*, 201; *1923–24*, 223, 226–27; *1924–25*, 244–45; *1926–27*, 268–69; *1927–28*, 291; *1929–30*, 385; Van Metre, *History*, 37, 70, 76.

181. Quotations are from McCrea, *Annual Report, 1933–34,* 347–48; see also *1932–33,* 300–301; *1935–36,* 262–63; *1936–37,* 345; *1937–38,* 255–56; Steven A. Sass, *The Pragmatic Imagination: A History of the Wharton School, 1881–1981* (Philadelphia: University of Pennsylvania Press, 1982), 119, 123–24.

182. McCrea, *Annual Report, 1934–35,* 305; *Columbia Treasurer Report, 1932–33,* 10–41; *1933–34,* 10–41; *1934–35,* 10–41; *1935–36,* 10–41; *1936–37,* 10–43; *1937–38,* 10–43; *1938–39,* 10–45; *1939–40,* 10–47; *1940–41,* 10–45; *1941–42,* 10–45; Daniel, *M.B.A.,* 136.

183. Van Metre, *History,* 83–84, 89–90, 96–97, 111–13. During the 1970s financial problems led Columbia to tax CBS heavily. Daniel, *M.B.A.,* 230–31; McCaughey, *Stand, Columbia,* 501.

184. Donham, *Annual Report 1937–38,* 228; *1923–24,* 123. See also Kimball, Interviews with John C. Baker and Deane W. Malott; US Commissioner of Education, *Biennial Survey of Education 1924–26,* 2:11.

185. Donham, *Annual Report, 1920–21,* 129–30; *1923–24,* 119–22; Lowell, *Annual Report, 1923–24,* 28–29.

186. Donham, *Annual Report 1922–23,* 123; see also *1920–21,* 130; *1921–22,* 84–85; *1928–29,* 129; *1933–34,* 180.

187. Butler, *Annual Report, 1921–22,* 6; Egbert, *Annual Report, 1917–18,* 201; *1923–24,* 223, 226–27; *1924–25,* 244–45; *1926–27,* 268–69; *1927–28,* 291; *1929–30,* 385; Van Metre, *History,* 37, 70.

188. Donham, *Annual Report, 1919–20,* 115, 123–24, 129–30; *1920–21,* 129–30; *1922–23,* 107, 123; *1924–25,* 120; *1923–24,* 119–22; *1929–30,* 141; Lowell, *Annual Report, 1914–15,* 24; *1915–16,* 5–6; *1920–21,* 7; *1923–24,* 28–29; David, *Annual Report, 1944–45,* 221.

189. McCrea, *Annual Report, 1934–35,* 305. See also *Columbia Treasurer Report, 1932–33,* 10–41; *1933–34,* 10–41; *1934–35,* 10–41; *1935–36,* 10–41; *1936–37,* 10–43; *1937–38,* 10–43.

190. Donham, *Annual Report, 1923–24,* 123; see also *1920–21,* 115; *1921–22,* 81–82; Lowell, *Annual Report, 1929–30,* 21.

191. Lowell, *Annual Report, 1929–30,* 21.

192. Quotation is from Donham, *Annual Report, 1923–24,* 120; see also 123; *1921–22,* 85.

193. Donham, *Annual Report, 1936–37,* 239.

194. Donham, *Annual Report, 1932–33,* 150–51; *1936–37,* 239; see also *1919–20,* 117; *1920–21,* 129; *1928–29,* 126; *1939–40,* 257; Gay, *Annual Report, 1912–13,* 112; *1914–15,* 124.

195. Donham, *Annual Report, 1920–21,* 129; Cruikshank, *A Delicate Experiment,* 199–200.

196. Donham, *Annual Report, 1937–38,* 230; see also 229–35, 341; *1935–36,* 218.

197. Egbert, *Annual Report, 1931–32,* 236; *Columbia Treasurer Report, 1930–31,* 10–40; *1931–32,* 10–43.

198. Egbert, *Annual Report, 1917–18,* 196–97. See also Butler, *Annual Report, 1915–16,* 17–18; Khurana, *From Higher Aims,* 127.

199. Butler, *Annual Report, 1915–16*, 4–5; see also *1928–29*, 59; Stone, *Annual Report, 1919–20*, 75; Smith, *Annual Report, 1927–28*, 92–93; *1931–32*, 7; *1933–34*, 105; *1936–37*, 89; *1937–38*, 76–77; *1939–40*, 84; *1944–45*, 11; Pound, *Harvard Law School* (1919); Pound, *Harvard Law School* (1925).

200. Conant, *Annual Report, 1947–48*, 11–12; see also *1944–45*, 15–16.

201. Hadley, *Annual Report, 1913–14*, 13–14.

202. Egbert, *Annual Report, 1920–21*, 211. See also Donham, *Annual Report, 1937–38*, 226.

203. Melvin T. Copeland, "The Genesis of the Case Method in Business Instruction," in *The Case Method at the Harvard Business School*, edited by Malcolm P. McNair (New York: McGraw-Hill, 1954), 25. See also Donham, *Annual Report, 1937–38*, 226.

204. Donham, *Annual Report, 1937–38*, 226.

205. Griswold, *Annual Report, 1947–48*, 381–82; Erwin N. Griswold, "Opportunities for the Future," *Harvard Law School Bulletin* 1 (December 1950): 3.

206. Daniel C. Tosteson, S. James Adelstein, and Susan T. Carver, eds., *New Pathways to Medical Education: Learning to Learn at Harvard Medical School* (Cambridge: Harvard University Press, 1994), 23, 88, 161–63.

207. Quotations are from, respectively, Ezra R. Thayer to Mark A. D. Howe, March 28, 1914, box 1, Dean Thayer Correspondence, Subject Files, Law School Dean's Office Records, President A. Lawrence Lowell Records, Harvard University Archives, Cambridge, MA; Pound, *Harvard Law School* (1919), 16; Griswold to Pusey, September 4, 1968.

208. Ludmerer, *Learning to Heal*, 4–5; Ludmerer, *Time to Heal*, 21, 27; Geiger, *Research and Relevant Knowledge*, 182–84.

209. Brian Z. Tamanaha, *Failing Law Schools* (Chicago: University of Chicago Press, 2012); "Symposium: Is Law School Worth It?" *Journal of Legal Education* 63 (2013): 173–246; Daniel R. Coquillette, "American Legal Education: Where Did We Come From? Where Are We Going?" *Bar Examiner* 82 (June 2013): 44–50; J. G. Leipold, "The New Entry-Level Legal Employment Market." *Bar Examiner* 82 (June 2013): 6–17.

About the Contributors

THOMAS ADAM is professor of transnational history at the University of Texas at Arlington and a former Humboldt fellow. He is the editor of the *Yearbook of Transnational History* and the editor of the book series Intercultural Transfer Studies with Anthem Press. He has published widely in the field of transnational history and philanthropy studies. His most recent publications include *Philanthropy, Civil Society, and the State in German History* (Rochester, NY: Camden House, 2016) and *Transnational Philanthropy* (Basingstoke, UK: Palgrave, 2016).

A. BURCU BAYRAM is assistant professor of political science at the University of Arkansas. Her research applies insights from psychology and behavioral economics to the study of international relations with a focus on international cooperation and global governance. She has published on global development and international law and organization. Her publications include "Due Deference: Cosmopolitan Social Identity and the Psychology of Legal Obligation" in the journal *International Organization* and "Aiding Strangers: Generalized Trust and the Moral Basis of Public Support for Foreign Development" in the journal *Foreign Policy*.

JAMIE M. BROWN received a BA in history from the University of California, Berkeley, and a JD from Harvard Law School, where she contributed to the historical research for chapter 5. She now works as a real estate attorney in the San Francisco office of Paul Hastings LLP. Her practice includes data center and mixed use development projects and commercial leasing.

DAVID C. HAMMACK is Haydn Professor of History at Case Western Reserve University. He served as president of the Association for Research on Nonprofit Organizations and Voluntary Action and received the association's 2012 distinguished achievement award. He edited the widely used reader *Making the Nonprofit Sector in the United States* (Indiana University Press, 1998) and has completed a three-volume series of books on philanthropic foundations in the United States: *American Foundations: Roles and Contributions*, edited with Helmut K. Anheier (Washington, DC: Brookings Institution, 2010); *A Versatile American Institution*, written with Anheier (Washington, DC: Brookings Institution, 2013); and *American Philanthropic Foundations: Regional Difference and Change*, edited with Steven R. Smith (Bloomington: Indiana University Press, 2018).

JORDAN HENSLEY is a policy analyst at the University of New Hampshire, with his role involving research, analysis, and engagement on a variety of policy topics, including economics, education, science, and health. He holds an MPP from Oregon State University and a BA in political science from the University of Idaho and is a former member of AmeriCorps VISTA.

STANLEY N. KATZ is professor of public and international affairs and director of the Center for Arts and Cultural Policy Studies at Princeton University. He is a specialist on American legal and constitutional history and on philanthropy and nonprofit institutions. He has authored and edited numerous books and articles. Among his many publications is the volume *Mobilizing for Peace: Conflict Resolution in Northern Ireland, Israel/Palestine, and South Africa*, which he coedited with Benjamin Gidron and Yeheskel Hasenfeld (Oxford: Oxford University Press, 2002). That book was awarded the Virginia A. Hodgkinson Research Prize for 2003. His recent research focuses on contemporary developments in American philanthropy, the relationship of civil society and constitutionalism to democracy, and the relationship of the United States to the international human rights regime. He is the editor in chief of the *Oxford International Encyclopedia of Legal History* and the editor emeritus of the *Oliver Wendell Holmes Devise History of the Supreme Court of the United States*. He is the cofounder and editor of the history of philanthropy blog www.histphil.org. Katz has served as president of the Organization of American Historians and the American Society for Legal History and as vice president of the Research Division of the American Historical Association. He is a member of the Board of Trustees of the Newberry Library and numerous other institutions. He is president of the Foundation of the Princeton Public Library. He also currently serves as chair of the American Council of Learned Societies/Social Science Research Council Working Group on Cuba.

BRUCE A. KIMBALL is professor in the philosophy and history of education program at Ohio State University and a former Guggenheim fellow. After serving as dean of Morse College at Yale University and then spending two years at Harvard Law School as a liberal arts fellow from 1985 to 1987, he began research on the history of professional education. In addition to studying the history of Harvard Law School, he publishes on the history of the finances of higher education. Among his most recent publications is *On the Battlefield of Merit*, coauthored with Daniel R. Coquillette (Cambridge, MA: Harvard University Press, 2015), which was awarded the Peter Dobkin Hall Prize for the most significant scholarly contribution to our understanding of the history of philanthropy in 2017.

JEREMY B. LUKE is a PhD candidate in the educational policy program at Ohio State University. He has performed research on the history of the finances of higher education and published articles with Bruce Kimball in journals such as *Social Science History*, *Historical Methods: A Journal of Quantitative and Interdisciplinary History*, and *Nonprofit and Voluntary Sector Quarterly*. More broadly, his research interests include the effects of marketization on modern-day educational organizations and institutional responses to competitive pressures in K–12 schools.

SAM STERN is professor of education and dean emeritus at Oregon State University, where he has been on the faculty of education since 1981 and between 2002 and 2011 served as dean of the College of Education. His teaching and research has focused on the relationships between learning and working and has had both interdisciplinary and international dimensions. He has taught in the Department of Systems Science at Tokyo Institute of Technology, the business program at the Athens Laboratory of Business Administration, and the Department of Economics at Harvard. He is the coauthor, with Alan G. Robinson, of *Corporate Creativity*, the 1998 Academy of Human Resource Development Book of the Year.

Index

Other Titles in the Walter Prescott Webb Memorial Lectures Series

African Diaspora
Alusine Jalloh and Stephen E. Maizlish

Creolization in the Americas
David Buisseret and Steven G. Reinhardt

Sacrifice and National Belonging in Twentieth-Century Germany
Greg Eghigian and Matthew Paul Berg

Beyond Black and White: Race, Ethnicity, and Gender in the US South and Southwest
Stephanie Cole and Alison M. Parker

Transatlantic History
Steven G. Reinhardt and Dennis Reinhartz

Traveling between Worlds: German-American Encounters
Thomas Adam and Ruth Gross

Lights, Camera, History: Portraying the Past in Film
Richard V. Francaviglia and Jerry Rodnitzky

Catholicism in the American West: A Rosary of Hidden Voices
Roberto R. Trevino and Richard V. Francaviglia

Baseball in America and America in Baseball
Donald G. Kyle and Robert B. Fairbanks

Manifest Destiny and Empire: American Antebellum Expansionism
Sam Haynes and Christopher Morris

Assumed Identities: The Meanings of Race in the Atlantic World
John D. Garrigus and Christopher Morris

Crossing the Atlantic: Travel and Travel Writing in Modern Times
Thomas Adam and Nils H. Roemer

Folly of Jim Crow: Rethinking the Segregated South
Stephanie Cole and Natalie J. Ring

Mexican Revolution: Conflict and Consolidation, 1910–1940
Douglas W. Richmond and Sam W. Haynes

Cold War Crossings: International Travel and Exchange across the Soviet Bloc, 1940s–1960s
Patryk Babiracki and Kenyon Zimmer

Contested Empire: Rethinking the Texas Revolution
Sam W. Haynes and Gerald D. Saxon

Currents in Transatlantic History: Encounters, Commodities, Identities
Steven G. Reinhardt

Deportation in the Americas: Histories of Exclusion and Resistance
Kenyon Zimmer and Cristina Salinas

CPSIA information can be obtained
at www.ICGtesting.com
Printed in the USA
BVHW080810070219
539571BV00016B/214/P

9 781623 497439